Living with the Queen

**Malcolm J. Barker with
T.C. Sobey**

Barricade Books Inc. • Fort Lee, N.J.

Published by Barricade Books Inc., 1530 Palisade Avenue,
Fort Lee, NJ 07024
Distributed by Publishers Group West, 4065 Hollis,
Emeryville, CA 94608

Published in Canada by McClelland & Stewart Inc. as
Courting More Disaster, 1991

Printed in the United States of America.

Library of Congress Cataloging-in-Publication Data

Barker, Malcolm J.
Living with the Queen: behind the scenes at Buckingham
Palace / Malcolm J. Barker : with T.C. Sobey.
ISBN 0-942637-75-5 : $18.95

1. Elizabeth II, Queen of Great Britain, 1926–   2. Great
Britain—Royal household—History—20th century.
3. Buckingham Palace (London, England)   I. Sobey, T.C.
(Timothy C.)   II. Title.

DA590.B263   1991   92-11345
941.085—dc20   CIP

Authors' Note

The events described in this book are factual. No names have been changed or altered with one exception, that of Mr. Humphrey. Artistic license and liberty have been taken with respect to dates, times of year, locations and the order in which some events took place. For the sake of continuity and clearer understanding of how the Queen's Court operates, events spanning several years have been condensed into one twelve-month period. A foreword, another chapter, and an afterword have been added to the paperback, hence *Courting More Disaster*.

Contents

Foreword   ix

1 Buckingham Palace   1
January 1st - April 15th

2 Windsor Castle   39
April 16th - May 15th

3 Buckingham Palace   59
May 16th - June 12th

4 Royal Ascot   93
June 13th - June 18th

5 Buckingham Palace   101
June 19th - June 30th

6 Palace of Holyrood   115
July 1st - July 7th

7 Buckingham Palace   133
July 8th - August 15th

8 Balmoral Castle   155
August 16th - October 15th

9 Buckingham Palace   187
October 16th - January 1st

10 Recollections from Ensuing Years   217
in Various Royal Residences

Goodbye to All That   255

Afterword   257
The Odyssey of Courting Disaster

later I presented myself at Buckingham Palace for an interview. I had had sufficient time to recover from being invited to the palace to discuss the possibility of a suitable position. There were many other applicants from both within and outside the Royal Household to be considered for the vacant post, which turned out to be for an Official in the Master of the Household's Department.

I was the last to be interviewed and endured a gruelling two hours with first the Deputy Master and then the Master of the Household himself. I outlined to them why it would be such a privilege to serve Her Majesty and explained why I believed my administrative and organizational abilities would help me to justify my selection, despite being only twenty-one years old.

Vice-Admiral Sir Peter Ashmore appeared to be impressed with what I had to say and promised to give very careful consideration to my candidature. I departed satisfied in the knowledge that I had given a good account of myself. But the elation of being informed some weeks later that my application had been successful was one of the happiest moments of my life. Shortly thereafter I proudly arrived at Buckingham Palace to begin my career, overflowing with enthusiasm. Little did I know what lay ahead . . .

Foreword

I have always been a staunch Monarchist. If th
leads you to suspect otherwise, then you are
it entirely in the wrong light. To me, the Royal
represents the best in tradition, continuity and
ity. In times of national crisis the British peop
invariably turned to the monarchy as a sy
hope and strength. At other times, they a
throughout Britain and the rest of the wo
wonderful advertisement for Great Britain, an
tion that will always be a reminder of decen
nity and consideration for others.

Upon leaving the University of Mancheste
I had a decision to make regarding my
realized a business career was not the right
me. What would I most like to do, I aske
There was never any question in my mind:
to serve the sovereign in some capacity. Pu
ambition into practice was of course anoth
Nevertheless, I resolved to ascertain what
prospects of employment for me in the Roy
hold and, after making various enquiries, I
the Queen's Master of the Royal Househol
my services. At least, I told myself, the w
would have to suffer would be a curt refus

To my utter astonishment, I received
reply indicating that there was a vacancy.

BUCKINGHAM PALACE

January 1st - April 15th

1

It went something like this.

It was 8 a.m. on a cold morning in January and the Royal Family had not yet returned from their two-month holiday in Norfolk. They would be in residence there at Sandringham House until early February. I, on the other hand, found myself standing in the White Drawing Room of Buckingham Palace, awaiting the arrival of one of Her Majesty's Senior Officials, a gentleman by the name of Mr. John Humphrey. He was responsible for giving me a tour of the palace and introducing me to the highest ranking men in the Court of Her Majesty Queen Elizabeth II.

As I waited for Mr. Humphrey, this senior representative of the Queen, I was naturally a touch anxious. After extensive interviewing and weeks of debate, the Queen's Master of the Household had finally made his decision. Unfortunately, I was so elated about my new job as an Official that during the previous evening's celebrations I drank one glass too many of Veuve Cliquot. As a result of this, I awoke on the morning on which my career at the palace was to begin, wishing I were dead.

Naturally, there was no way out. I realised that. One just could not turn up at Buckingham Palace on one's first day of work an hour or two late. It simply wasn't done. I therefore told myself I was going to the palace and that was that. But I was feeling so *dreadfully* ill. However, with fortitude and will I was able to pull the show together, and there I now stood in one of the most exquisitely elegant rooms I have ever been in, and awaited the important man I had an appointment with this day.

I was alone in the magnificent White Drawing Room and surveyed my surroundings. Everywhere there was gold: walls, embroidered chairs, desks, the ornate ceiling, vases, even the screen in front of the fireplace was made of solid gold. In one corner of the stately room I passed my fingers lightly along a French Florentine cabinet inlaid with panels of semi-precious stones. In front of the ceiling-to-floor French doors, which looked out onto the garden, stood graceful marble statues and tall ivory vases overflowing with white lilies. Above me and in the very centre of the drawing room hung a breathtaking tiered crystal chandelier. All around there was overwhelming beauty.

When the hour for my meeting had come and gone I wondered if I had made an error. Surely not, I thought. I waited a few moments longer, but Mr. Humphrey did not come. Thirty minutes later when he still had not shown I began to fret, and when almost an hour had passed and I was on the verge of despair, wondering if perhaps this was all a terrible joke and the palace had not wanted me after all, Mr. Humphrey finally entered my life.

Now, before we go any further I want to supply you with a little background on the man I was about to meet. Mr. Humphrey was not what one would normally expect to find in such an elevated position as a Senior Official to the Queen, especially considering the fact that he was also regarded by her as a personal friend. This was, as I knew, largely due to their shared passion for horses. The Queen regularly asked him to break in some of her most valuable stock from the famous Lippizaner stables in Austria. She was an experienced buyer herself and naturally had access to the very best advisers in the field. Mr. Humphrey was considered to be one of them.

I recalled seeing frequent photographs in the press of him with the Queen and the Duke of Edinburgh, deep in discussion during one of the numerous horse events held in Great Britain throughout the year. I believe the last picture I saw was of Mr. Humphrey with the Duke at the Royal Windsor Horse Show.

No matter. You will appreciate this long-winded history of a man you do not even know yet when I tell you of my surprise when he finally arrived. Entering the White Drawing Room, this scruffy, stupefied, gargantuan man proceeded to traipse across the burgundy and gold Persian carpets to where I was standing, clad in old rubber boots laden with horse shit!

It was extremely awkward for me. As a newcomer, I did not feel in the position to question, yet I felt compelled to say something of the matter when, across the splendid room, I could see a trail of sticky footprints extending outside the White Drawing Room and down the full length of the East Gallery which Nash had so lovingly designed! Mud, straw, and evil smelling manure were everywhere as Mr. Humphrey rambled on in an equally unexpected coarse cockney accent about the investiture which was to be held there the following day.

Mr. Humphrey, as I have said, was not a small man. At roughly 250 pounds and over 6 feet tall, he was like a giant compared to myself. Clinging to his head was a nest of sandy hair, possessing that unmistakable quality which suggested it had not seen a wash in quite some time. With huge round cheeks and still larger bags around his eyes, Mr. Humphrey gave the impression that he was half asleep. (I would soon learn that he was.) As if this were not enough, one of the most remarkable features about him was his sideburns. They were thick and untamed and circled their way down towards the corners of his mouth, where they came to a halt in narrow points. To accompany this were large ears and violin sized feet, everything panoramically producing a sight that reminded one of a poorly groomed bear standing on his hind legs.

A more unlikely candidate for Buckingham Palace, I could not have imagined.

But then I do not like to prejudge.

As we left the royal apartments that housed the Queen and Royal Family, I looked down at the brown muddied footprints in front of us. It had been a whirlwind tour. As I saw it, the main damage was sustained to the White Drawing Room in which we had first met. Apart from the odd patch of muddy grass that Mr. Humphrey left in the Queen's sitting-room, it was the White Drawing Room that concerned me most. Was it possible that this was acceptable behavior for a Buckingham Palace Official? I really didn't know what to think. But surely one couldn't parade about Her Majesty's beautiful palace spreading horse shit on the marble corridors and hand-sewn carpets? What should I say? Were we not going to be in some trouble for this mess? The thoughts tumbled through my aching head until I at last hit upon a tactful approach.

"Mr. Humphrey," I asked politely when the moment seemed right, "have you noticed these footprints on your way in?"

With vague apprehension of what I was saying he looked down and exclaimed with what I thought mild disinterest, "Oh ya… so there are. I better get someone onto that sometime." As I have mentioned, Mr. Humphrey had a thick cockney accent and made use of an alphabet that excludes the letters T and G at the end of his words.

As we retraced our steps I could not help but think my tour somewhat abridged. Certainly it was less informative than I would have expected. I mean, half an hour for over seven hundred rooms? I barely knew Mr. Humphrey, but I became aware that something was awry when we returned to the White Drawing Room for a weathered case he had forgotten.

"Look at that silly tart over there Malcolm!" He pointed to the portrait of Queen Charlotte over the mantle.

Somewhat taken aback I replied faintly, "Oh? I always thought she was quite a respectable monarch in her time. Didn't you?"

"Heh heh heh!" he chuckled deep like a bear, "I don't care about that, heh heh heh! I wouldn't mind havin' a good go at her, that's what I mean!" (This was a Senior Official to the Queen, I thought again?)

Now, I had been informed that owing to a shortage of space I would be temporarily sharing an office with Mr. Humphrey, and upon leading me to his spacious room on the second floor of the palace, and showing me to my desk, Mr. Humphrey disappeared into the private washroom en suite. Two minutes later he appeared in the office wearing nothing but his underwear, and then promptly settled himself comfortably into an armchair, replete with a huge mug of coffee, three bags of potato chips and a daily paper. I believe it was the Daily Express.

Quite unashamedly this Senior Official sat in his Buckingham Palace office with his unappetizing body proudly displayed to all. I would discover in time that this was his way. Every morning he would come in from his stables, undress in the washroom, spend an hour or so in his stained and torn underwear eating and making telephone calls, and then just before ten o'clock he would drag out a brown wrinkled suit which he kept on the floor of the closet.

A telephone call came in while I sat there listening and watching Mr. Humphrey gorge himself noisily on his supplies. My head was hurting again. After the twelfth ring he reached a fatty arm across his chair and gruffly picked up the telephone. "Hello?" he growled, diving simultaneously into a freshly opened packet of smoky bacon chips. It became evident early into the telephone call that the trail of footprints had been discovered, apparently by a passing footman or someone I could not for certain tell whom, and attempts were now being made to rectify what was considered by the caller to be a serious *faux pas* on the part of 'somebody' in the palace. That individual was rumored to be John Humphrey, Esquire. A serious telephone discussion was now hotly taking place.

"How do I know how they got there?" Humphrey declared defensively several times. "It's not my problem. Someone must have had dirty feet, heh heh heh!" But even Mr. Humphrey realized the gravity of the situation eventually, for the Department of Environment which handled all the maintenance within the palace had to be called in, and a senior government representative was already onto the matter. They explained to Mr. Humphrey that the damage to the White Drawing Room was being viewed as something of a catastrophe. It wasn't possible to get out a broom and pan and simply sweep it all up. There was serious damage done to some priceless rugs.

Having concluded with the contents of the last packet of chips, and as I have already said, clad only in his underwear, Mr. Humphrey stood up and angrily denied any responsibility for the mysterious footprints. "Look, Bill, I really can't help ya. If I hear anythin' I'll be sure and give ya a call. It's the best I can do." With that, he slammed the telephone down and scratched his crotch.

"Hmmmmm..." he said thoughtfully, "think it's time to change me undies." From the sight of them, it most certainly was.

Just then the door flung open and in marched an extremely haggard looking man who was even larger—much to my surprise—than Mr. Humphrey.

"Good mornin', Peter," Mr. Humphrey said congenially. "How are you doin' today?"

"Oh I do feel rough," the gigantic beast of a man growled in yet another cockney accent.

"I'm sorry to hear that," Mr. Humphrey replied sensing the shabby man's bad temper. "Did you have a rough night or somethin'?"

"No, I didn't have a rough night," he barked, looking anxiously around the room as though he had forgotten what he had come in for. "I haven't had any bloody Scotch yet, have I!" With that, he marched out of the office.

"Who was that?" I asked curiously. Surely it could not have been another Senior Official I thought.

"Oh, that's the Royal Chef, heh heh heh! He's off to the palace bar, heh heh heh!" he chuckled in his deep booming voice once more.

It was now nine thirty a.m.

At ten o'clock I met with Sir Peter Ashmore. Sir Peter was the Queen's Master of the Household and had been in charge of this crucial section of the palace since 1973. He was a member of a group of six or so who made up the Queen's closest advisers, very similar to the senior statesmen who surround the President of the United States. These individuals were known as Household and included, in addition to Sir Peter, men such as the Earl of Westmorland, Lord Maclean, Sir Rennie Maudsley and Sir Geoffrey DeBellaigue.

I belonged to the department called Officials who carried out the orders of Household. We were their aides and basically the engine room of Buckingham Palace, responsible for the needs of the Queen and the Royal Family in every conceivable way. Approximately eight Officials in my department supervised over 150 servants in the section known as Staff.

Now the pecking order of Staff was very important to them. There was a definite hierarchy and it was rigidly adhered to by everyone. If the Yeoman of the Silver Pantry, for example, in totalitarian charge of the four pubescent underbutlers, was not referred to as *Mister* Fletcher, then there would be cries of outrage and damnation throughout the palace that I cannot even begin to describe.

My actual duties were far too multifarious to list precisely, however they could range from the very smallest matter to the gravely important. An example of the former was the occasion shortly after I began when Her Majesty sampled a dish of what she thought were her favorite macadamia nuts. She discovered to her horror that they were not what she had wanted at all and subsequently sent them back.

"Please tell the gentleman in food branch that I do not want a macadamia nut from Australia!" the Queen declared greyly to her footman.

One soon learns in the Royal Household that only nuts from the Island of Hawaii will do!

This, quite obviously, is not earth shatteringly important, but at the other end of the spectrum I was one of only five men in the country to have security clearance to enter the Queen's personal apartments when she was not at home. This included the Earl of Westmorland, Lord Maclean, Sir Peter Ashmore, Mr. Michael Tims and myself. We were the only ones.

When warranted, I would be taken into the city in one of the Queen's fleet of ten Jaguars, each bearing the license plate 'B P' with numbers one through ten. Sometimes I would visit shops to choose new wall coverings which I thought Her Majesty might approve of, possibly calling in at Colefax and Fowlers near Claridges Hotel.

I remember one day I made a telephone call to a clothing shop we had not dealt with before and spoke to an assistant there, indicating that I wanted to order some goods and open an account. It was ordinarily a quick procedure and businesses were usually thrilled to be asked to supply Buckingham Palace, particularly when it included the possibility of a royal warrant should they remain with us for three years. When I attempted to open an account with this particular clothiers, however, I was told bluntly that they would do nothing for me unless they were provided with a bank reference first—a bank reference for the Queen of England! Needless to say, we looked elsewhere for our requirements.

One of my most demanding responsibilities was the Queen's footmen. They were always requiring some attention either with their schedules or their behavior problems (mostly the latter). The footmen also belonged to the section of the palace known as Staff. Lowest on the Staff ladder were the toilet cleaners, porters and housemaids. Towards the middle of the ladder were the pages, valets and footmen who performed everything from walking the Queen's six corgis to serving her meals, and attending to her laundry. At the top of the Staff infrastructure were long-serving men such as the Sergeant Footman, the Palace Steward and the Royal Chef. In between there were as many titles as jewels in the State Crown, with wonderfully ancient ringing names such as Yeoman of the Glass and China Pantry, The Queen's Dresser and The French Polisher.

There were receptions and banquets to attend, State visits and investitures, garden parties and audiences, as well as attending the countless other functions held at the palace every week. In addition, I would receive the daily agenda for the Queen and each member of the Royal Family. For example, if an ambassador was arriving for a meeting with Her Majesty, I would be there at the Grand Entrance to greet him before he was led to her.

2

I was beginning to feel familiar with the way the palace functioned when the Queen and Duke of Edinburgh returned from Norfolk in early February, and my life in the Queen's Court truly began. It was also around this time that I was at last able to find my office without having to embarrass myself asking for directions.

At half past ten one morning, shortly after the Queen and Duke were back in residence, the Royal Chef arrived outside Her Majesty's Audience Chamber where I was speaking with her Private Secretary, Sir Philip Moore. We were discussing some last minute preparations concerning the upcoming visit of the King of Norway, when we were abruptly interrupted.

"Mornin', mornin'," the Royal Chef grumbled irritably.

"You cannot go in there yet, Mr. Page. Her Majesty is not ready for you." Sir Philip looked tightly down his nose at the Royal Chef, and then cast his full attention back to me. The Royal Chef was not in a good temper.

Two minutes passed and then the Queen's secretary spoke to the Royal Chef. "You can go in now, Mr. Page," Sir Philip gestured ceremoniously. The Royal Chef rolled his eyes, opened the door to the Queen's Audience Chamber, and shut it with a slam. There was little love lost between the two, I sensed.

Inside, the Royal Chef took a seat in one of the golden silk-covered chairs next to the Queen. The pale green sitting-room where she met the Royal Chef every morning at this hour was bright and cheery and commanded lovely views onto Constitution Hill and Green Park. Here they discussed food requirements for the day as well as arrangements for important functions in the days ahead. Typically, their meeting might concern a luncheon with friends, a visit from one of the London ambassadors, or possibly a State banquet given in honor of an important leader, as was the case with the upcoming visit of the King of Norway.

The Queen is not forced to attend to such mundane matters, of course, but during her residence in the palace she has always taken a keen interest. As with other hostesses, Her Majesty takes an interest because she enjoys it immensely, possibly due to the fact that it is one of the few decisions within the palace she is allowed to make completely on her own. Unlike a vast majority of others around Her Majesty, the Royal Chef is not appointed by the government.

He was huge. There is simply no other way of putting it. At 6 feet 2 inches, a chest of 54 inches and a waist about the same, he weighed in at over 300 pounds. He towered over the Queen and everyone else in the palace, with the possible exception of Mr.

Humphrey who was but a fraction smaller. At the age of sixty the Royal Chef was mostly bald, with strokes of greyish black hair at the sides and back. Usually he could be spotted sporting the sloppiest of attire. And I mean the *sloppiest*!

His massive face was usually brilliant scarlet and layers of fat cascaded from his jaw. His stomach was also enormous. One could not call it a paunch. It was on a much larger scale than that. Perhaps a paunch times twenty would be more accurate. When he sat down he liked to unzip his fly to release some of the pressure exclaiming, "Oh, that's better" in the same gesture. Although he refrained from doing this in the presence of Her Majesty you could be certain that lurking beneath his white chef's coat, which he wore to see her every day, the situation was the same. He picked his nose in public, chain smoked and produced the most alarming belches. I often gasped at the thought of any mortal having to deal with this particular specimen, let alone the Queen of England!

In preparation for their meeting each morning, Her Majesty would always have a large Scotch awaiting the Royal Chef and a footman standing nearby would replenish his glass as the meeting necessitated. During the course of their twenty-minute discussion, the Royal Chef would typically down at least two stiff measures to aid his concentration, and in longer meetings as many as three or four might be required. Of course there were not always footmen running around to top up his glass throughout the day, so the Royal Chef carried a small flask in his hip pocket. Thus, wherever he happened to be in the palace he could be assured of a constant flow, and there was lots more in his kitchen if a topping up was in order. It was a rare day indeed when the smell of Scotch did not accompany the Royal Chef in his audience with the Queen.

Despite the Royal Chef's shortcomings, though, somehow he existed and was considered by the Queen to be one of her most valuable members of Staff. While I was at the palace, she always took him with her when traveling to foreign countries on tours or State visits. He prepared her meals when she was not required to attend State functions.

Her Majesty has definite likes and dislikes and when in a distant land she prefers to dine on what she is used to having at home. This policy also aids in preventing some of the nastier bugs which one is liable to pick up in certain parts of the world. Therefore, the Royal Chef is always at hand, and to give him credit, his skills in the kitchen would rival that of any five-star London hotel.

"Mr. Page?" the Queen's Private Secretary called sternly to the Royal Chef, as he left the Queen's chamber and again slammed the door shut behind him. "I have asked you several times to please close the Queen's door quietly."

The Royal Chef stopped in his tracks, scowled at Sir Philip, took a swig from his silver flask, and then stomped off without saying a word.

Sir Philip Moore became Private Secretary to the Queen in the late 1960s and was exactly what one would expect to find in someone considered to occupy the most important job in the palace. An aristocratic, well-bred and well-attired man in his early sixties, Sir Philip performed his duties to perfection. I would soon learn that he had that rare quality of zest combined with a flare for quiet efficiency. Exactly what was called for in a high-level job such as this.

Although the Queen could not have been happier with the way Sir Philip performed his duties, it was common knowledge within the palace that their relationship was purely a business one. Being appointed by the government, the position of Private Secretary is one of many close to the Monarch over which she has no control, and often the appointments are the total opposite of what Her Majesty wishes.

Sir Philip handled Her Majesty's affairs along with an assistant and an elderly lady who acted as his own secretary. His main responsibilities were organizing and managing the Queen's daily timetable, as well as handling all her private correspondence. The two worked very closely together. So exalted was his role that no one within the palace was permitted to see Her Majesty without his permission. The only member of the entire Royal Household who was exempt from this rule was the Queen's public relations man, Michael Shea.

Sir Philip entered the Queen's Audience Chamber and I headed back to my office. Along the Queen's corridor I proceeded, down the Minister's Staircase, through the Marble Hall, up the Grand Stairs, down the East Gallery and finally into the Master of the Household's corridor where my office was located. Dominated by red carpet and graceful teak cabinets this hallway led to eight other offices which made up the Master of the Household's department. It had taken me many weeks to find it easily.

3

Just before noon one morning near the beginning of March, the telephone rang in my south wing office, which I was still sharing with Mr. Humphrey. It was an urgent call from the Queen's policeman at the Grand Entrance. The King of Norway, I was informed, was wandering aimlessly around in the Grand Hall and would I please come immediately and see to him.

Apparently no one in the palace had remembered that the King was due to arrive that morning as a guest of the Queen. I quickly telephoned various departments to advise them of the situation, and then dashed through the Master of the Household's corridor and down the staircase where I found the King standing around under the piercing glare of the palace policeman, who was voraciously attacking a cheese sandwich.

The King, a dignified elderly man, was dressed in a dark, two-piece suit, sombre in profile and looking very much like a London businessman, except for that extra measure of rank and dignity befitting royal blood. He patiently tapped his finely-crafted wooden walking-stick on the red carpeted surface of the marble Grand Hall, pacing back and forth and somewhat bewildered, and perhaps, I thought, confused at the lack of attention his arrival had caused. After all, he was the King of Norway and one of the Queen of England's closest friends!

Swallowing my horror at this appalling oversight, I determined to ensure that he was not subjected to any further distress. I smiled with genuine pleasure and warmly welcomed His Majesty.

"If you will forgive the delay, sir, I'm afraid we have had a slight problem today in the palace. This doesn't usually happen. I hope you will accept my deepest apologies."

The King looked unruffled, bemused, even.

"That is quite alright," he stated regally, and then with a slight shrug, "I can find my own room if you like. I have been here enough times you know."

"That is very good of you, sir, but you won't have to do that. I will take you there myself. Again, I am dreadfully sorry about this."

The King followed me and was remarkably good-natured about the whole incident. That was a relief. However, it began to occur to me that he seemed almost amused. Perhaps it was only my imagination, and shrugging off my feelings of apprehension I hastily led him to the Queen's elevator, up to the second floor of the palace, through the Picture Gallery and Green Drawing Room and into his suite overlooking the palace gardens. On this occasion the King was staying in the Belgian Suite; a vast and exquisitely furnished apartment comprising three bedrooms, three dressing-rooms, two sitting-rooms, an audience room, five bathrooms and a swimming pool.

15

Little touches provided by the palace were all around, especially in the master bedroom where King Olaf would be staying. In his expansive marble bathroom he would find twelve crystal cologne bottles, each draped with a solid gold chain and tag describing the contents.

King Olaf walked over to the impressive ornate bed and placed his briefcase on it. Above it hung Peter Paul Rubens' *The Farm at Laeken* which was acquired by George IV in 1821. On the opposite wall, a Rembrandt Van Ryn signed in 1603.

His Majesty turned to me. "What is your name, young man?"

"Malcolm...Malcolm Barker, sir."

"Malcolm... Malcolm..." he thought deeply for a moment. "You are new here, are you not?"

"Yes, that is correct, sir."

"Well then, Malcolm, I shall remember to call you should the need arise."

"Yes, of course, sir, extension 273. You will find it next to your telephone." I turned to leave. "Once more, sir, I do apologise for the inconvenience."

"Oh please do not worry about that," he told me happily. "Last time I arrived here it took twice as long for someone to come and get me!"

The King had indeed been here before.

Ensuring that he was comfortably settled, I bade the King good day. Then I headed straight to the office of the Queen's Sergeant Footman to ascertain why he had failed to send someone to meet the King upon his arrival. This was tantamount to telling Prime Minister Thatcher when she arrived for her weekly meeting with the Queen that Her Majesty was not at home and would she please go away and come back later. It just was not done.

In his office, the Sergeant Footman explained to me that moments earlier both senior footmen he had assigned to assist the King had been discovered very drunk and fast asleep in their room, apparently seeming to take a liking to the same bed. As the seamy story unfolded, his lips trembled with fear. He was obviously aware that the incident was serious enough to cost him his job. Assuring me that this would not happen again, he gave me a gushing farewell and expressed the hope that this isolated occurrence might be forgiven.

"I will let it go this time, as it is apparent it was out of your control, but in future I expect you to make certain your lads are in position well before they are required. This cannot be allowed to happen again."

"Of course, Mr. Barker. You have my word."

I turned towards the door and added, "You had better hope the King doesn't mention this to the Queen. I won't be able to help you if he does, you know."

Fortunately for the Sergeant Footman, the King never did.

The entire palace was now fully immersed in the visit by the King of Norway. I was sitting at my desk which was piled high, as usual, with mountains of paperwork, my own, as well as an ever increasing proportion of my colleague's, Mr. Humphrey. Apart from the outside mail that arrived each morning and afternoon, there were four daily internal deliveries from Her Majesty's other principal residences in the United Kingdom. Mr. Humphrey was now unashamedly dumping all his mail on my desk as soon as it arrived and expecting me to deal with it for him. Letters incorrectly addressed to "Mr. John Humphrey, Crown Equerry," or "Mr. John Humphrey, Master of the Queen's Household," would be delivered with regularity, always to be passed off by him as "a fluke" or a "natural mistake." I was not so sure.

It was around this time that I decided to tactfully mention to Mr. Humphrey that my share of the workload seemed somewhat excessive compared to his own.

"John?" I approached the subject carefully. "Something funny seems to be going on here."

Mr. Humphrey looked up from his newspaper and bit into a McVities chocolate biscuit. "What do ya mean 'funny' Malcolm?"

"Well if I may be totally honest, I seem to be doing most of the work around here and it isn't much fun, I can tell you."

Chuckling he replied, "Ya, that's right... you do all the work and I have all the fun, heh heh heh," and he returned to his reading. I could see I would have to try another tactic.

The telephone on Humphrey's desk gave several short rings. I answered his line.

"Mr. Humphrey, please, Malcolm," came the familiar request from the voice at the other end.

"If that's for me, Malcolm, I'm out to lunch." Humphrey rushed out the door.

"I am afraid he's out to lunch, Mr. Tims," I reluctantly obliged.

"What do you mean 'out to lunch'? It's past two thirty." The line went dead. Tims was not falling for it this time.

Mr. Michael Tims, a tall wisp of a man in his late fifties, was Assistant Master of the Household and attempted to rule our department as though we were all junior accountants in the days of Charles Dickens. His tenure at the palace had not been the smoothest. Joining the Royal Household some thirty years earlier it was unlikely he would rise beyond his present level as assistant to Sir Peter Ashmore. Not only was he unpopular within the palace, he was also intensely disliked by the Queen herself, for the simple reason that she considered him arrogant and totally incompetent.

A few years before I arrived, Tims had suffered a nervous breakdown on the job, and had to take an extended leave of absence. After convalescing, he returned to the palace and although supposedly completely recovered, it often appeared as though he might have another breakdown at any moment. Much of his day was spent making telephone calls on behalf of the Christian Science organization of which he was a devoted member and an enthusiastic fund-raiser.

It was well known that one of the main causes of his harried mental state was my colleague, Mr. Humphrey. To be blunt, he was the bane of Tims' existence; for although Mr. Humphrey's file was chock full of official reprimands, warnings and black marks, due to his popularity with the Royal Family, nothing he did, no matter how serious a breach of rules, or even laws, would see him dismissed.

The situation was not helped by Mr. Humphrey constantly falling asleep in his meetings either. When his head dropped into a penetratingly deep coma Tims would snap him into consciousness with, "MISTER Humphrey! ARE YOU WITH US?"

"Oh...ya, ya, Mr. Tims. I'm with ya." Drowsily he would shake himself awake.

"Well, do you agree that we should regild the Queen's Ballroom at Windsor Castle, Mr. Humphrey?"

"Oh, *absolutely*, Mr. Tims, *absolutely*. Couldn't agree with you more on that. In fact, I've been lookin' into that very matter meself."

Tims' expression would chill the air to an uncomfortable temperature. In his opinion, Humphrey was the ruination of his life.

Consider, for instance, the frustration Tims must have encountered over the years when faced with a man who not only was well liked by Her Majesty, but was also equally unsuitable to serve her, in his eyes. Tims was therefore forever on the prowl, determined to catch him in the one act that was so horrendous the palace would have no choice but to relieve Mr. Humphrey of his duties on the spot. The only problem was Tims' moment of glory seemed always to be only just out of reach.

4

The King of Norway departed after four successful days.

I had just seen Princess Alexandra safely to her car following a casual luncheon with Her Majesty and Prince Charles. The Prince's idea of casual was a single-breasted suit. In our office, Mr. Humphrey was asleep in his chair while I busied myself rearranging some of the cluttered and confused files I had inherited on joining the palace. It was an ongoing project. In one cabinet I found several empty packets of chips, and in another, one of the largest and smelliest socks to which I have ever been so unfortunate to bear witness.

The door opened suddenly. The Assistant Master of the Household, Mr. Tims, gleefully bolted into the office to find Mr. Humphrey collapsed in his favorite armchair still fast asleep. All was lost. Surely even Mr. Humphrey would not be able to talk his way out of this one, I thought.

"Mr. Humphrey!" Tims barked angrily. "What are you doing in that chair?"

Humphrey bolted up immediately and looking around somewhat stunned said, "Oh oh oh...Mr. Tims, sir, what are you doin' here?"

"Mr. Humphrey, the question is what are you doing *there*?" Tims pointed an accusing finger to the red leather chair.

"Oh, um, actually, Mr. Tims, I was just takin' a break. I've been awfully busy here this afternoon. Been on the phone all day about that shipment of white shirts for the new footmen," Humphrey pleaded.

"Mr. Humphrey, I am not interested in shirts at this present time. I want to know exactly what you are doing in that red armchair you stole from the Queen's storeroom? It is only two thirty in the afternoon and you are fast asleep. Her Majesty does not pay you to sleep, Mr. Humphrey, she pays you to work. Why aren't you doing any?"

"Ugh…well ya see, Mr. Tims, like I just said…it's been very rough for me today and I just thought I'd take a few minutes to rest me weary eyes before I get on to that tailor shop again. I really can't understand why Her Majesty puts up with this lousy service, Mr. Tims. Do you know what's up with them lately?" Mr. Humphrey was hoping to change the subject.

"*Mister Humphrey.* You are not answering my question," Tims snapped now with teeth clenched. "I know that you were sleeping in that chair when you should be at your desk working, and nothing you say will sway me from that belief. You have only just come back from lunch. Now get to work and understand that I am going to note this incident in your file. In fact I think I had better see you in my office in five minutes." With that Tims slammed the door angrily and stormed off.

Thirty minutes later Mr. Humphrey appeared sheepishly through the door looking miserably dejected. I felt compelled to ask what had happened to make him so downcast. "John, you look terrible. What happened in there?"

"Oh, Tims gave me a real bollockin' and threatened me with the sack if I get another black mark," Humphrey said forlornly.

"That is terrible, John," I replied sympathetically. "You will have to watch yourself from now on."

"It's worse than that…" he bellowed remorsefully, appearing as though he may break into tears. "He told me I have to get rid of my chair!"

True to Tims' word, two porters appeared the following morning with instructions to remove Mr. Humphrey's chair forthwith. Mr. Humphrey was horrified and I must admit, I had to feel just a bit sorry for him. To Humphrey it must have been terribly humiliating and he was unusually quiet during the following few days. A close attachment between the two had obviously taken place over the years and he was having difficulty coping with the loss.

"I really miss that chair o' mine, Malcolm. It's just not fair. Bloody Tims!" he would moan several times a day. But one week later, while Tims was on another of his 'breaks' and Humphrey was put in charge of Her Majesty's Household, the armchair mysteriously appeared back in our office, where it stayed for ever more. When it came to having a snooze, there was no one with a better excuse for not doing any work than Mr. Humphrey. He was a master.

5

A call came in from Sir Peter Ashmore.

"Hello, Malcolm? Sir Peter here. Prince Andrew has just rung me and it seems he requires a safe for his apartment. I told him you would look after it for him."

"Yes of course, Sir Peter, I will attend to him right away," I replied willingly. It was always well advisable to be as obsequious as possible to the Queen's senior advisers! I left Humphrey adjusting a harness on his desk.

The Prince was indeed in need of a safe and after two weeks of investigation, measuring, and countless discussions, he finally decided upon the exact safe that he wanted. When it was delivered to the palace I dispatched two elderly porters and instructed them to place the safe in the Prince's apartment. I met them just outside the entrance of the Prince's suite. His apartment had recently been redecorated under his personal guidance, and the once elegant and stately rooms were now awash in a sea of purple, orange and green. It resembled more closely the residence of an opium-smoking hippy rather than the second eldest son of the Queen.

Prince Andrew arrived to inspect the safe more closely. All the time he was in his dressing room the porters were huffing and puffing, moaning and grunting their disapproval outside. They did not like the task I had asked them to perform at all.

"I wish ya had of told us like how heavy the bleedin' safe were, Mr. Barker," one of them said suddenly and very much out of breath. "There should 'a' been four of us to manage that ya know. I'm not puttin' my back out for some bloody snotty-nosed Prince!"

"Really Powers," I said disapprovingly. "You must watch your language in the presence of an Official, especially when it concerns a member of the Royal Family."

Prince Andrew called something from the bedroom. "No, no, I've changed my mind about this," the Prince muttered as he came out of his suite. "Malcolm, have them take it away for me will you. I don't think I want it after all."

"Oh...um...yes, of course, Your Highness. Would you like me to find you another one?"

"No...I can't be bothered with it now," he replied firmly. "Take it away!" And with that he marched briskly down the hall towards his sister's wing. So much for two weeks of work.

"Well, you heard him lads. You will have to remove that safe before the Prince returns," I informed them sternly.

Neither was impressed.

"The bloody ponce," Powers sniveled angrily, and all the way down the staircase and towards the storeroom they muttered and grumbled and complained of their harassed and troubled lives. Thankfully I was able to leave their most disagreeable company and pop into the Officials' dining room for a much-needed cup of coffee.

I did not see much of Prince Andrew during my first few months at the palace. Most of the time he was away at naval college and only returned on special occasions and holidays. When he was around, the Prince was extremely difficult to deal with. He threatened and bullied those who served him and laughed about it afterwards in the company of his friends. He was

23

not concerned at all about what anyone thought—not even his mother!

While still a bachelor, Prince Andrew brought different women into his palace apartment just about every night of the week. Parties and drinking sessions would last to the small hours of the morning, and more often than not, the lady he was entertaining would spend the entire night in his bedroom. The Prince had an extensive list of regular lady friends so there was never any shortage.

One of my first experiences of the Prince's behavior was the night he held a dinner party for twelve of his navy friends. As dinner progressed in the State Dining Room, the evening began to get out of hand. Prince Andrew started showing off by grabbing fistfuls of vegetables and throwing them at his pals seated around the table. Encouraged, they replied with more of the same. Then the Prince thought what fun it would be to see the footmen's reaction if he pelted them with his dinner. In the end, their livery was splattered from head to toe with potatoes, sauces and drink. The more they drank the rowdier Prince Andrew and his friends became, and by the end of dinner they were smashing beautiful wine glasses against the priceless canvases that graced the walls, making an absolute shambles of the entire dining-room.

Her Majesty was less than pleased when she was informed of her son's behavior and gave him a severe reprimand the following day. No change, however, was noted in the Prince's attitude.

Of all the Royal Family it was Prince Edward that I became closest to, and he would soon begin to call me personally when he wanted something accomplished. As one of the youngest Officials in the palace, I was somewhat closer in age to the young Prince, and I believe he felt it easier to approach me rather than some of my older and more institutionalised colleagues.

While passing through the red and gold East Gallery I came across a group of six porters attempting to remove a large painting from the wall. Apparently, Her Majesty had decided that this should be exchanged with another presently in storage. Spotting Ged Powers, the same porter who had been complaining to me earlier, I was naturally apprehensive and decided to supervise the proceedings.

The six men conversed amongst themselves regarding what best method they should employ, and then set about positioning themselves in what soon appeared to be the very worst comedy of errors. As they were about to remove this very sizeable and celebrated work from the wall, I noticed with alarm that Powers, who was also the oldest of the porters, was not very steady on his feet and his eyes were extremely glazed. Suddenly his grip on the painting slipped and although he attempted to grab it, the giant work went crashing to the floor with a horrifying thud.

All stood back in disbelief.

There, in the very centre of the canvas, was a hole the size of a cricket ball. The old porter had put his fist clear through! My ulcer gave a nasty twinge of pain as I realized with horror the magnitude of what had just happened. Not only was this particular work a favorite of the Queen, it was painted by a relatively well-known artist—Rembrandt—and was considered irreplacable!

The Queen was furious at the needless damage to the work of art. In his defense, the porter named Powers explained that he was emotionally distressed because his girlfriend with whom he had been living in the palace had left him. To recover from this traumatic incident in his life he was given six weeks leave of absence with full pay, believe it or not!

"Now Mr. Tims come along with me," the Queen commanded. "I want you to order me some new wall coverings for my suite. Sir Peter has informed me that the work should be concluded soon and I want to have this done quickly. We have all had just about enough noise and confusion since the renovations began several months ago."

"Yes, Ma'am," he purred sycophantically, nervously collecting up the books of material and color samples he had brought along for her to peruse, and then scurrying out the door after her. "I think you will find the colors I have already circled along the lines of what you are looking for, Ma'am."

"Yes, I'm sure I will," Her Majesty replied dryly. "I just want to be assured that you, Mr. Tims, know exactly what I want so that this mess can be cleaned up as swiftly as possible. Do you understand me?"

Mr. Tims was not having a good day. As they made their way down the Queen's corridor, towards where I was standing inspecting the plasterers recent efforts, I couldn't help but feel just a little sorry for him. Granted he was detested by just about everyone in the palace, but he had tried hard to make amends. Unfortunately, "trying" isn't good enough when you work for the Royal Family. Things have to be done right the first time, and as far as Her Majesty was concerned, Mr. Tims had long ago run out of second chances.

"Good morning, Malcolm," Her Majesty called pleasantly, and then more coldly to Tims, "Now, see that you get this down properly, Mr. Tims. I do not want any mistakes."

I stepped back while they discussed patterns and fabrics and when they were finished and Her Majesty had departed for the sanctuary of her apartment again, I drew a little nearer to Tims, who was busy making notations from one of the wall covering catalogues. He wasn't going to risk any errors this time.

Two weeks later a call came in from Sir Peter.

"Malcolm? Come up to my office at once and should you come across Mr. Tims perhaps you'd bring him along as well."

I headed out the door forthwith and met Tims outside in the Master of the Household's corridor. "Sir Peter wants to see us both immediately," I said urgently, leading him along with me as I spoke.

"Wonder what for?" he replied perplexed.

Once inside his naval-like office, a very agitated Sir Peter instructed us both to sit down.

"Now I do not know what has transpired between yourself, Mr. Tims, and Her Majesty, but I received a call from her a few moments ago and she wants to see you upstairs now. I suggest we all go there as I assume you were both involved in this decorating matter."

Upon arrival we were greeted by a very sour-faced Monarch.

"Mr. Tims," the Queen wailed, "just what is this paper doing on my walls?" She pointed angrily.

"Well, Ma'am, this is the wall covering that you requested I order a few weeks ago. Don't you like it?"

"Like it?" Her Majesty squeaked with frustration, in the manner that had earned her the palace nickname of 'Squeaky Liz.' "This is not what I wanted at all. You have got it all hopelessly wrong again, Mr. Tims!"

Tims went powder white pale. "No, Ma'am, I can assure you that I wrote down just as you wished. It was Malcolm who dealt with the wallpaper company. I'm afraid Malcolm that you have ordered an incorrect code." All eyes now turned towards me.

Flipping quickly through a file of receipts and orders I had brought along with me, I came up with the relevant document and compared it to the one Tims had asked me to order.

"No, I'm sorry Mr. Tims, but if you look here I have only ordered what you asked me to. This is your writing is it not?"

The Queen was fuming. "No, Mr. Tims, it is not Malcolm who is in error here, it is you! You again! It is this pattern that I wanted," she said pointing fiercely at the open book I was holding, "and now it is going to take another two weeks to have it shipped in. Thank you very much for your help, Mr. Tims, but I will now ask that Sir Peter take the matter in his own hands from this point."

Her Majesty stormed off in a heated rage.

Tims looked around the corridor meekly and then up at Sir Peter, whose glare was now embedded in him. Tims had done it to her again!

8

Shortly after this little episode, I received an invitation to dine with the Queen's Chaplain, Canon Anthony Caesar. It had been a particularly long afternoon and around four thirty I said good night to Humphrey, and moved towards the door.

"Where are you off to then, Malcolm?" Humphrey bellowed at me, receiver in hand.

"Oh, the Queen's Chaplain has invited me for dinner this evening so I'm going to knock off a little early. Awfully thoughtful of him, don't you think?"

"Very thoughtful, indeed I do. Very good then Malcolm. Enjoy yerself and I'll see ya tomorrow."

As I proceeded through the door I thought I detected some laughter after me. Couldn't be? What could possibly be so funny about having dinner with Canon Caesar? After all, he was sub-dean of the Chapels Royal and assistant to the Bishop of London. Nothing humorous in that, surely?

Arriving at St. James's Palace at seven o'clock that evening, I found Canon Caesar to be in excellent spirits...literally speaking.

"Oh, come in, gorgeous," the Canon gushed as he greeted me at the front door of his Friary Court apartment. "What's a hunk like you doing out in this miserable weather?" (Not quite what I had expected.)

We chatted for a time over drinks in his sumptuous residence and then spent a leisurely two hours enjoying dinner. We had naturally come to the topic of the Queen and Buckingham Palace, and the Canon began telling me some of his more memorable tales. Following the excellent cuisine which Canon Caesar had prepared himself, he decided it was time to adjourn to his sitting-room for after-dinner drinks. He smiled at me as he lowered the lights.

"Brandy, Malcolm?" he invited, placing a crystal decanter and two glasses on the elegant cocktail table.

"No thank you, Canon. I think I have perhaps had enough to drink this evening. I must be going shortly anyway as I have an early morning coming up tomorrow."

"No, no, you can't go now. We are having such a fun little talk, you and I." He poured out two stiff measures and handed me one.

"That is very kind of you, Reverend, but I will just have a sip of this. I really must say good night to you," I reiterated, glancing at my watch and noticing that it was well after the hour I had intended upon leaving.

"Now Malcolm. I am going to insist that you stay. Sleep here, if you like." He sat down next to me and topped off his glass.

"Again, that is most kind of you, Reverend, however I see it is already past my bedtime and I do want to be fresh in the morning." I moved up from the sofa and out towards the small cluttered cloakroom adjacent to his front door.

"Malcolm, come back!" he called pleadingly after me. "You cannot leave in your condition. You must stay here tonight!"

I was putting my scarf tightly around my neck in preparation for the biting cold outside. "No, Reverend, I assure you I am fine."

Suddenly he was behind me. "You cannot leave!!" he proclaimed and grabbed me around the waist and pushed me up against the closet wall. "I won't let you go!" With that he spun me around, and before I knew what was happening he planted the moistest kiss on my lips that I had to that date ever received.

"Really Reverend!" I exclaimed very much out of breath and still pinned firmly against the closet wall. "I want to go home now, and if you do not allow me to leave immediately I will have to break a window."

Canon Caesar reluctantly released his surprisingly firm grip and opened the door. Thankfully, I was able to depart.

The next morning with this encounter all too fresh in my memory (as well as the taste) Canon Caesar came hurriedly into my office, slamming the door shut behind him. Humphrey had telephoned earlier to say he was taking the day off.

"Malcolm," he began quickly, "I am so dreadfully sorry about last night. I have never done anything like that before and I feel very much ashamed. Will you ever forgive me?"

The Canon was dressed as the evening before, in a black clerical suit, and was really very youthful and charming with his short jet-black hair, but he possessed the most penetrating brown eyes. He appeared smaller then I remembered, about five feet six inches tall, and his veiny hands shook as he waited expectantly for my reply. He looked melancholy and truly regretful.

"Of course I will, Canon. These things do happen when one has had a little too much to drink. It's all forgotten." I hoped this would encourage him to leave.

"I hope you mean that, Malcolm. Will you come again for dinner sometime?" he asked hopefully, now sitting himself down on the corner of my desk and aiming his crotch directly towards me. I did not know it at the time but this was a habit of the Canon's, aiming his crotch that is, and for a chaplain he certainly wore the most restrictive of trousers.

"Yes, I'd be glad to. You really are a wonderful cook."

"Good...good..." he replied a little too quickly and then, "What about tonight?"

"Oh...tonight? I couldn't possibly —"

"Fine, then it is all settled. See you around eight o'clock." Then he was gone before I could protest any further.

I couldn't believe my own stupidity. Normally I would not have even contemplated another meeting with him but I was new and after all, he *was* the Queen's Chaplain. I don't know why it came as a surprise later that night when I found myself being embraced by Canon Caesar on his sitting-room sofa, however I vowed to accept future dinner invitations from the Queen's Chaplain with a little less enthusiasm.

At ten forty-five the next morning Humphrey came ambling into the office. "Enjoy yer dinner with the Reverend the other night then, Malcolm?" He smiled with enjoyment. "No need to say anythin'. You'll learn all about him in time. He's probably got a bit bored with jumpin' into bed with the footmen." The laughter he had been containing now broke free.

About an hour later I was returning from the Queen's apartment where I had been checking, as I did every day, on some important *objets d'art* in the Buhl cabinets. Here were kept some of the most valuable and finest pieces in Her Majesty's possession, many having been personally collected by Queen Mary.

"Oh there ya are, Malcolm. What do ya think of this?" Humphrey handed me a letter before I could even close the office door. It was addressed to a senior government attaché, commonly referred to in Britain as a government actuary. Mr. Humphrey was replying to a letter he had received from the gentleman concerning an umbrella he had left behind following a diplomatic reception hosted by the Queen. Humphrey's reply went as follows:

```
     Dear Go%ern ant Actuary -
  No luck so far. Will keep looking.
   Best wisges - John Humphrey
```

"John, you can't send that out like that," I told him bluntly.

"Why not?" he asked annoyed, giving the top of his head a vigorous scratch.

"I shouldn't have to tell you. Can't you see that it is not suitable? You haven't bothered to correct your spelling and it isn't even centred properly."

"Give it 'ere," he growled, grabbing the letter out of my hand. "He's only a bloody queer anyway." With that, the letter was sealed and firmly placed in the outgoing tray.

The following morning it was pouring with rain and as Humphrey arrived with his handsome black umbrella it struck me that I had never seen him with one before. Umbrellas were most definitely out of character for him.

"That's a nice brolly you've got there, John. I haven't noticed you with it before."

"'Course ya haven't," he chuckled. "It was turned into me by one of the footmen last week."

"John! That probably belongs to that government official who wrote to you. Don't you think you should give it back?"

"No, I bloody well don't," he said giving it a good shaking over my desk. "He shouldn't be so careless. I can just do with a brolly like this. Kind o' suits me don't ya think?"

The brolly was never returned despite numerous calls by the actuary's secretary impressing upon Mr. Humphrey how important it was. Even when she told him that it was a special gift from his mother who had recently passed away, Mr. Humphrey remained unmoved. "Oh well," he chuckled heartily after the call. "If his mother's dead then she won't know the difference anyway. Heh heh heh."

9

It was now approaching Easter and one morning a large box arrived at the palace from my mother in Yorkshire. I had a busy day ahead of me so I only had a moment to open it and inspect the lovely selection of Easter eggs inside. There were six huge Suchard of Switzerland dark-chocolate eggs, each measuring about six by nine inches, as well as a dozen other assorted small cream eggs which my mother knew to be a favorite. I put the box to one side and left the palace on business.

A painting had been lent by the Queen to the Tate Gallery for an exhibition. Whenever valuable pieces of art were borrowed, I had to see to it that they were returned in perfect condition to the appropriate royal residence.

When I arrived back at the palace about two hours later, I found, much to my distress, that the box containing my eggs had been violently ripped apart and the wrapping paper and cards strewn all over the office floor. I shuffled through the debris and wondered what on earth could possibly have happened. Of the original six large eggs I counted only four. The twelve little ones were reduced to six. Who could have done such a thing I gasped to myself? Then I spotted some of the wrapping paper sticking out of the waste basket next to Mr. Humphrey's desk. Near the bottom of it, on closer inspection, I found the remnants of the two missing big eggs. Surely even Mr. Humphrey couldn't have consumed both, I tried to rationalize. One would be ill after eating all that chocolate.

Humphrey returned a few minutes later.

"John? Do you know what happened to my Easter eggs? I've just come back and found some missing."

"Ya, 'course I do. I ate them, didn't I."

"John, they were a present from my mother. I wanted them for myself."

"What do you want with all them, Malcolm? You'll never get through the whole lot."

"That is not the point, John. They were mine to do with as I wished."

"I didn't eat them all, did I?"

33

"No, I see that, but there are eight missing...eight!"

"Oh? Didn't seem like that many."

"John, I have to tell you I am not very pleased. I know normally I am willing to have a good laugh at anything but I find nothing humorous in breaking into my private package, delivered by Her Majesty's mail no less, and then deliberately stealing the contents. Now I really am very cross."

I hurtfully packed up all the papers that had been so lovingly placed as protection around their valuable cargo—namely MY EASTER EGGS. What remained of them I placed under my desk. Realizing that nothing was to be gained from lamenting further over my dear mother's thoughtful present, I sat and buried my head in the mound of paperwork that was forever threatening to take over my desk.

Mr. Humphrey was aware that I was annoyed and began busily preparing himself a cup of coffee in the corner. A few short moments later, he was standing sheepishly in front of me with a look of deep deliberation on his face. I waited for the apology I felt certain was to come.

"Malcolm...?" he began pensively, "mind if I have another of those Easter eggs of yours?"

10

"Hello there, Freddie!" Mr Humphrey greeted the tiny big-bosomed woman who walked into our office without knocking. "What are you doin' here today?"

"I've come to persuade you to take me for a little lunch, love."

Humphrey beamed with delight. "Right-o then. I'll be with ya in a couple of secs."

"Hello, Freddie," I said to the character I had come to know so well in the preceding three months. Freddie walked over to me and held out a tiny hand. Her ample breasts jiggled with a life of their own, making up a little for her petite five-foot-two figure. With her overly made up face and tall imitation-leather boots I thought she resembled a hooker the first time I was introduced—a hooker who appeared not to be taking in too much business. However it soon became apparent that this was the mysterious Freddie I had heard Mr. Humphrey talking with so much on the telephone during my first few days at the palace, someone I had mistakenly assumed to be his wife.

"Come on then, my little red rose," Mr. Humphrey beckoned to her, pulling on his wrinkled coat, and they left for lunch hand in hand.

Many of you would be forgiven for thinking otherwise, but Freddie did not work in the Queen's Household. Her full name was Mrs. Freddie Gentle and she did not appear under any department on the palace payroll. No, Freddie was Humphrey's girlfriend, whom he had picked up at the MacDonald's on Regent Street one afternoon during an extended lunch—which all his luncheons were—and ever since that time she had taken on the task of doing an awful lot of Mr. Humphrey's work. (What little there was left.)

After a heavy lunch and a good roll in the back of his car in Battersea Park the two of them would appear back at the palace around three in the afternoon, at which point Humphrey would sit Freddie in front of the typewriter with instructions on what she was to accomplish for him that day. Then he would curl his bulky frame into his favorite armchair and promptly go to sleep.

There was quite a scene one afternoon when Tims unexpectedly appeared at the door to find Freddie sitting at Humphrey's desk , busy typing away and taking no notice of the man staring at her in utter disbelief.

"Hhhhhhm!!" Tims quietly cleared his throat expecting to attract her attention away from the typewriter.

No result.

"Hhhhhhhhm!! Hhhhhhhhhm!!" quite a bit louder.

Still no result.

And then, "Excuse me, madam!" in a highly stern and snotty tone.

"Ya? What ya want?" she replied still typing without looking up.

"Well, madam, I would first of all like to be appraised of exactly what you are doing in this office."

"I'm typin', ain't I," she whined, bursting a bubble of bright pink chewing-gum in the process.

"Look here, Madam, you know to what I am referring. Why are you typing here in this office? You don't belong here, do you?"

"I'm doin' some work for Mr. Humphrey, ain't I, and if ya don't stop botherin' me, like, I'm never goin' to finish?"

Tims turned a deep, dark purple and then spotted Humphrey snoozing in his chair. "Mr. Humphrey!" he spoke loudly down at the blissfully sleeping body sprawled luxuriously half way to the floor, "Wake up! Wake up!"

Humphrey bolted to his feet, straightening his hair at the same time, chortling, "Oh oh oh, Mr. Tims, sir, what are you doin' here?"

"Mr. Humphrey, the question is what is this woman doing *there*?" Tims pointed a manicured finger at the desk. "She is not an employee of the palace. She should not even be on the premises!" Tims was in utter astonishment.

"Oh, well, ya see Mr. Tims," Mr. Humphrey began earnestly, "this is my girlfriend, Freddie. She's been helpin' me out with me work."

"I can see that, Mr. Humphrey, but this is *your* work and I expect to see *you* sitting at this desk when I come into the room, not a strange woman! We can't let people off the street simply come into the palace and start routing through our desks. There is sensitive and confidential material here. She is to leave immediately and I think I had better see you in my office...now."

Mr. Humphrey had not fully awakened and was having some difficulty in comprehending what was happening. Tims added before leaving, "I am certain Mrs. Humphrey would find it interesting to learn that you now have a *girlfriend* helping you out at the palace."

Freddie, obviously unaware of Mr. Humphrey's marital status, was finally distracted from her typing. "Hey you!" she shouted angrily, grabbing Humphrey's stained yellow tie and pulling him tightly down to her face, "What does he mean by *Mrs.* Humphrey then, ehhhh?"

WINDSOR CASTLE

April 16th - May 15th

1

President Reagan was grinning from ear to ear as he waited for his wife, Nancy, to step out of the helicopter which had just landed in the palace gardens. Although the Queen and the Duke had departed for Windsor Castle the day before, and would in fact be holding a state banquet for the Reagans there, it is traditional to welcome a visiting Head of State at Buckingham Palace first. On this occasion, I had been asked to perform the official welcome on behalf of the Queen. I stepped forward to greet them as the American President and the First Lady cleared the whirling blades of the helicopter.

"Good day Mr. President...Mrs. President...I mean Mrs. Reagan." (Oh God, how did that come out? I mentally chastised myself.) "On behalf of the Queen, I would like to welcome you to Buckingham Palace."

I shook hands with President Reagan and his wife. Then, Mr. Reagan, turning around to look back at the helicopter which was now lifting off the ground, said, "This is sure the biggest landing pad I've ever seen. Ha ha ha!"

No one laughed. Not even Nancy.

As I reclined in the rear of the silver Jaguar bearing the license plate 'B P 3,' I leafed through the program of the two-day State visit at Windsor Castle. Windsor is Her Majesty's favorite home and she is always most relieved to leave her London residence which she and her husband regard as their office. However, State visits are not the only occasion when Her Majesty makes use of Windsor Castle. Every Friday afternoon at about two o'clock the Queen's number one Rolls Royce departs the palace gates en route for a peaceful weekend there. The trip takes approximately thirty minutes, and I would be arriving shortly at the castle myself.

It was unusual to hold these important visits by political leaders or reigning royalty anywhere but Buckingham Palace, but as Her Majesty and the American President had such similar interests, namely horses, it seemed a logical choice to invite the Reagans there on this occasion. In actual fact, it is the greatest of honors to be asked anywhere but Buckingham Palace and certainly Windsor was more appropriate than the time Queen Beatrix of the Netherlands came to stay. She had insisted on giving the Queen a banquet at Hampton Court—one of the Queen's very own homes! This was not standard practice and naturally the Queen thought the request rather odd, but one does not want to offend a royal associate. When Queen Beatrix arrived from the Netherlands she brought over one hundred servants with her and then set up house in Hampton Court as she had requested. Her Majesty (the British one) was not impressed. Royal protocol, however, essentially forbade her from saying anything to the foreign Queen, and she put up with the strange arrangement to the very end.

The Queen, the Duke, Lord Maclean and Sir Peter Ashmore were in place at the castle to greet the Reagans. Having arrived, the traditional shaking of hands took place, but Nancy wouldn't curtsy, and then a few moments were alloted for press photography. This concluded, the party turned to enter the castle. Now, normally at this particular point it is the Head of State who walks in front with the Queen, while the spouse follows behind them with the Duke. However, on this occasion Nancy pushed ahead of her husband, took a firm hold on Prince Philip's arm and proceeded to walk him into the castle, ahead of the Monarch! A highly bewildered and annoyed Queen obliged, no doubt to keep any embarrassment for Mr. Reagan to a minimum. Her Majesty and the President were forced to walk several paces behind Nancy and the Duke!

Later on, when the Queen and her husband were alone, Her Majesty was heard to remark to her husband, "That woman! Who on earth does she think she is?"

3

Later that afternoon I picked up the telephone receiver in my Windsor Castle office. "Yes, hello?"

"Mr. Barker?" came the concerned voice of the castle operator. "I'm afraid there seems to have been a bit of an accident."

"What sort of accident?" I asked with alarm.

"A motorist has just called in from a pay phone to say that a few moments ago she came across a car in the river."

"Well, what does that have to do with us? Tell her to call the police."

"Yes, well, she says that she has already done that and they told her to call the castle."

"Why would they do that?" I was naturally baffled.

"Because when they stopped to see if they could lend a hand the gentleman inside the car told them that he was the Crown Equerry. I think it is Sir John Miller, Mr. Barker!"

Indeed it was.

Sir John Miller presided over the Royal Mews which is situated behind Buckingham Palace. Although the Mews is considered part of the palace, it is in reality almost a little village unto itself. It houses Her Majesty's fleet of Rolls Royces and Jaguars, her vast collection of Hanover Grey and Cleveland Bay horses, all the royal carriages, and the hundreds of other vehicles in her possession.

When I began service to the Queen, Sir John had been part of royal life for more than three decades and was approaching retirement. In addition to running the Royal Mews he was also Crown Equerry to the Queen, which meant that he was one of her most senior advisers. In his early seventies, Sir John was a graceful man. Slim and blessed with plenty of snow white hair and a moustache to match, he was as aristocratic as they come. The Crown Equerry, as he liked to be referred to, possessed twinkling blue eyes and an ability to dress immaculately. Like certain members of the Royal Family, he was also noticeably bowlegged caused by his enthusiasm for riding.

The Crown Equerry was one of many close to the Queen who was living in another era; an age where if you were a member of Household at Buckingham Palace everything was done for you, including the driving! As a result of this, Sir John was prone to allowing his mind to wander when he was out in his Jaguar, when his attention ought to have been cast fully in the direction of the road and the steering wheel. This was no doubt the cause of his little mishap today.

I dispatched a crew of men from the castle, and when they appeared on the scene of the accident, they found Sir John sitting calmly in his car, precariously situated roughly half in and half out of the Thames river. It seemed that when Sir John should have been turning right at a sharp bend his mind was heading in a straight line. "Oh blast!" Sir John said to the police officer and the castle crew. "It appears as though I'm in a spot of bother."

"Well, what happened sir?" The policeman looked perplexed.

"How on earth should I know, man? Nothing to do with me. Ask the car. It landed me here!"

Sir John left his automobile to be attended to by the castle crew, the policeman, and the local towing service. Another Jaguar which I dispatched from the castle brought the Crown Equerry back.

"Have that car seen to, young man," Sir John sternly ordered to the driver. "Tell them to fix it. It isn't working properly."

"What shall I say is the problem, sir?"

"What's that you say?" Sir John's mind was wandering again.

"What shall I say is wrong with your car, sir?"

"Well I don't know, for God's sake, man. If I knew that I wouldn't have ended up in the water now, would I?"

Sir John's troubles were not over. Later on in the day his male secretary heard a cry for help while sitting at his desk outside the Crown Equerry's office. Rushing in, he discovered Sir John struggling with a painting that had fallen off the wall and landed on him. The secretary ran over and helped him remove the heavily framed piece of art that was lying on his back and pinning him to his desk.

"Oooooh..." Sir John cried dramatically. "Get this thing off me please! Ooooh...Ooooh...I don't like this at all. Oh please, please, someone help me!"

Sir John was not having the best of days and it took many hours, several hot water bottles and a visit from the Queen's physician to help him get over his fright.

4

Another senior member of the Queen's Household, Lt. Colonel Blair Stewart Wilson, arrived at Windsor Castle for the State banquet. The Colonel, Deputy Master of the Household, walked into the Queen's elevator in the main entrance of the castle. The ancient iron gates slowly slid across and then the cage began its steep climb. The Colonel was going to the second floor of the castle. The elevator stopped shortly before. Confused, he waited for thirty seconds, and then when no sign of movement was in evidence he began pushing the buttons. Any buttons. Still it would not budge.

Two or three minutes elapsed and when it became apparent to the Colonel that he was trapped, he hesitantly, if not a little reluctantly, called down to the deserted lobby below. "Hello...Hello...Is there anyone down there? I need some help!...Hello...I want to come out of here...Oh blast! What am I going to do now?"

A few minutes later I was passing through the lobby and heard the Colonel's cries. Unfortunately it took two hours to find the only man who could service the special elevator and another three quarters of an hour to get the Colonel out. Colonel Stewart Wilson moaned with grand drama the whole time, and even after his release he was heard to remark as he disappeared up the stairwell, "What is going on? I just don't understand this modern world." The man was totally baffled. He had not wanted to use the wretched contraption in the first place.

5

The following morning the Queen went riding with President Reagan while the Duke, in the company of Nancy, went driving in Windsor Great Park. He would be showing her the four-in-hand horse carriage which he would be using in the upcoming Royal Windsor Horse Show.

The Queen waited patiently atop her horse in the courtyard, while President Reagan chatted neverendingly it seemed with the press. Hordes of photographers and reporters had literally set up camp outside in the castle grounds days before the President had even arrived. Now that he had, the noise and confusion was much worse.

Her Majesty was still waiting for President Reagan to stop talking. She was not pleased at all with the way the Americans had taken over her castle. She had agreed that security could be stepped up while the Reagans were in residence, but she had no idea it was going to be quite this intolerable. Secret Servicemen were scattered throughout the castle, taking all the spare rooms (even some of the Staff's), carrying out bugging tests at irregular intervals throughout the day and placing an extraordinary burden on all who worked there. But the aides and security team that accompanied the President did not care. They were obnoxious and unruly to Staff, especially to the footmen and maids, and as an added burden to all went to the lengths of having hundreds of additional telephone lines installed prior to their arrival. As one White House aide said to the Queen, "The President has to be in touch with every movement back home." Every movement perhaps; but this was more along the lines of every pulse.

There the Queen sat, outside Windsor Castle, waiting. No indeed she was not happy. She had not come out to talk with reporters; she had come out with the explicit purpose of going riding, and the latter was exactly what she intended to do. Lips pursed into a tight little circle, she pulled at the reins and headed her horse off in the other direction. Her patience was gone.

President Reagan was not aware, apparently, that one simply does not put the Monarch on hold while one attends to something else. One has to remember that she *is* the Queen.

In all Her Majesty's years as the head of the Windsor Household, I am certain she has never met anyone quite like Ronald Reagan. Although she obviously had a soft spot for him, he was definitely quite a departure from other world leaders she has entertained.

Mr. Reagan suddenly sensed that something was wrong and decided, at last, to cut off the banter. Apprehensively he sauntered after her, grinning ridiculously at the Queen when he finally caught up.

Meanwhile, Nancy was looking very uncomfortable in the Duke's carriage as he drove her around and around and around, explaining in depth about the carriage driving competition in which he would be taking part on the following day. Poor Nancy had not even heard of the damn sport before and she wasn't finding it terribly fascinating. Of course, not many outside of England would.

6

The beginning of May features an important date in the royal diary: the annual Royal Windsor Horse Show, staged in Windsor Home Park. A three-day extravaganza, visitors to this equine 'not to be missed' event flock to indulge their tastes for such thrilling competitions as the National Carriage Driving and Gymkhana Championships. Competitors in these pulsating events invariably include such sporting giants as the Duke, Sir John Miller, and Mr. John Humphrey. It is therefore always advisable to arrive early to avoid the disappointment of being caught up in the stampede for a ringside seat.

There is far more to the Royal Windsor Horse Show, however. It is a major social gathering for many members of the Royal Family and their Household, and is always eagerly awaited. Sadly, though, Windsor is not the best location on the planet for fine weather at the beginning of May, and the action-packed horse show is frequently disrupted and rescheduled by rain.

This does not deter the majority, however, and invariably the liquid refreshments marquee in the royal enclosure will be patronised by many stalwart members of Household and Officials, with their unquenchable thirsts. The less fortunate in the public enclosures must content themselves with warm beer in plastic cups and limp, tasteless ham sandwiches, or wander around the vast collection of private stalls offering such tempting merchandise as garden furniture, teddy bears and candyfloss.

I was in attendance this year in an off-duty capacity, and relishing the entertainment.

Never having been victorious before in the carriage driving championships, Mr. Humphrey decided to make an extra push for glory and the much-coveted first prize. In the six months prior to the competition, Mr. Humphrey spent much of his valuable recreation time building a new and improved carriage. Great care and attention were lavished on its construction as this dedicated horseman devoted hundreds of hours of his own time, as well as the Queen's, to the completion of his ambitious project.

Two weeks before the event his task was complete, and he was delighted with the result. He built an obstacle course in Windsor Great Park and took his team of Windsor Grey horses round it twice each day. Finally, he declared to all that he was satisfied with his preparation, and in the palace office there was a ring of confidence around his armchair as he slept off all his exertions. I was impressed; such self-assurance could not be dismissed lightly.

I began to look forward to the championships, for the Duke of Edinburgh had a new team of Cleveland Bay horses, and Sir John Miller was coming out of carriage driving retirement for the event.

The day of the competition was damp and windy, but I took my seat in the royal enclosure early, having just witnessed the unfortunate Duchess of Grafton, the Queen's Mistress of the Robes, being splashed with muddy water, as a rather over-zealous competitor drove his carriage through a large puddle close to her. The Duchess's response was not one of total apprecia-tion, and she stormed out of the Home Park, reducing the Queen's entourage by one. Someone in the royal enclosure shouted after her, "Serve the stuck up old granny right!"

Upon consulting my program, I was happy to note that carriage driving was one of the first scheduled competitions and due to start at eleven-thirty following the current riveting event called the dressage. I stifled a yawn and looked across to the royal box where the Queen seemed to share my opinion of the spectacle, preferring to converse with Lord Porchester, her racing manager, doubtless in the hope that he would be in a position to assure her there would be some potential winners in the stable for next month's Royal Ascot race meeting.

Beyond the Queen were Prince Edward, reading a book, and Princess Margaret eyeing the large cocktail which was being placed beside her. "Good idea," I said to my companion and headed for the bar.

I didn't spend long over my drink, hearing an announcement that the carriage driving event was imminent. Now surely, I thought, the apathetic atmosphere would evaporate as the multi-tudes grew tense in anticipation of their favorite cosmic mega-stars performing their incomparable skills.

The first two aspirants set a good standard to follow, dextrously weaving their four horses and carriage in and out of the closely grouped poles, splashing successfully through the three-feet-deep water stretch, and then going on to cope with the cross-country section, consisting of rough terrain, awkward hil-locks and finally a tricky wooded area. The latter is a difficult section of the course, and many a fine horseman has come to grief trying to cut too fine a corner around the thick trees with their exposed bony roots.

Next to appear in the carriage driving event was the first of 'the big three,' Sir John Miller. This septuagenarian had retired from the sport ten years ago, but clearly had decided that his many adoring fans deserved one more chance to revel in his redoubtable abilities. Would the old master still have what it takes? Would advancing years take their toll? Had he recovered sufficiently from his back injury a few days earlier? Certainly he had selected for himself some of the finest horses in the Royal Mews to aid his prospects, and for further assistance in realizing his goal, some generous measures of his favorite whisky.

When he appeared I was disappointed that his arrival in the arena failed to inspire an adulatory greeting, but I put this down to tension. Indeed, with her hands clasped together, the Queen seemed to be praying for divine assistance as the venerable gentleman somewhat shakily maneuvered his vehicle towards the starting line, grinning amiably at the royal box.

Sir John got off to a bad start. As he tried to weave his team through the first set of poles, he dropped the right hand rein, resulting in the two pairs of horses trying to move in opposite directions. Three poles went down and, fighting to regain control, he lurched forward and demolished another four poles, losing his silk top hat in the process. A groan from the crowd did nothing to help him, and he turned and brandished his whip angrily at his groom who was standing behind him on the carriage footplate.

Emerging from the pole obstacle, however, Sir John's team were able to reform and thus enjoyed two hundred metres of ponderous but safe progress on approach to the water stretch. The next few minutes would dictate his retirement from carriage driving. His carriage raced towards the water, horses and carriage plunged in, and then abruptly stopped! No amount of cajoling would encourage his stubborn foursome to move. The old maestro, spluttering hoarsely with humiliation and rage, stumbled from his carriage seat only just avoiding an unwelcome soaking in the ditch. He shook a frustrated fist at both groom and horses yelling, "What the deuce is going on you stupid fools? I am going back to the castle. Clear this lot up at once, do you hear me?"

With that somewhat inconciliatory statement, Sir John hobbled from the arena and headed for the haven of his comfortable castle rooms. Groom, horses and carriage humbly retreated to lesser surroundings.

There was, of course, considerable sympathy for the aged knight's misfortunes, but there were still more débâcles to come. Four more teams performed with varying degrees of success and mediocrity before the adjournment for lunch.

The talk in the bar and luncheon rooms was very much centred around Sir John's undignified withdrawal. "Damn fool for trying again," was the acerbic observation from the Earl of Montgomery, while waiting impatiently to be served some lunch. "Wouldn't know a horse's head from its arse," was the more agricultural comment from Royal Mews head coachman Arthur Showell, fortified by several pints of extra strength ale.

I wandered out of the royal enclosure, past the swarms of bedraggled spectators attempting to enjoy their picnics on the sodden grass, and headed for the paddock, where the afternoon's drivers were carefully making final adjustments to harnessing, reins and saddles. I had a purpose for being there: the first team to start in the second half of the carriage driving championships was that of my eminent palace colleague, Mr. Humphrey, that paragon of all things non-work orientated. I found him easily enough, clad in a voluminous overcoat, faded breeches and boots. The gentleman's attire was completed by an undersized top hat perched precariously atop his head.

"I just came to wish you good luck, John," I called.

"Luck?" he replied brazenly. "I don't need luck ya silly bugger. Just watch! There'll be no contest."

"I'll be watching you all the way round," I answered him loyally, trying to banish the nagging apprehension inside. Surely the body of his carriage was made of plywood, I thought to myself? And were not the rear wheels rather on the small side? Time would tell…

In pure Hollywood style, a loud thunderclap followed by streaks of lightning provided the fanfare as Mr. Humphrey's ample form balanced on top of the carriage swept into the arena and shuddered to a halt in front of the royal box. He dipped his hat to an amused Queen, and then trundled off to the starting line. The glares of Sir Peter and Tims burnt into his back.

More by luck than skilled judgement, the team managed to come through the pole section with only two down—one of the best starts of the day. Could the man keep it up? The hushed crowds waited with bated breath.

I looked along the front row and saw his mistress of the moment, Mrs. Freddie Gentle, take a long, large drink of amber liquid. Clearly she was feeling the tension too.

Mr. Humphrey now appeared to be in trouble. He was having difficulty lining up his team for the water stretch. One of his horses had had enough, and was trying to rear-up on its hind quarters. A loud crack of the whip, followed by "Get on with yer" from their master, was the chosen discipline. In contrast to Sir John's team, Mr. Humphrey's trotted sedately towards the water stretch, ignoring all impassioned bellows to the contrary. This was serious, as slow times would be penalised.

The actual progress through the water made matters worse, as the horses, clearly finding the weather too humid, decided to quench their thirst. More embarrassing, as they imbibed at the front, they relieved themselves at the back. Laughter drifted from the spectators' terrace. Then, catching Mr. Humphrey unawares, all four horses charged out of the water, causing the groom, Mr. Humphrey's son, to fall off the carriage and collide with an elderly judge who had to be stretchered out of the arena in shock.

Having come to a stop, which meant more time faults, Mr. Humphrey was able to reform his team, but his fortunes slipped from disastrous to impossible. His horses were now frightened, his groom stunned, and as they headed for the first hillock on the cross-country section, a forecast of doom seemed quite the most sensible. Three quarters of the way up, the Windsor Greys had finally had enough. They baulked, faultered, and the combined weight of carriage, groom and, more especially, Mr. Humphrey, dragged them back down the slope. The carriage reached the bottom with a loud "CRACK" — and to gasps from the spectators the structure split in two with the distinguished horseman falling through the centre.

The horses were terrified. Mr. Humphrey was still holding the reins as they charged forward, churning their hooves in the sodden turf and dragging the broken wreck of a carriage with them. His son ran around to the front and stoically managed to grab the leading pair of horses and halt them.

Partial order was restored. As concerned members of the Royal Family and the Royal Household looked on, several spectators rushed up to help. The fallen idol stiffly rolled out from beneath the debris, gingerly easing his arthritic tree trunk legs into a vertical position. In a similar manner to Sir John, he shook an angry fist above his mud-splattered body, bellowing, "Sod this bloody lark… Ya can keep yer rotten horse show. It's all a poof's piss-up anyway!" Her Majesty and those who were within hearing felt for the man. But wasn't that one of her very own mares out there in Mr. Humphrey's team, the Queen thought suddenly? Couldn't be. No, surely she was mistaken?

The spectators gave Mr. Humphrey a sympathetic reception, but the mood in the royal enclosure was very different. I had been unable to witness the scene without a considerable degree of mirth, but this was soon drowned by the raucous shrieks of amusement from several palace Officials present: "Great entertainment!" and "Lose some weight!" echoed around the stands, attracting disapproving glares from the Queen and Princess Anne. Prince Edward was still involved in his book. Princess Margaret was being handed a fresh drink.

True to form Mr. Humphrey did derive some pleasure from the weekend after all, as Their Majesties the Queen and Queen Mother decided to pay a visit to his stables the next morning, to commiserate with him on the tragedy. The man was never down for long.

The final hopeful in the competition was the Duke of Edinburgh. On paper he had an excellent chance, having won the event before, and the best score so far was no better than acceptable. But with such uncertain weather conditions who could tell what might happen? Would the Duke be able to provide us with an exhibition of brilliant world-class carriage driving?

Well, on the obstacle course the Duke sent the poles flying, and then he overran and went out of bounds, for more time faults. One consolation for him was a flawless approach and procession through the water stretch, but he was clearly in a bad temper. Flicking his whip impatiently and sending baleful looks up to the rain-filled skies the carriage rattled and bumped across the saturated cross-country terrain, knocking down markers with alarming regularity. But he was determined to extricate his rug, which had fallen from his lap and become tangled in a carriage wheel. When his right wheel stuck in a rut behind a tree it seemed he would finally concede defeat, however he was miraculously able to deal with that and managed to complete the course to rapturous applause.

As the commentator announced the scores over the loudspeaker, the Queen studied her program closely, making the calculations for the day. How did her husband place in the National Carriage Driving Competition this year? Well as far as she could tell, the Duke finished last!

On the final evening of the State visit of President Reagan and 'Queen' Nancy, Her Majesty and the Duke gave a banquet in their honor. It was held in St. George's Hall, a magnificent Gothic-style structure regularly used for ceremonial functions. Dating back to the reign of King Edward II, it was an ideal setting for such a grand occasion.

Mr. Humphrey and I were attending the banquet in a supervisory capacity, checking to see that the state apartments were in order and that the Staff were behaving. The banquet was being televised by the BBC so there should be no question of repeating a performance of a previous embarrassing incident during one such event. This occurred at the banquet for the King of Nepal where a number of porters and cleaners created such a disturbance while the Queen was raising a welcoming toast that they had to be forcibly subdued.

As the Reagan banquet was getting under way, Mr. Humphrey stomped rapidly round the banqueting rooms, ensuring that all the Queen's senior advisers, such as Lord Maclean and Sir Peter Ashmore, realised that he was amongst those present. Then he announced, "Right then Malcolm. I'm off home for a few hours snoozin' time. I'll be back later, but if Tims or anyone else wants me, say I'm in the castle somewhere checkin' up on Staff."

"Alright then, John," I acknowledged. I knew I would be far better off without the man anyway. Conveniently his home was only a few minutes drive from the castle, and Humphrey would never miss a golden opportunity like this to sneak off.

Shortly afterwards, Tims came up to me and asked if I had any idea where Mr. Humphrey was. I replied as requested and went off to keep an eye on the Pages who were setting up drinks in the Grand Reception Room.

Just before the royal party was due to proceed into St. George's Hall to join the guests for dinner, Tims tackled me again. "Have you seen Mr. Humphrey yet?"

"I am afraid not."

"Dear me. This is intolerable. He has a duty to be here, not wandering round the castle." He gave me a slightly suspicious glance. I just shook my head.

The banquet was a great success. The Queen and her 170 guests enjoyed superb food skillfully prepared by the Royal Chef who, unlike some previous occasions, managed to get through the evening without letting inebriation affect his performance. Throughout the evening Tims repeatedly asked me for Mr. Humphrey's whereabouts, and I was able to say, quite truthfully, that I did not know...exactly.

As after-dinner speeches were about to begin, Tims caught up with me again. "Malcolm, it's perfectly obvious that Mr. Humphrey has chosen to be elsewhere on this very important evening and I shall make further investigations in the morning. I might add that this reflects very badly on the department."

The Queen began her speech, immediately stressing Anglo-American ties and friendship. Then one of the BBC cameras on this live broadcast zoomed in for a close up on Her Majesty. There, standing directly behind her chair in full state livery was the Palace Steward, Cyril Dickman, leaning on the back of Her Majesty's chair, swaying unevenly, eyes glazed, his face matching the color of the red wine on the table. He also decided at that moment to treat the audience, estimated in the millions, to an exhibition of how to pick one's nose in public.

As soon as the speeches were over, the banquet came to an end. The royal party departed for liqueurs and coffee, and guests began to leave. Tims' face was almost the color of Cyril Dickman's, but through sheer rage, not intoxication. Suddenly out of the darkness a corpulent figure strode up the Grand Staircase and tapped Tims on the shoulder. "Oh, so there ya are,

Mr. Tims. I've been searchin' for ya all evenin'. Where have ya been?"

Tims spluttered with convulsed anger, "What do you mean, Mr. Humphrey, where have I been? I have been here doing my job. Where have *you* been? That is the question!"

"What do ya mean Mr. Tims? I've been everywhere checkin' that the Staff have been doin' their part properly. Ya know how careful you've got to be with them. I thought the whole evenin' went very well, didn't you?"

Tims seethed inwardly. "In future, Mr. Humphrey, I want you spending more of your time around here where everything is happening, instead of drifting off to remote parts of the castle."

"OK then, Mr. Tims. I'm tired and hungry now so I'm just goin' for a sandwich in the dining-room and then I'm off home. Cheerio!"

Tims' cold, beady eyes flashed with hate. Oh that Mr. Humphrey could be so infuriating!

The following morning the Queen and the Duke bade farewell to President Reagan and Nancy in front of the castle. They were leaving for London where Airforce One was waiting to take them back to the United States.

"Bye Mr. Reagan. Thanks for everythin'. Silly old fart!"

Now who could that have been yelling from a castle window, we all wondered?

BUCKINGHAM PALACE

May 16th - June 12th

1

Shortly after arriving back at Buckingham Palace I received a letter from a lady who was extremely upset over an incident involving some of the palace staff. She had been traveling from Windsor to Waterloo on the same British Rail train as two of Her Majesty's personal footmen. Prior to arriving at the station, the footmen had been partaking of refreshments in a Windsor pub, and by the time they were ready to board the train, they were already becoming quite inebriated.

Once the train departed, the two footmen soon became rowdy and aggressive in a manner that was quite unbecoming to young men in their position. On the way back from the bar, at the rear of the far reaching train, they started harassing and taunting a young girl who was quietly waiting to use the washroom. She attempted to brush off their attention but they were relentless. When she would not give in, the footmen started making filthy suggestions, one putting his hands to the young girl's breasts and pulling at her school sweater. Fortunately for the girl, an astute male passenger soon realised what was going on and told the boys to go away. Begrudgingly they departed.

As they made their way through the train back to their own seats in a compartment further along, they accosted and made rude remarks to every girl they came across. The letter writer detailed how, once back in their seats directly opposite her own, the boys began making abusive remarks about working in the Royal Household and then equally maligning the Queen. They swore and ridiculed the entire Royal Family and when the woman had finally heard enough and told the footmen to be quiet, they turned their hostile attention towards her, until she was finally forced to find another seat.

She considered the possibility that the boys were not actually employed at Buckingham Palace and perhaps only acting out of drunken rage, but she stressed that the boys were so outspoken in their comments on the Queen that if they were from the palace, someone ought to know about their behavior. When I brought the letter into Sir Peter Ashmore, he read it swiftly and then without hesitation said, "Sack them." It was one of the few firings I ever witnessed at the palace.

Most letters that arrive addressed to the Queen never make it to her desk. Sir Philip Moore, her Private Secretary, had his own secretary who saw to it that all important incoming mail went to him, while the remainder was handed over to another lady in the Private Secretary's department, the wife of a London doctor named Mrs. Valerie Rose.

Letters that might be brought to Her Majesty's attention include requests for appearances from charity organizations, openings of new buildings, launching ships, or perhaps making a special trip to a private school summer fête. Numerous other organizations vie for her attention, and all this in addition to her other official obligations.

The Queen discusses each request with her Private Secretary and if it is for a good cause and she is available at the time, then she will do her utmost to attend. Whatever she decides to take on, these dates have to be fitted in to her already crowded diary. This is why her Private Secretary is so indispensable. He essentially organizes her life.

Once in a while school children send touching letters to the palace which Sir Philip might want Her Majesty to see. Most letters however appear on Valerie Rose's desk. The Queen, even if she wanted to, could never reply to the thousands of letters she is sent every year.

Valerie Rose handles less urgent correspondence: letters that ask the standard questions which have been posed by loyal subjects a thousand times before. There is really no need for the Queen to see these, and Valerie will respond with replies that are in keeping with Her Majesty's wishes. For instance, a request for signed pictures or queries regarding the workings of the palace would be handled without the Queen ever being informed. It is usually thrill enough for most royal fans just to receive a written reply on the beautiful red crested Buckingham Palace stationery, each signed by one of Her Majesty's ladies-in-waiting, of which she has six. Ladies-in-waiting to the Queen take up their palace duties in turn, without remuneration, usually for a month at a time.

While many of the letters are relatively simple to respond to, others are not. You would not believe some of them. There are regular letters from elderly ladies in the provinces, detailing how their husbands have just died and explaining to the Queen that they don't know if they can go on living. Some will tell the Queen of other hardships that life has dealt them, expressing their frustrations with high food prices or the cost of good clothing. It is not uncommon for these desperate people to demand that Her Majesty do something for them immediately! These are sad to receive, but there is little she can do other than sign a letter of sympathy and wish them better fortune in the months to come.

Letters do not just arrive from British citizens, hundreds are received every year from the Commonwealth countries, especially Canada, New Zealand and the Caribbean. Often, these have a better chance of being seen by the Queen than the letters from England.

There is one gentleman in Australia who has been writing to the Queen for over ten years. The first letter received from him was one of admiration and respect for her. So lauding in his praise was he that Sir Philip Moore decided to show it to the Queen that same day. It would certainly cheer her up! Her Majesty was naturally touched by the Australian's compliments and she promptly dispatched a lovely one page letter to the man in Sydney, thanking him for his kind words.

But then the following week another letter arrived from the same individual in Australia, but this time he told the Queen that she was "a fucking bitch," "a lying cunt," and "a whore." Believe it or not, the Queen actually replied, saying that she was sorry he felt that way about her and that she would try harder to please him in the future. In one letter which Valerie showed to me the Australian actually suggested to Her Majesty that she should be beheaded for treason!

The Queen no longer sees the Aussie's letters, but her secretary's department is under firm instructions from her to make sure an answer is sent out to each and every letter that is received from him. This wish is carried out. One week the man is full of praise for the Queen, the next, vehemently lambasting her or another member of the Royal Family for something they have done to displease him. And so once per week for over a decade, a letter goes out from the Queen to the strange man in Australia who is so persistent.

2

Valerie Rose and I entered the Officials' dining-room on the second floor of the palace. It was one o'clock. Each day at this time Officials gathered in their private dining-room, elegantly comfortable in its soft red and white silk wall covering and meticulously laid out white linen tables.

Valerie's daughter, Melanie Rose, was already seated at one of the eight tables collected about the lovely room, and we took the two chairs next to her. We were soon enjoying the first course of the Royal Chef's ample and delicious four-course luncheon.

Melanie Rose was a shy, petite little girl. She was smaller then her mother, not much beyond four feet ten inches. Her nickname was 'the dwarf' and she had been brought in to help with the present heavy workload in the palace. I had been a guest in the Rose household more then a dozen times since I had arrived at the palace. At first I thought that Valerie was simply fond of having me around. That was quite accurate. I later learned however that it was more specifically for her daughter. I soon put an end to that!

As the first course plates were removed from the table, I eased my chair back for a moment of relaxation in the comfortably upholstered chair. Paul Almond, a Senior Official in the Royal Mews, stood up at the adjacent table and peered over in our direction. Paul was known throughout the palace not so much for his work, but for his pranks. He was forever dreaming up ways of playing tricks on people. Today, it was Melanie Rose's turn. Paul came walking up to our table, stood directly in front of the timid young girl, calmly unzipped his fly, outlined his John Henry with a hand and bluntly said to her, "Get your gob round that!"

Melanie turned bright red, burst into tears, and ran from the room. Humphrey, sitting nearby, roared with laughter, immensely enjoying the show. Melanie's mother later reported the incident to Sir John Miller but nothing came of it. In fact, he couldn't understand what all the fuss was about. "What did you expect from him?" the old knight said unsympathetically. "A bunch of roses?"

It was a cruel joke though and not the least bit funny to most who witnessed it. When Humphrey and I were alone in the office following lunch, I asked him what he found so amusing in humiliating an innocent young girl. "Serve the silly little tart right," he roared with glee once again.

As I have said, Paul Almond was always planning new assaults on the Royal Household. Roughly once a month he would call Major Marsham in the Royal Mews and leave a message for him to call the Queen's husband regarding an urgent horse matter. The problem was the Duke did not want to hear from Major Marsham at all. Aside from the frequency with which he telephoned him, the Duke always thought he was an obsequious little blighter to begin with. The continual and incessant telephone calls only proved his thoughts further. But no matter how often the Duke told Major Marsham that he had not left him any message, the Major would not give up. He was convinced and determined that one day the message to call the Duke would be for real, and he did not want to miss his golden opportunity.

Paul Almond gave this a rest for a few months after the last phoney message he had left. When the Major dialled the Duke's private apartment and told him he was replying to his message, the Duke flipped. "Look, you damn little man, you...I have not left a message to call. Don't you have the brains to realise that somebody is having you on? Now STOP calling me—please!"

Paul was particularly fond of phoning up important people in the palace, though not in the manner in which they have grown accustomed. When they answered, Paul would stick his tongue between his lips and then blow loudly and prolonged into the receiver. This is commonly referred to as blowing a 'raspberry.'

One of his favorite people to taunt in this way was the Queen's Mistress of the Robes, the Duchess of Grafton. The Duchess was a tall woman with a pronounced stoop and wore clothes that were thirty years out of date. With her greyish-brown hair forced into a maid style bun at the back and a large aquiline nose, the Duchess resembled an old mare that had been retired to the pasture for grazing. Never satisfied with anything or anyone, she was eternally difficult, and in addition possessed a high-pitched voice that reminded one of a far-too-strict school teacher gone completely mad.

The 65-year-old Duchess was constantly complaining and possessed that annoying ability to find fault with just about everything. She was forever calling me for a lengthy moan and once she actually telephoned me in my office to complain about the temperature of her tea.

"It is not hot enough, Mr. Barker. It just is not hot enough!"

"What is that, ma'am?"

"My tea, Mr. Barker, my tea! Your footmen are too slow. "What are you going to do about it?"

I refrained from suggesting she blow on it, as she certainly had an abundance of hot air; instead, I instructed a footman to deliver another freshly brewed pot.

A former nurse, the Duchess was the Queen's closest confidante and friend. Her official title, 'Mistress of the Robes,' is an ancient one that once must have had something to do with managing the Queen's wardrobe. Now though it is simply a lady of position who accompanies her to openings, walkabouts and on foreign tours. Traditionally this position is always awarded to a Duchess. Similar to Her Majesty's ladies-in-waiting, there is absolutely no remuneration, but Her Majesty is at least allowed to offer this position to someone of her own choosing, and in the Duchess' case, they got along very well.

The Duchess was rarely in appearance at the palace. More often she could be found with her husband, the Duke of Grafton, at their ancestral home located deep in the county of Norfolk. When she wanted to visit the palace she simply telephoned the Queen on her private number, known to only a few people, and her room was prepared. She always stayed in room number 232, reserved for her personal use, and while in residence she performed the important tasks of taking luncheon with Her Majesty and attending any banquets or private dinner parties which might be scheduled during her stay.

When not in the palace, the Duchess still made her presence known. She often telephoned me from Norfolk asking that the

Queen's cabinet maker or her French Polisher drive up to Norfolk and see to specific pieces of furniture in her home. Toni Bonici, Her Majesty's highly experienced craftsman, was forever complaining that he was forced to work around the Duchess's home, in his spare time, without her ever so much as giving him a shilling for his efforts. This intruded into his Bible-reading sessions as well and he was not happy about it. Besides, Buckingham Palace salaries were minimal as it was. A man such as he, in service for fifteen years or more, could count on a yearly salary of about three thousand pounds (roughly five thousand U.S. dollars) at the very most. At the other end of the scale, a man such as Sir Peter Ashmore would be paid roughly forty thousand pounds. For the poorly paid Staff, such as Toni, the palace salary was hardly conducive to taking on charity work, especially for those as financially well endowed as the Duke and Duchess of Grafton.

Another member of the Queen's Household who was at the receiving end of more then his share of Paul Almond's raspberries was Sir Rennie Maudsley, Keeper of the Privy Purse. As the treasurer of the Royal Household, Sir Rennie was in one of the most important positions. He was responsible for all expenditures incurred by the Queen, as well as those of the palace. However, for a man in such an exalted position, Sir Rennie had the odd habit of never paying his own bills. He would order braces of pheasants and Christmas crackers, amongst other items, and his cheque was always the very last to come in, if at all. When payment did arrive, it was only after months of pursuit, and even then the funds had to be practically dragged out of him.

Sir Rennie's career at the palace was not one of the glossiest. A hard man with ice cold features to match, he was extremely bad tempered and almost impossible to work with. He took enormous liberties, even expecting the Royal Chef to pluck his pheasants for him (as did the Duchess of Grafton). As a senior member of the Queen's Household, Sir Rennie was provided with a beautiful apartment in Mayfair, one of the best residential areas in all of London. Having persuaded the Queen to allow him to redecorate the apartment at palace expense, he promised to pay the money back to her at a later date. Years after he resigned, however, we were still trying to get some sort of reimbursement from him, but he refused to pay; this, even though he is an enormously wealthy man. Interestingly enough, although he owes the Queen thousands of pounds, he is still an Equerry to her, which means that on special occasions, such as a royal wedding or an important State visit, he will be brought in to provide assistance to Her Majesty as the situation requires.

One of Paul's very favorites for the raspberry treatment was the Queen's Dresser; a lady now in her seventies who began service as nanny to Princess Margaret and the then Princess Elizabeth. When she gave up her duties and 'retired,' she continued to live in the palace as a favor from the Queen. Bobo Macdonald is her name and as long as anyone can remember she has been living in the palace ruling an imaginary court of her own.

When I first met Bobo she struck me as bearing a remarkable resemblance to the Wicked Witch of the East in the tale of the Wizard of Oz. She was crabby and wrinkled and walked with an alarmingly arched back. She had the most tiresome voice and droned on in the most affected of accents, and with her dark Victorian dresses and bloodshot eyes, a more perfect character for the above mentioned theatrical role I cannot imagine. Basically harmless, but strong with the knowledge that Her Majesty would do practically anything to keep her happy—and quiet!—Bobo could make an otherwise cheery day miserable even for the Queen.

After each State visit it is customary for the Queen to give one bottle of good French champagne to each Official in the palace, and one half bottle to each member of Staff. Problems arose though when Bobo, who technically didn't do anything in the palace anymore, called me about the allocation she herself had received following one such event. She was miffed because she had only received a half bottle when she felt entitled to a full one, in light of her many decades of service to the Queen. I explained that the rules were the same for all Staff and that there was nothing I could do; it was after all a policy agreed to by the Queen herself. But Bobo was furious and threatened to call the Queen if I did not oblige her.

Ordinarily one could afford to laugh at such a threat, but not with Bobo. You see she really did have that sort of control over Her Majesty and her calls were always taken by her personally. But there was nothing I could do. Rules were rules and that is the message I conveyed to Bobo.

A few minutes later I received a telephone call from Sir Peter Ashmore, who instructed that a bottle of "the very best" champagne be sent up to Bobo right away, by order of the Queen herself! Naturally this was done. However no one in the palace could stand Bobo. She was a real old bat. I didn't feel she deserved a bottle of the Queen's very best and so I had a bottle of Asti Spumante delivered instead. As I didn't receive a call of complaint I congratulated myself on the assumption that Bobo didn't know the difference.

Another time Bobo called the Royal Chef and requested a light afternoon snack consisting of tea and some pâté de foie gras. As the Royal Chef refused to talk to her, one of his assistants took the order. Unfortunately, Bobo had to be told that they were completely out of the pâté and would she like something else instead?

No she would not like something else instead thank you very much! Immediately she called the Queen to complain and twenty minutes later a Harrods' delivery truck arrived at the palace with a shipment of fresh pâté de foie gras for Bobo.

The most memorable, and I confess most enjoyable experience I had involving Bobo Macdonald curiously enough occurred after Bobo went away on holiday. For almost two years

Bobo had refused to allow any of the maids into her room to clean it. She said that she kept the place tidy herself and she didn't want anyone "nosing around," as she put it, in her belongings. She really was quite adamant that the room should not be touched. The chief housekeeper on the other hand saw the matter somewhat differently. She felt that it was her duty to ensure that not one room in the palace went without proper attention and in the case of Bobo, her time had come.

With Bobo safely away on the train to somewhere everyone agreed had to be pretty awful, the chief housekeeper decided to make a thorough inspection of her room. When completed, she declared that a cleaning was definitely in order and two housemaids were assigned to the task. When they finished the job they informed the chief housekeeper that Bobo's room had been given a complete cleaning...with one exception: they could not open the large solid cupboard in her room. It was securely locked.

I went up to the room to lend a hand but even with the aid of two burly porters, the doors to the cupboard just would not open. Finally the palace locksmith had to be called. Arriving back in Bobo's room, the housekeeper and I stood in front of the imposing six-foot high cupboard as I slipped the key into the ancient lock and pulled the two doors open.

Down came a torrent of empty bottles with such a force that one housemaid screamed and the chief housekeeper and I had to fling ourselves out of their path. Gin, vodka, Scotch and sherry bottles flooded the floor of Bobo's bedroom and were littered everywhere. Miss Martin and I—hearts beating rapidly from the scare—both looked at each other and knew instinctively now why the Queen's Dresser wanted absolutely no one in her room.

Poor Bobo must have thought she was the only one in the palace who did any drinking.

Now as I have said, Bobo was an abrasive woman. She was the only member of Staff to have her own footman. This assistant lived with the other footmen on the attic floor above the royal apartments in the west wing of the palace. One day Her Majesty informed Sir Peter that she intended to give an inspection of the living quarters pertaining to the footmen and the housemaids. Sir Peter, in advising me of this upcoming event, added that I should ensure that anything hanging on the walls that could be considered "insulting" to Her Majesty should be removed. This was carried out.

The following morning, when she had completed her menu consultation with the Royal Chef, Her Majesty arrived on the Dressers' floor for the big tour. Sir Peter Ashmore and myself were there to meet her. All went well in the maids' quarters and there were no hitches. We then moved on to the footmen's lounge and this was found to be equally satisfactory. Proceeding to the pages' main floor, Her Majesty found everything there to be in order and thoughtfully mentioned to Sir Peter that some new paint for their kitchen might be a good idea to brighten it up. Sir Peter smiled willingly. He was relieved that there were no problems for a change. Her Majesty was more than happy and the inspection really was progressing extremely well.

Eventually we came to the footmen's bedrooms and as we made our way along the corridor that was for some reason called the London Bridge, Her Majesty peered into several bedsitters to check on what sort of condition they were in, stopping once or twice to ask a question or chat with a favorite young boy. At last we neared the end of the hallway and soon were standing in front of the very last bedroom, the room occupied by Bobo's assistant.

Her Majesty paused in front of the closed door, and looked up at the banner in bold red lettering tacked across.

SEX LESSONS GIVEN HERE. FIRST LESSON FREE
INQUIRE WITHIN

The Queen looked sharply around at Sir Peter and began twisting the wedding ring on her left hand—a sign that warned all who knew her that she was *not at all pleased!*

"I believe I have seen enough, thank you," the Queen spoke icily, and with that led a highly agitated Sir Peter off towards her apartments, no doubt for the lecture he knew he was about to receive.

Bobo's assistant was simply given a reprimand later that day, and nothing more was said of the matter.

3

The President of Nigeria and his party were due to arrive at London's Victoria Station at twelve o'clock noon. Unfortunately they were late, obliging the Queen who was there to meet them to stand waiting on the platform wondering what to do next.

It was a dull, gloomy, miserable May day, the train station was damp and draughty, and Her Majesty, despite her usual display of fortitude and resilience, had her patience sorely tried. Anxious Royal Household Officials, shivering with apprehension and cold, constantly checked their watches and murmured their frustrations. There was widely felt relief when the President's train finally arrived more than thirty minutes late.

The Nigerian party was small by comparison to some State delegations I have witnessed. The King of Morocco, for instance, liked to bring as many as 120 dignitaries from his country. The Nigerians were about fifteen in number, including the President's wife, the Prime Minister of Nigeria and other eminent dignitaries.

Considering the expected calibre of the group, their behavior was surprising. Not only did they seem to relish leaving their palace suites in the most disheveled heaps imaginable each day, but in a move that can only be described as avaricious at best, they succeeded in taking the royal wine cellars to the cleaners! My colleagues and I were amazed at the amount of alcohol which was being consumed.

There was an awkward scene when the President of Nigeria spotted a copy of *White Man's Country* by Elspeth Huxley next to his bed in the Belgian suite. Mr. Humphrey had personally selected this tale of white colonialism for the visiting leader, for whenever a monarch or leader stayed at the palace it was required that either Mr. Humphrey or I select several appropriate books from Her Majesty's library and place them in the rooms. Normally this was not a difficult task. As part of my role, I would do a little research prior to the arrival and, for example, if a certain King had a particular interest in cricket or a Sultan in British history, I would make the appropriate choices.

When Sir Peter was told of the book incident, Mr. Humphrey was summoned into his office for yet another vituperation. When I entered the office around ten o'clock the following morning he was reposing comfortably in his besmirched pale blue under-wear, a fleshy buttock exposed, unaware of the mephitic aroma he was creating. As this Senior Official to the Queen paraded happily around his desk tackling a broken harness, his only answer when I asked him why he chose such inappropriate reading material for the Nigerian leader was a vociferous, "I thought he might like somethin' different. How was I to know he'd get so upset?"

To be truthful, no one was really too concerned about the Nigerians anyway. Of all the State visits, Her Majesty and the Royal Household found the Nigerians and Zairians the most difficult. Rather than behaving in the dignified manner that is expected in the Queen's home, they acted as though it was *they* who were in charge and treated the palace as they would a London nightclub.

Chaos was not confined to the privacy of the Nigerian suites however. On the final evening of the Nigerian State visit, at the banquet given by the Queen, the Nigerian president proceeded to criticise both Prime Minister Thatcher who was in attendance and President Ronald Reagan, who was not. Because this criticism

73

was levied in the presence of Her Majesty it was considered an absolute scandal by the press.

As a final insult to the Queen, the President of Nigeria and his entourage stole everything they could lay their hands on. They stripped their rooms of valuable books, radios, priceless ornaments and anything else they felt inclined to swipe. They even removed the leatherbound London telephone directories from their rooms. Now I cannot deny that it must be a great honor to have one of Her Majesty's beautifully bound telephone books in your very own home, but it must prove terribly awkward, say, if one wants to look up a friend's number in Lagos!

Suffice to say the Queen was not amused, and it was a very long time before the Nigerians were invited back to Buckingham Palace for another visit.

4

A more serious insult to Her Majesty occurred, however, when she was paying a visit to Morocco.

On the day of the Monarch's arrival in Morocco, she was invited to a be guest of honour at a banquet at the King's palace. Leaving the British Embassy promptly at seven o'clock, she endeavored to arrive at the front entrance of the palace precisely on time at seven thirty-five. She was alone in the rear of the maroon Rolls Royce which had been specially sent ahead from the Royal Mews in London. Passing through the gates of the King's pretty little palace, Her Majesty was delivered to the main entrance. King Hassan's secretary greeted her and then informed the Queen that she would have to go away: His Majesty was still fast asleep in bed!

The Queen considered this information for a moment and the ramifications that it held. Then she issued instructions to her driver to "drive around a bit." When she returned to the palace fifteen minutes later, as agreed upon with the King's secretary, he again told her that the King still had not awakened but optimistically added, "It should be any time now!" So, the Queen and her driver headed out once again into the streets of Rabat.

With the suggested fifteen minutes once more depleted, the Queen proceeded back to the palace, where she was now more eager than ever to proceed with the banquet. Stepping from the car on her own, and beginning to close the door for herself, the King of Morocco's secretary shouted at her from the entrance, "His Majesty has still not awakened and no one is allowed to disturb him while he is asleep. I don't know when he is going to wake up." (They had very strict rules about that, he told her.)

So, once more, the Queen wearily climbed back into the Rolls Royce and sank into the plush interior, perhaps casting a thoughtful eye at the mahogany cocktail bar in front. "Drive on!" she instructed. "They tell me not to come back for an hour!"

That night, the Queen saw more of Rabat than she ever knew existed, or even wanted to know. But she had to kill an hour and she was too polite—unlike some monarchs—to simply go home and forget the banquet.

After a very long hour had elapsed, the Queen was again driven to the front entrance of the King's palace, where this time she waited inside the comfort of her Rolls Royce for the little man whom she had come to know so well.

"Are you ready for me?" the Queen asked through an open window, not even bothering to get out.

"Yes we are, Your Majesty," the secretary announced triumphantly. "The King is up!"

His Majesty, it was true, had indeed awakened. But as usual after only just taking a nap, he required a little time to gather his thoughts before dining. As a result, his guests did not sit down to dinner until eleven o'clock that night. The Queen had expected to be home and in bed by that time and she was not in the best of moods.

Her Majesty, however, is always prepared for the unexpected. Customs and ways vary throughout the countries she visits to such an extent that she never knows what might happen.

At a ceremony welcoming her to Sark in 1949, a gatecrasher in the form of a mongrel dog wandered up to the royal chair on which the Princess Elizabeth was seated and for one horrifying moment appeared as though it was—yes—going to take a leak on the leg of the royal chair! But the Princess snapped her fingers at it authoritatively and, avoiding embarrassment, it mercifully moved away where it took up position next to the British Home Secretary standing immediately behind her.

On a trip to several of the British-owned Caribbean islands once, Her Majesty attended a banquet unlike any other. Traditionally, as the guests of another country, the Royal Family are given a welcoming banquet. At these glittering affairs the fanciest foods are prepared for them by the very best chefs in the land. Often, hosts will go to great lengths to find delicacies that might be uniquely associated with their own part of the world. In Nova Scotia, for instance, Her Majesty might be served smoked salmon, or in India it might be a special curry dish.

At the banquet given in her honor on one particular tropical island though, the delicacy was one that she had not sampled before. As she sat in the guest of honor position at the table, a large dinner plate was placed in front of her. Chatting amiably with those around her, it took a few moments before she picked up her cutlery. Upon inspecting the main course more closely, it became apparent that what she had in fact been given to dine on was their island version of what we commonly refer to in England as a rat!

With her usual fortitude and disciplined state of mind Her Majesty skirted around the plate and managed to have a tiny pick at the unpalatable item that was placed in the very centre. In the end, unable to digest the thought of what she saw in front of her any longer, she pushed the plate to one side and cast her glance firmly away. (And she thought the sheep's eyes which were served to her in Saudi Arabia were bad!)

Fortunately for the Monarch, most host nations are inclined to a more conservative menu.

5

I received a call from Heathrow Airport. Above the din of the passengers and loudspeaker I listened to a man telling me in broken English that he had flown in to see the Queen and no one had arrived to pick him up. I put him on hold and telephoned Sir John Miller at The Royal Mews. Sir John realized instantly that it was the Emir of Qatar who was expected in on his private jet from the Gulf, and told me to advise him that a driver would be at the airport for him as quickly as possible. In the meantime, he was going to find out why there had been a mix up.

"Where's Hawkes?" he inquired icily arriving in the building that housed the chauffeurs.

"I think he's in his room, sir," a young apprentice driver replied.

"Yes, well just lead me to it now," he ordered.

Having arrived at the bedsitter door he dismissed the chauffeur and began knocking rapidly. "Hawkes...Hawkes? I want to see you now please... Come on, I want to talk to you. What are you doing? Come out of there at once." Rapid knocking turned to blatant pounding.

Finally, movement was heard from within and then the door opened ever so slightly. "Yes? Who is it?" came a deep, groggy voice.

"It's me. Sir John. Open the door I want to talk to you." The door swung open to reveal Hawkes in undershirt and briefs, hair askew, and breath reeking of Scotch. "What are you doing still in bed?"

"Ugh...I had a rough night. Only got in at four."

"Yes, well, I'm not interested in that," Sir John said pointedly. "Why were you not at Heathrow? You were supposed to pick up the Emir of Qatar. He is there now waiting for you."

"Ugh...but it's me day off sir." Hawkes scratched his head sleepily.

"No it is not," Sir John popped angrily. "You were supposed to be there for him at eleven."

"I was? Oh no...I thought I did that yesterday!"

Later that afternoon Her Majesty had made arrangements with Sir John Miller to come to the Royal Mews and view a new horse she had purchased. She arrived through the garden entrance at the back of the palace and met him in the stable yard of the Mews. The Duchess of Grafton accompanied her.

The Queen was dressed casually in a tweed suit, with a pale-blue head scarf tied loosely under her chin. Sir John trotted in, riding proudly atop the graceful Cumberland Bay. A more thoroughbred specimen I have yet to see. Her Majesty came up and gently took hold of its reins, affectionately patting the Bay's nose and calming it with her quiet words.

"Careful, Your Majesty. He's still a bit timid."

"Really, Sir John. He is fine." The Queen well knew how to handle a horse.

Sir John, feeling renewed confidence as the thoroughbred steadied for the first time, suddenly gave it a much too hard slap on the rear. He took the horse by surprise, and in its new surroundings, it was nervous. The thoroughbred broke away from the Queen's hold and she stepped back in good time, watching as it bucked and whinnied and shortly sent a startled Sir John sailing to the ground.

The Queen and the Duchess of Grafton laughed hysterically, the more so when they saw that the Queen's knight was not hurt. Sir John, looking humiliated, gruffly brushed the dirt from his clothes.

"Bloody horse!" he muttered more then a little annoyed.

The Queen, well satisfied with her new purchase, headed back to her apartments in the palace. No doubt for another good chuckle with the Duchess.

Sir John Miller had been at the Royal Mews for as long as anyone could recall and as I have already said, could never quite adjust to life in the eighties, preferring to live in an earlier and much simpler time; in this case, the mid-nineteenth century.

I recall one afternoon when Sir John drove into central London and parked his Jaguar outside the Army and Navy store on Victoria Street. He wasn't on an official visit however; he had gone to the department store to do some personal shopping. Occupying the important position of Crown Equerry, one of the most senior posts to the Queen, he assumed that he was more or less impervious to the rules and regulations that applied to the ordinary citizen.

Coming out of the Army and Navy store when he was finished, Sir John strolled briskly towards his royal blue car parked illegally in front of the main entrance. Standing next to his car was a policeman in the act of placing a ticket on the windshield.

"Officer, officer, what are you doing to my automobile?" Sir John came rushing up to him.

"I'm afraid you have parked this car in a no parking zone, sir. I've had to give you a ticket."

"A ticket, a ticket?" Sir John asked with astonishment. "What on earth are you talking about, man?"

"I've just told you. You have parked this car in a zone that is not for parking," the policeman replied, probably as he had done a thousand times before.

"No, I am afraid you cannot give me a ticket," Sir John stated to him arrogantly.

The policeman looked mystified. "Why not?"

"Because I'm the Crown Equerry, you fool."

"The who?"

"The Crown Equerry. I always park here. I'm on business for the Queen."

The policeman was not impressed. "I don't care who you are. You still can't park here," and with that he snapped the Jaguar's wiper blade firmly onto the ticket and walked away.

A very perplexed and jolted Sir John arrived at his office in the Royal Mews half an hour later and began hurriedly trying to explain to his secretary what had just happened to him. Familiar with Sir John and his somewhat archaic lifestyle and beliefs, the secretary attempted to console him by stressing that nowadays it doesn't really matter who you are—laws are laws. But this didn't help and a thoroughly exasperated Sir John headed towards his inner office exclaiming, "I'm going to call the Queen about this. They cannot talk to me like that."

One can only imagine Her Majesty's reaction to that.

Sir John was an institution in palace life but as he grew older he had less and less to do with riding, or for that matter, anything at all. Mr. Humphrey was therefore given an ever increasing amount of the Queen's horse training to perform.

Humphrey had a highly respected stable at his home in Windsor in addition to his position at the palace. But he also ran another business: a private carriage business. How did he find time to do this as well? Very simple. He ran the carriage business from Buckingham Palace itself and his services were especially appreciated in the wedding business, which was thriving particularly between the months of May and October. All the London wedding shops had Mr. Humphrey's Buckingham Palace telephone number (930-4832, extension 274).

Telephone calls were always coming in and he advised the switchboard that any inquiries concerning the carriage business should be put through to him immediately. Being a Senior Official, this order was naturally never questioned. After all, he was their boss. However, the palace was not totally oblivious to this little operation of his. Tims had reason to suspect that Humphrey was doing something wrong. There were rumors going around about some sort of business or other, but he was never able to catch him at it.

One afternoon a call came in for John Humphrey Carriages and as Mr. Humphrey and I were both out of the office, the switchboard operator took it upon herself to put the call through to our immediate supervisor, Mr. Tims. He was naturally outraged and indignant when he took the call and was asked if he could "do a wedding on the 29th?" Angrily he told the caller that there was no such business to be found at Buckingham Palace and that they should not call again.

Taking advantage of Mr. Humphrey's absence, Tims entered the office and had a look through his briefcase and around his desk. In a drawer, he found what he was looking for—stationery with the Buckingham Palace crest and insignia, and underneath it the words "John Humphrey Carriages Ltd., Buckingham Palace."

Naturally he was aghast at what he had come across, but with some excitement realized that he now had the proof he wanted so badly. What once was only a rumor was now a fact.

Confronting Humphrey later in the day Tims informed him that he knew all about his clandestine little business and had been through his desk and found the incriminating evidence. He told Mr. Humphrey that he had no choice but to inform Sir Peter of this infraction. Mr. Humphrey, as expected, denied the allegations point blank and told Tims that they were "bloody rubbish." Tims jubilantly waved the proof in the air. But as with previous violations, Tims was not going to be taking any action at all.

Thinking quickly, Mr. Humphrey told Tims that if there were any reports concerning his carriage business, then he would have to raise the matter of Tims' illegal and equally serious excursion through his desk with the Queen herself. Amazingly enough, Tims fell for the ploy.

This enterprising project continued on uninterrupted, run entirely from Buckingham Palace and conveniently disguised as a service which it officially offered. Customers were under the impression, and indeed bragged about it to their friends, that the carriage transporting their beloved bride on her wedding day was in fact one of the Queen's very own. Wasn't it awfully good of Her Majesty to be so kind and generous with her subjects?

6

Something far more serious than Mr. Humphrey's carriage business though was happening at this time, and it involved two of the Queen's footmen and some explosives.

The drama was just drawing to a close. A few weeks earlier, during a routine inspection of rooms in the palace, police found explosives hidden in the recreation room of the Staff quarters. Two boys, Stephen Beevis and Andrew Gildersleeve, were apprehended and confessed to the whole scheme. Their story was that they had bought the explosives to reopen a disused goldmine in Gloucester, and they claimed they had no intention whatsoever of bringing any harm upon the Royal Family.

However, investigations by police found no such mine and led to still further questions when a stolen jeep belonging to the police was found near the spot to which the two boys had led them. It contained belongings clearly identified as being the property of the two footmen. Their story was extremely far fetched and both footmen were given six-month jail sentences and relieved of their duties at the palace.

I met one of the footmen's mother, Mrs. Beevis, a short time later when she arrived at the palace to collect her son's clothes and property. Leading her to Stephen's room in the footmen's quarters, I left her there alone to do the packing up and returned to my office.

An hour later the policeman called from the Grand Entrance to advise me that Mrs. Beevis was leaving. I went down to say goodbye. She was obviously a very warm and kind-hearted lady and the trip to the palace had quite noticeably been terribly embarrassing for her. I left Humphrey, feet up, watching a small television set he had recently and mysteriously acquired.

Mrs. Beevis was waiting for me beside the policeman's desk in the foyer with two large boxes at her side. I asked politely if she had found everything she had come for. "Yes," was her reply, "except for a little color television set we bought Stephen for his birthday. I can't seem to find that anywhere in his room."

Humphrey immediately popped into mind. But what could I say? I certainly couldn't admit that one of the Queen's Senior Officials had stolen it for himself. That wouldn't look very good. I promised her I would do my best to find the television for her and said I'd call if it was handed in.

I returned to my office and confronted Humphrey, now well into another packet of chips and enjoying immensely his new acquisition. "John," I asked seriously, "is that Stephen Beevis' tele you are watching?"

"'Course it is," he replied nonchalantly, taking a gulp of coffee.

"Well, don't you think it should be returned to him? Mrs. Beevis has just asked me about it and I didn't know what to tell her."

"Don't tell her nothin'. Her son's a crook anyway," and he continued on untroubled with his chips, coffee and television; the latter, Mrs. Beevis was never to see again.

The Queen's footmen were always up to some mischief. There were about twenty in all and the faces were constantly changing. At least two or three times a year a footman would depart, having had his fill of a job that soon lost its initial thrill and glamor. Another would arrive to take his place. Salaries were impecunious, especially during the footman's first year, in which

83

he was not even allowed to personally serve the Queen. When the time arrived that he could serve her, an increase in wages of approximately five pounds per week was about the maximum he could look forward to.

Most of the footmen ranged in age from seventeen to twenty-two. The majority, of course, were still quite immature and possessed that school boy ability of constantly testing the rules. When not on duty the boys would normally remain in the palace and it was natural for deep friendships as well as deep resentments to build up over the course of time. I was always having to haul one of the footmen into my office every few days to remind him that he was no longer in prep school and that he should monitor his behavior, both on and off the job.

One of the most responsible senior footmen I met was a young man by the name of Keith Magloire. He was one of two members of the fold who were Her Majesty's personal footmen, and he had been with her for several years. One of the two was always on call to her, whether it be standing nearby while she was dining in her private apartments, or bringing her a bedtime drink before she retired. Keith performed his job well and was highly relied upon by the Queen. There was just one problem: he was having a torrid love affair with a former Russian count who lived in the fashionable residential area of Belgravia.

Keith made no attempt to hide this relationship and would tell palace employees all about the love interest of his life. I discreetly made it clear to him that this was just not on, but the answer I received from him was, "Everyone else in the palace is doing it, so why can't I?" Of course, I assumed he meant everyone was having affairs, not necessarily with Russian counts.

Another footman, named Michael Fawcett, was extremely unhappy with his accommodations in the palace. He had served Princess Anne as a nursery footman, and when she married and moved on he was kept on as a general footman. This he regarded as a demotion and he complained bitterly to the Princess at every opportunity.

The footmen's living quarters were located on the second floor in the west wing of the palace, well away from the royal apartments. They were not considered luxurious by any stretch of the grey matter, but neither were they a shambles as Fawcett seemed to think. Princess Anne eventually offered him a job as a butler in her own home and Fawcett was happy. So was Buckingham Palace.

It didn't surprise me at all to witness the strong bonds that frequently developed between Staff and the Royal Family. It had been that way between the Queen and her former nanny, Bobo Macdonald, Prince Charles and his valet, Stephen Barry (who later died of Aids), and it was that way between Princess Anne and Fawcett. But his new position in Princess Anne's home did not last long. She reluctantly had to ask him to leave shortly after he began in her Gatcombe Park residence. She was very glad she did when, a few months later, it was revealed that he had gone totally mad and stabbed his grandmother several times in a fit of rage.

Princess Anne did not have the best of luck when it came to her employees. A young underbutler in her silver pantry was going through a difficult time. After receiving countless death threats in the mail, he told the Princess about his fears that someone out there was really after him. Naturally the police were brought in and started some investigations.

He was a good-looking boy and performed his duties to the Princess admirably. Even when he was found in bed more then a dozen times with other male members of her Staff, she still wanted to keep him on. She liked him very much and wanted to do all she could to help him through his period of distress. After all, receiving death threats can be quite a terrifying experience.

The police worked for weeks trying to solve the mystery of who was sending the death threats to her underbutler. Although concerned with the underbutler's life, they were naturally worried for Princess Anne and her family as well. The young servant showed them half a dozen notes he had received, each compiled through the use of characters cut out of newspapers. A couple of the threats he received though were written by hand and when the police could find no lead or clue, they resorted to taking the letters to a handwriting expert.

Suspicions were raised when the handwriting expert asked for a sample of the underbutler's writing. After comparing this to the threatening letters, the expert told the police that there could be no doubt in his mind...the letters had been written by one person—the underbutler himself!

When confronted with this new information, the boy broke down and admitted that, yes, he had sent the life threatening letters to himself. He had only wanted some attention he explained in his defence. That he certainly received, and a dismissal notice from Princess Anne the same day.

7

There was another serious dilemma for me to deal with towards the end of May and it had nothing to do with Russian counts, granny stabbings or death threats. No it did not. The problem was what was to be done about all the peeing that was going on in the Royal Household, namely, on the Queen's property.

Believe it or not, peeing in the Royal Household occupied a fair amount of the servants' time, and they were forever being caught at it even by the Queen herself. A kitchen porter had been caught by a policeman one evening peeing against the palace. The young porter was returning from a favorite pub around eleven thirty and just could not wait a minute longer. He had to go and he had to go now! To make matters worse he chose the Queen's Picture Gallery where many of her prized paintings are hung on display to the public. This also happened to be the sight of the private Royal Chapel prior to its bombing during the Second World War. For this offence, the porter was given notice the following morning; coincidentally, the same day the manager of the palace bar was fired for embezzling funds. No charges were pressed for either offence. But the peeing went on.

In an apartment building in the Royal Mews, directly behind the palace, another incident had taken place. One of the Staff residing there with his wife and family opened his second-storey window around midnight and proceeded to relieve himself out of it. Unfortunately, Crown Equerry Sir John Miller was coming out of his office on the ground floor at the same time and narrowly missed a good drenching by only a few inches.

The next day Sir John investigated the matter further and when it was discovered who the offender was, the employee responsible explained that his wife had been mad with him and locked him out of their bedroom. As the bedroom led to the only bathroom in the apartment what was he to do? Nothing, of course, and that was exactly the action taken by Sir John.

Children of Staff living with their parents in apartments provided by the palace treated the grounds around them as contemptuously as they would a public lavatory. Fifteen and sixteen-year-olds would ride their bikes in the Royal Mews quadrangle, use foul language, torment other children and, yes, frequently have a good leak against a wall when the need arose.

There were other Staff problems as well.

A seventeen-year-old apprentice chauffeur to the Queen Mother had recently threatened members of the public with a knife in a London bus shelter. Although he did not harm anyone, he was relieved of his duties; but because the boy's father was a farrier in the Royal Mews, an ancient title for a blacksmith, this meant that even after the boy was convicted of possessing a dangerous weapon, and dismissed from his job, he continued to live with his parents in a grace and favor apartment behind

Buckingham Palace...within walking distance of the royal apartments!

He was a difficult youth and would walk about the Royal Mews grounds lugging a large tape player on his shoulder, blaring acid rock music which didn't fit in at all with the gracious surroundings. One afternoon he came strutting into the centre courtyard, stereo in tow as usual, the sounds of Michael Jackson's 'Billy Jean' announcing his arrival. Just then, the Earl of Westmorland came out of Sir John's office and when met with the din stopped in his tracks quite bewildered. He was either shocked by what he heard or this was evidence that the Earl had not yet received his copy of the album 'Thriller.' The boy knew he disapproved, and took great delight in gathering a large mouthful of bile and then spitting it casually on the ground in front of the earl as he passed him by. His Lordship, understandably, was appalled, but again there was nothing to be done. Times had definitely changed.

The lower end of the Staff section of the palace was difficult to manage in other ways too. Most of the porters, old pages and basement cleaners had been working in their jobs for thirty or forty years, and with no possibility of ever gaining a promotion, they basically stayed in their rooms in the basement drinking Scotch and gossiping their days away.

When I was still quite new on the job, I remember I had cause to enter the royal kitchens in order to check menus with the Royal Chef. I was still finding my way around the palace and inadvertently walked into the wrong kitchen. The sole occupant of the room was an old woman who was bent over a sink peeling potatoes. "Excuse me," I called politely.

The old woman turned around, tossed her mop of unkempt hair and glared at me. "What do you want?" she rapped hoarsely.

"I am looking for the Royal Chef, but I seem to have come to the wrong kitchen."

"You're new here, aren't you?" she said, totally ignoring what I had just explained to her.

"Well...Yes I am new but—"

"Well, what do you think of this beauty?" she laughed sinisterly and without further hesitation lifted up her filthy skirt. Unfortunately, she wasn't wearing any knickers underneath and I found myself in full view of her unsightly credentials.

I left the kitchen feeling slightly squeamish and returned to the office where I hurriedly explained to Mr. Humphrey what had happened to me. He told me all about the crazy lady named Miss Ivy Hoaen and casually stated that this was nothing out of the ordinary. Apparently she was always exposing herself around the palace and usually several times a day. Mr. Humphrey told me about the time Ivy flaunted into the Staff dining room at Windsor Castle, and with a coarse shriek, she peeled of all her clothes and then sat down at one of the tables with her lunch. This was considered so normal that the Staff continued to eat as if nothing had happened.

Mr. Humphrey's final comment on the matter was, "Well, Malcolm, I'd have her myself, but she's gettin' a bit past it these days."

Now as I have said, servants who performed the most mundane of tasks were paid very poorly. To recompense them, they received accommodation within, or around, the palace and were provided with all their meals. Most were satisfied with this arrangement.

However one servant, a basement cleaner in the palace, was an exception to the rule. It wasn't that he was dissatisfied though; he was quite happy. For although he was poorly paid, he was always talking about his upcoming trips which he was looking forward to, and I don't mean to Brighton. No, this basement cleaner traveled the world. One year he would be off to the United States, another to Italy, and then a few months later he would be winging his way to Switzerland. Even more of a surprise came when he told me that he was shortly leaving for New Zealand and that he wasn't quite sure whether he should take Air New Zealand's First Class, or British Airways' Crown First Class, going on to add that he found the latter not quite up to par on his most recent trip.

Through this worldly traveler I became familiar with many of the exotic sounding names commercial airlines use to attract passengers. Some of them are highly inventive, if not verging on the pretentious. For instance, the basement cleaner thought highly of South Africa Airways' Diamond Class, but was not very keen on their executive cabin service, called Gold Class. (He didn't try their economy cabin, called Silver Class.) Air Portugal's Navigator Class was acceptable, while Kenya Air's Lion Class and Gulf Air's Golden Falcon Service were disappointments. Of course, as he pointed out, not every airline is this original, and most simply make do with the mundane nomenclatures of First or Business Class. Under this same system, I suppose, one could provide their own name if they so desired. For example, if you happen to be flying with Areoflot you might consider yourself to be traveling Crash Class.

This lowly servant was quite a character and I liked him very much. The majority of his brethren were so well lubricated most of the time that it was difficult to get a courteous word out of them at all, so he was naturally very much appreciated on the premises. The mystery behind this man's good fortune was solved when he told me that his mother had died a few years earlier and left him an unexpected fortune in stock. Despite his wealth, and when not flying the globe—First Class, of course—he was content to sweep the basement floors of the palace and move the Queen's furniture when the need arose. A lovely, simple man, whose good fortune I could not have wished on a better soul.

Low-ranking staff were not the only ones who caused problems. A Senior Official at the palace had recently been found in possession of drugs. On a tip-off from an anonymous caller the police raided his apartment in Kensington Palace, a short distance away from Princess Margaret's. There they found marijuana as they had been told. But although a far more serious crime then relieving oneself against a Buckingham Palace wall, he was only given a stern lecture by the Queen's Master of the Household and told not to do it again.

All of the above happenings pale though to an incident which occurred at Sandringham House one year. It was an evening in early January, around eleven-thirty, and one of Her Majesty's long serving pages who took care of her personal needs while in residence there was on his way back from the pub, an establishment he headed for at every available opportunity.

He was in his customary state of total intoxication when he arrived back at the stately manor, and after letting himself in through the Queen's private entrance he staggered around the maze of narrow corridors completely unable to locate his bedroom. Finally he came to a door he had not yet tried and began fumbling unsuccessfully with the handle. Then, as if by magic, the door opened for him.

It was an unfortunate choice.

As he stepped forward into what he thought was his bedroom, he plunged rapidly down a steep semi-darkened staircase. Muttering obscenities and grasping hopelessly at the air for some support, he collided heavily with the Queen, who was slowly ascending the stairs to retire for the evening. Her Majesty was knocked flying and found herself lying at the foot of her private staircase with the drunken page on top of her!!

Managing to free herself with some difficulty, she stood up with as much decorum and dignity as she could possibly muster and addressed the page who was clinging to the bottom step.

"I suggest you take yourself to bed immediately!" the Queen ordered in frigid tones, "that is, if you are capable of doing so!"

Looking untypically disheveled, the Queen of England, Defender of the Faith, Head of the Commonwealth, then took herself to bed.

ROYAL ASCOT

June 13th - June 18th

MEMO

DUE TO A SHORTSIGHT THE 150 TICKETS NORMALLY
AVAILABLE TO STAFF FOR ROYAL ASCOT RACE WEEK
HAS BEEN REDUCED TO 75.

THERE WILL BE A RAFFLE TOMORROW SO THAT THESE
LAST FEW TICKETS MAY BE FAIRLY DISTRIBUTED.
%
J.S. HUMPHREY ESQ.

Thus commenced Royal Ascot Week.

It is customary for Royal Household employees to be allocated two tickets each for a day's racing of their choice, and one of Mr. Humphrey's duties was to ensure that the distribution was fair and non-discriminatory. This assignation could be deemed by many as most injudicious by Sir Peter Ashmore, as it was well known that Mr. Humphrey took an unofficial week's leave of absence and invited relatives and friends by the score to a four-day racing booze-up in a private quarter of the racecourse paddock. Of course his guests needed tickets, and Mr. Humphrey had promised almost eighty of them this year to his nearest and dearest friends. He concluded that he must draw generously on the Staff ticket allocation if he were to meet his commitments and, of course, consoled his conscience by reasoning that the Staff did not need all those tickets in the first place. The admission to the race meeting meant much more to him and his mates.

So, Mr. Humphrey did up a standard coffee-stained memo with the announcement, constructing it with the unique skills he had acquired in the department of ambiguity. No one would even notice, he told himself. But they did.

Staff were outraged and cornered my abundant friend for more information and details on why such an error could be allowed to occur. However, even with their combined efforts, they were unable to secure any reason from the man himself, who sympathised with their plight and told them how upset he himself was when he learned of their misfortune this year. With resentment and hostility they at last relented, and Mr. Humphrey was able to pocket the tickets that he required so badly.

The English summer social season really gets under way in the middle of June when the Royal Ascot Race Meeting takes place. Four days of excellent racing, high fashion, and of course a strong royal presence makes this one of the principal events of the entire year. The royal enclosure is the place to be, where at least a year's notice is normally required when requesting tickets for admittance, and many eminent people are disappointed.

Wednesday dawned bright and clear and after dressing in morning attire I took the train from Waterloo to Ascot. The fine weather had certainly ensured a huge attendance, and a very brightly colored one too. Women were in pretty silk dresses of turquoise and greens, lemons and hibiscus, while the gentlemen were dressed in long morning coats, cane and top hat. All were carrying the ubiquitous race card, peering at lists of runners and riders with furrowed brow.

Having enjoyed an excellent lunch, I settled myself in a good vantage point to view the two o'clock royal carriage procession up the racecourse. It was a glittering spectacle. The Queen arrived in a highly elegant emerald green silk dress with matching hat, smiling and waving; Lady Diana Spencer in a stunning peach silk creation, looking radiant with pre-marriage bliss; the Queen Mother in a pretty lilac outfit; Princess Margaret was dressed in pink, and was beaming away happily, her mind perhaps on the excellent Pimms which are served in the royal enclosure. Only the Duke of Edinburgh and Prince Charles looked somewhat bored, as neither father nor son share their family's passion for horse racing.

The afternoon progressed most pleasantly. The first race, the St. James's Palace Stakes, was a very tight finish but I was happy to start the day with a winner, having been given a tip by the Marquis of Northampton. I headed to the betting shop to collect my winnings. A corpulent individual dressed in a baggy tweed suit appeared to be having an argument with the girl behind the window. I smiled as I recalled that the Royal Chef took his racing most seriously.

"Having a spot of trouble, Peter?" I inquired in cheery tones. With a belligerent "Thank's a fuckin' lot for nothing" to the distraught girl the Royal Chef swung around, almost lost his balance, and stepped heavily on my foot. I winced, but managed to maintain my composure.

"Well, it's this stupid bitch here who wrote down the wrong horse" he growled dangerously. "Now I've lost ten quid when I should have won fifty!" The usual Scotch haze emanated from his mouth and clung to my nose wickedly. For the second time I winced.

"Never mind, Peter. Better luck in the next race." I passed on, collected my winnings and headed for the refreshment marquee to enjoy a cool glass of Pimms.

I found, most unsurprisingly, Mr. George Jenkins, Comptroller of Supply at the palace, making full use of the bar facilities, clutching a rapidly emptying beer glass in one hand and a squashy egg sandwich in the other.

"Hello there Malcolm. How's your luck going so far?"

I told him of my success, and the Royal Chef's lack of it. Mr. Jenkins, having taken a large bite of his sandwich, threw back his head and with a raucous bellow of laughter, sent pieces of chopped egg flying from his mouth onto the back of the Duchess of Westminster's satin dress.

The Duchess was not slow to respond. "Oh, just look what you've done, you vulgar man, you," she stormed indignantly.

"Never mind, love. We'll soon wipe it off with a hanky, eh!" he chuckled, and produced a soiled rag from his jacket pocket.

"Oh put that revolting article away. You have ruined my afternoon." With that the Duchess left to do her own repair job in the comfort of the ladies powder room. I beat a hasty retreat.

I passed Sir Peter Ashmore and his wife, Lady Ashmore, the latter chattering away non-stop and clearly embarrassing her husband. She always wore the most inappropriate dresses. I strolled down to the paddock where the throngs of people were gathering to watch the runners for the next race. The Queen Mother was in evidence and stood talking to Viscount Whitelaw, the Deputy Prime Minister, who appeared very unsteady and had a face the color of an enlarged beetroot. Clearly the sun was affecting him. He staggered again and his wife, Lady Whitelaw, decided it was time to take some action. Making apologies to the Queen Mother, Viscount Whitelaw was escorted towards the tea rooms for reviving refreshment.

The first three races were now over and still people were pouring through the turnstiles, though the royal enclosure was now becoming somewhat overcrowded. I spotted Princess Anne emerging from the royal box in company with Lady Diana Spencer. Lady Diana's brother, Viscount Althorp, was also with her. Althorp did not seem affected at all by the recent press revelations that he had been discovered in an East London gay discotheque, dressed magnificently in brown leather sex gear and chains. He certainly did not look the part today in his handsome and dignified silk morning wear.

In direct contrast was the Queen's Palace Steward, Cyril Dickman, who came stumbling through a door dressed in a shabby three-piece suit with the buttons of his vest craving release from his extensive paunch. He nodded and walked straight into the Duke of Northumberland.

"Just look where you are going, you damn fool!" protested his Lordship.

"Sorry, sir, but I've got to get to the betting shop," responded an irritated Dickman.

"Well of all the nerve..." The Duke's voice faded out incredulously.

I was just listening to some cynical remarks concerning lunch from Royal Mews superintendent Major Phelps about "stuffed penguins" and "mutton dressed as lamb," when the Royal Chef made a dramatic re-appearance, clutching a near empty bottle of champagne and looking decidedly queasy. Was the Royal Chef about to succumb to the evils of liquor, despite his unrivalled capacity? He swayed past me mumbling something about "champagne" and "muck" and then put in an extra gear and charged over to the fence bordering the racecourse, regurgitating the contents of his considerable stomach. Horrified members turned their faces, and even Larry Hagman was unable to find a smile. I retreated for the refreshment marquee, once again determined not to be put off my strawberries and cream.

"Daaaaaaaarling!" I looked up from the freshly whipped cream at the lady who bore the voice that sounded strangely familiar. "Darling, that's enough champagne. You won't get me back to the Savoy in one piece!"

Over at the champagne bar, a well known 'Dynasty' star was making the most of her appearance and laughing hysterically.

"C'mon honey," another American offered, staggering dangerously close to a butler with a tray of glasses above his head. "Let's make this tent roll!"

An outraged snort from behind made me turn. "Can't go anywhere without meeting these damn American film stars," blasted the Earl of Home.

Finally it was time for me to depart. I had an important meeting in London regarding the upcoming trip to Scotland and I had seen enough for one day. My final sight in the royal enclosure was that of Lord Napier and Ettrick, Master of Princess Margaret's Household, looking harassed and rushing towards the royal box. What was the Princess up to now, I wondered, but did not stop to find out.

On my way out of the gate a voice hailed me. "Had any winners then, Malcolm?" Mr. Humphrey was holding a plate piled high with sandwiches and cakes, grinning at me affably.

"Just the one, John. How about you?"

"Four winners out of four," was the triumphant reply.

"Well if you keep that up you'll be able to retire early," I suggested, reflecting for the one thousandth time how fortune seemed to favor the indolent.

"You must be kiddin'? I know when I'm onto a good racket," boasted my elated colleague. "I'll see ya in the office next week, Malcolm."

As Mr. Humphrey tore off back to the royal enclosure to be with his wife, another voice from behind demanded my attention. "'Ere you!" the tiny lady called me. "Have you seen that man a mine?" It was Freddie Gentle.

"No, I'm sorry, Freddie. I haven't seen him for...oh...quite some time."

"Just you wait until I get my hands on him. Just you wait!"

Damn, I thought to myself. Now there was a show I would love to have seen.

BUCKINGHAM PALACE

June 19th - June 30th

1

It was Monday, the nineteenth of June, and everyone was occupied with the Court's approaching visit to Holyrood Palace in Scotland. Around eleven in the morning Crown Equerry Sir John Miller attempted to telephone Mr. Humphrey in the palace. In his absence I took the call. Sir John informed me that the Queen was anxious to hear about the progress of one of her newly acquired horses which was being trained by my colleague at his own private stables in Windsor Great Park. Where was Humphrey, he wanted to know. As usual, I did not know either.

Sir John Miller was in a state of restless boredom as he sat frowning in his office wondering where he would find Mr. Humphrey. It was a busy time of year but as Sir John had little to do himself he decided to inspect the re-painting of the Staff quarters in the Royal Mews quadrangle. With any luck the work would be unsatisfactory, allowing him to have a moan to his comptroller about shoddy workmanship and declining standards.

Closing his office door behind him, Sir John ambled across the forecourt, passed beneath the magnificent Doric arch and patroled into the quadrangle, narrowly avoiding an errant tennis ball from the racket of a boisterous and unruly child. "What on earth...?" began the Crown Equerry.

Royal Mews superintendent Major Phelps came puffing up like an obese bull elephant. "What the bloody hell do you think you're playing at, Sir John?" he yelled. "Look where you are going."

"Alright, alright. Stop acting like a distraught chicken," responded Sir John. He glanced round at the offending child. "Send that miserable creature indoors at once."

Sir John began his inspection. He frowned at the uneven brush strokes on the crimson doors, tut-tutted at finger marks on the newly painted walls, and pursed his lips when noticing the black paint splashes which had dripped from the railings onto the tarmac. Yes, there would be plenty of scope for complaints here, he chuckled to himself. Now what else could he find?

"Swoooooosh..." It came without warning.

Sir John had been standing beneath one of the upper Staff apartments and the next instant he found himself totally drenched with soapy water. "Ach...Gff...Piff," spluttered the now aquatic Crown Equerry, as the cold water penetrated his Gieves and Hawkes suit, Jermyn Street shirt and took up residence against his skin. "What has happened to me?"

It took him some moments to gather his feelings which passed into outraged disbelief and absolute horror at his condition. "Just look at my shoes," he wailed. He gazed up at the apartment building helplessly, then his face darkened. Whoever had decided that he required a pre-lunch shower would have some explaining to do!

He walked gingerly up the outside staircase leading to the apartment that he suspected was responsible, dripping water onto the drying black paint. Arriving, he rapped loudly on the door. A corpulent, buxom woman with a forbidding expression appeared on the threshold. "Now who the bloody? — Good heavens, Sir John! What have you been doing?"

"It's what you have been doing that warrants explanation, Mrs. Du Pont," retorted the enraged, shivering Crown Equerry.

"How dare you cover me from head to foot with your domestic washing requirements."

"Well, how was I to know you'd be underneath me kitchen window? Me sink's blocked and I'd nowhere else to get rid of the water." Mrs. Du Pont narrowed her eyes accusingly. Unsympathetically she continued, "What were you doing there anyway?"

"That is neither here nor there, you impertinent woman," Sir John lambasted her, almost dancing with anger. "I demand to see your husband immediately."

"Well, you will have to wait till he gets back from pub, and you won't get any sense from him then anyway." Mrs. Du Pont was defiant. "Perhaps you'd like to try and fix sink for yerself? I'm sure it wouldn't take long with a clever man like you."

Sir John decided it was hopeless to continue the conversation, especially when he recalled that her husband, Mr. Du Pont, was the culprit who had taken a piss out of the same window a few weeks earlier.

Mr. Du Pont was a gatekeeper and he liked going to the pub; not usually for beer though. No, Mrs. Du Pont was the beer drinker in the family. Her husband preferred Scotch. Recently Mr. Du Pont had shown such a keen interest in the product that he had to be removed from his position as farrier (blacksmith) because he could no longer function efficiently—or for that matter, at all. Now he spent his days sitting in a gatehouse in the Royal Mews quadrangle, watching his TV and keeping his spirits as high as possible.

Sir John wasn't getting anywhere with Mrs. DuPont. He could see that. Water sodden and weary he retraced his steps and ambled across the quadrangle to the comfort of his house. At least there he knew he would be in for a more sympathetic reception from his housekeeper, who liked to indulge him.

Later, and a little drier, Sir John called Tims looking for Mr. Humphrey for a second time. I was in Tims' office discussing some arrangements regarding the upcoming visit to Holyrood. It was a glorious day and I looked longingly out of the window at the brilliant sunshine I was missing. I made a mental note to take a walk in Hyde Park after lunch.

"Where is Humphrey?" boomed Sir John over the speaker phone in Tims' office. "The Queen wants to know about her horse."

Tims did not know either. Highly embarrassed, he pledged to ascertain Mr. Humphrey's whereabouts for him and began dialing the number to the Senior Official's Windsor home, a number he had committed to memory many years ago.

Sure enough, Humphrey answered the telephone at his Windsor residence.

"Good morning, Mr. Humphrey," Tims said somewhat surprised to reach him so easily. "Why have you failed to appear at the palace today?"

Despite the scorching June heat Humphrey replied, "Well, ya see Mr. Tims, I'm afraid that the snow's so thick here I can't get the car out."

"Can't get the car out? What on earth are you talking about, Mr. Humphrey?"

"Like I said, Mr. Tims, sir, the snow's got me car all blocked in so I won't be in today."

"Mr Humphrey," Tims only just managed to keep his temper in check, "Windsor is only twenty miles from London and it is a beautiful sunny day here. It cannot possibly be snowing in Windsor!"

"Ya, well um, Mr. Tims, it must be some kind of freak snowstorm or somethin'."

Mr. Tims, who as I have said had already suffered one nervous breakdown while serving at the palace, was losing his grip on his patience.

"Humphrey, get here within thirty minutes otherwise you will explain this pathetic story to the Lord Chamberlain. Now I am telling you, it is not snowing in Windsor!"

It took Humphrey over an hour to appear, just in time for a large four-course lunch in the Officials dining-room. When I finally had a chance to question him on the inadequacy of his excuse for not showing up to work, Humphrey looked at me with his usual impudent swagger and simply said, "Oh piss-off you!"

2

As the end of June came upon the Royal Household, Sir Peter Ashmore was busily making arrangements for the Court to have as comfortable a stay in the hinterlands of Scotland as possible.

The Queen did not always get along with her Master of the Household, finding him autocratic even with her. Besides, she wasn't terribly fond of navy people in the first place, having received more then a fair dose in her own family, particularly the Duke.

There were two days remaining until the Court moved to Scotland and Sir Peter would be briefing us after lunch. I was relaxing in the palace bar with a gin and bitter-lemon. I left Mr. Humphrey in the office composing a note to the Queen concerning the horse she was anxious to hear about. My weighty colleague had scratched out a rough and shoddy few sentences on a stained and crinkled sheet of paper. I reminded him that when a member of the Royal Household wishes to write to the Monarch, any correspondence must be prefaced 'With my humble duty'. Mr. Humphrey had simply scrawled 'Your Majesty' and this could be considered most offensive. "Give it here," he growled when I pointed out his error, and snatched the paper out of my hand. "The Queen's not interested in all that crap." Of course, she most certainly is.

Paul Almond, the phantom raspberry blower, was sitting next to me in the bar and was in a foul mood. As we were talking, Sir Peter walked past the entrance of the bar. "What a fucking prat," yelled Paul, taking his frustrations out on the nearest person who did not meet with his approval. Sir Peter stopped in his tracks and peered into the bar. It was not one of his favorite territories. He had obviously heard the remark and glared at Paul saying, "Keep the noise down in here please," and then disappeared. Still within hearing range Paul loudly shouted, "That will bring the boring old sod down to earth," and then roared with laughter. Sir Peter did not come back for a second dose.

At four o'clock that afternoon Sir Peter held the meeting in his office. The most senior of Officials gathered to hear his final remarks concerning the visit to Holyrood. Myself, along with Tims, a gentleman by the name of Michael Parker, and Mr. Humphrey sat in a semi-circle in front of his desk.

Sir Peter was a tall, elegant man in his mid-sixties; elegant, that is, except for his large ears which were even more protruding than those belonging to Prince Charles. Previously a vice admiral in the Royal Navy, Sir Peter ran the palace very much like one of his ships. He was fond of using navy metaphors and would frequently call me requesting that I come and see him on "the bridge."

Sir Peter was dressed in a dark pinstriped suit, once splendid, now threadbare and tired. He scratched his nose thoughtfully. "Now then, gentleman," Sir Peter began from behind his enormous teak desk, "I want you to all take note of these final remarks I have regarding our upcoming visit to Holyrood." Sir Peter shifted in his chair in the comfortable room overlooking Buckingham Palace Road. The office was warm and inviting with its pale pink Persian carpets and naval pictures dotted all around. "Now as you can see from the sheet I have provided you all…Ah…Humphrey? Are you paying attention? This is for your benefit you know." Sir Peter raised his eyebrows quizzically in my colleague's direction.

"Oh what's that, Sir Peter?" Humphrey looked up from his lap.

"I said, are you paying attention, Humphrey?"

"'Course I am, Sir Peter. Why do ya ask that?"

Sir Peter returned to the paper in front of him without answering. "Um, now where was I? Oh yes here we go...As you can all see from the sheet I have provided you with, there are still one or two matters which concern me about...Mr. Humphrey? Is there something I can help you with over there? You seem to be awfully busy."

Humphrey put his newspaper under his chair. "What's that, Sir Peter?"

"I asked you if I could be of any assistance?"

"In what?" Humphrey scratched a sideburn thoughtfully.

"In reading your newspaper. I am not blind you know."

"Sir Peter," Humphrey began defensively, "I want you to know that I've been listenin' to every word you've said."

"Oh really, Humphrey?" he replied scornfully. "What was I talking about then? Tell us all if you would."

"You was talkin' about the palace in Scotland."

Sir Peter looked exasperated. "Yes? Well? What about it then?"

Humphrey scratched his head with puzzlement.

"In what regard was I referring to Holyrood Palace?" Sir Peter prodded helpfully.

"What do ya mean, Sir Peter?" Humphrey was now stalling.

"Oh never mind, Humphrey. If everyone else will cast their attention in the direction of the sheets in front of them—*please*."

Sir Peter took a moment to collect himself.

"Now, as I was saying. There are one or two points I wish to make here. First off, what progress have you made with that shipment of food we have been discussing the past several months Parker? Is everything in order?"

Parker screeched to attention in his chair. "I'm dreadfully sorry, Sir Peter. What was that you said?" Parker always spoke far too loudly, far too quickly and with a heavy emphasis on each word.

Sir Peter sank to the back of his chair shaking his head in disbelief. After a brief pause he proceeded. "I would like to know, Parker, if you have finalized arrangements to provide Holyrood Palace with all the essentials the Queen is going to require for her week-long stay?"

Parker barked confidently, "Yaaah, Sir Peter! I most certainly have, Sir Peter! All is in order, Sir Peter!"

Sir Peter looked unconvinced.

"I see. You are quite sure?"

"Yaaah, Sir Peter! All taken care of, Sir Peter! All is in order, Sir Peter!"

"Parker you do not have to call me 'Sir Peter' all the time. One will do."

"Of course, Sir Peter!"

Sir Peter pushed on. "Alright then, Parker. But just let me warn you that I have telephoned Forsythes in Edinburgh and told them that due to a rise in their prices, Her Majesty will not be needing their usual shipment this year. I am counting on that freighter you are sending up from London."

Parker gave another quick, "All taken care of, Sir Peter!" and resumed studying the carpet.

Michael Parker, head of the Food Branch at the palace, ran an important department. He was solely responsible for all the Royal Family's food requirements, for State occasions as well as for their personal needs. Approaching forty years old, Parker was an odd one. Prior to working for the palace he had been in management—God help them—at the Savoy Hotel. A thoroughly bedraggled looking character, with black, receding, greasy hair, he always walked with his hands in his pockets and in the hunchback department would have given Bobo Macdonald a run for the bottle...I mean money.

The Queen despised him. She felt he was incompetent and a total waste of time. There were only a very small number of duties which he managed to actually carry out without something going wrong. Worse still, Her Majesty thought him a bit of a peeping Tom, for he was always spying on her whenever he had the opportunity. Often she would catch him peeking at her from behind a bush in the palace gardens, or through the doors of the state banquet room when she was dining with her guests.

Most of the time, we Officials simply laughed off his inefficiencies and ineptness and accepted the fact that he was not going to change. But an incident that occurred shortly after he arrived somewhat changed the picture. You see, there had once been a kindly old man who worked in the palace as a kitchen porter. His name was John Cleminson and although he did not directly work in Parker's department, Parker was in charge of assigning him living-quarters. Now, normally a man in John Cleminson's position received one of the less comfortable rooms available to Staff. He was, after all, about as low on the Staff pecking order as one could possibly be. However due to a problem with his heart, his doctor had recommended that his patient not climb stairways or exert himself in any unnecessary way.

For months the kitchen porter was housed in a room on the second floor of the palace, and this worked out well as it was so close to where his duties lay. Problems arose, however, when another sous chef was added to the Royal Chef's Staff and accommodation had to be found for him. As the kitchen porter was occupying one of the rooms normally reserved for the high ranking chefs, and these were all taken, Parker decided that the porter would have to move. And move him he did.

Although aware of the man's heart condition, Parker somehow came upon the idea that he was only exaggerating his

110

medical condition, possibly in the aspiration of acquiring a better room than he was otherwise entitled to. So Parker callously designated him a shoe box of a room, not on the first floor, or the second, or even the third. No he did not. He assigned him to the attic floor!

Being a meek sort of fellow and not the trouble causing kind, the lowly kitchen porter accepted the order without complaint and continued on with his job. Two weeks later he was dead. The strain of ascending and descending stairs that would give a twenty-year-old something to think about proved his undoing.

Sir Peter Ashmore was stunned with incredulity when he was informed of the tragedy as he had been responsible for securing the aged porter better accommodation in the first place. That order had not been rescinded. Parker had disobeyed his instructions, and now one of the Queen's servants was needlessly in his grave. Incredibly enough, Parker was not asked to resign. The whole incident was covered up from the press and everyone was led to believe that the cause of the kitchen porter's untimely demise had been natural.

"Sir Peter?" I called, wanting to get on with the meeting so I could go home, "I forgot to mention that I will be taking John Humphrey's place at Holyrood this year if that will be alright?"

"Why aren't you going, Humphrey?" Sir Peter looked at him suspiciously.

"What's that, Sir Peter?" Humphrey said, reluctantly removing his eyes from his newspaper.

"Oh now, Humphrey, you really are going too far. Haven't you been listening to me at all?"

"'Course I have, Sir Peter." Humphrey sounded hurt. "I really do find that insultin', I do. I've heard every word you've said." Humphrey was a master.

"Alright, Humphrey. Never mind." Sir Peter had had enough. He wasn't going to waste any more time on him. "Malcolm has just told me that you cannot make it to Holyrood this year. Why is that?"

"Oh oh oh...ya,ya...well...actually, Sir Peter, I'm glad ya asked me that question."

"Well? Why aren't you going?"

"Ya, ya, I'm with ya now, Sir Peter. I can't go this year cause...cause...um...oh ya, one of the mares has come down with a bit of a cold ya see, and I promised Her Majesty that I'd keep an eye on it for her."

"Well, why can't one of your employees do that? You have enough of them."

"Oh no, no, no, Sir Peter. I couldn't shirk my responsibility. When I give my word on somethin' I have to keep it. It is for Her Majesty ya know, Sir Peter."

"If it is for Her Majesty, Humphrey, then I suppose I will let you off. In answer to your question, Malcolm, that is quite alright. Delighted to have you there." He glared at Humphrey.

Parker hiccuped.

Sir Peter received a call from the Queen's Private Secretary in the middle of the meeting and had to leave for a few minutes. Tims majestically took over and positioned himself firmly behind the Master of the Household's desk. Humphrey raised his hand and interrupted shortly after Tims began speaking.

"Excuse me, Mr. Tims."

Tims ignored him.

"Mr. Tims... Excuse me, Mr. Tims."

Tims answered coldly, "Yes, Humphrey? What is it now?"

"Mind if I go and take a slash?"

Tims was perplexed. "A slash?"

"Ya. That's right, a slash. Mind if I go and take one?"

Tims looked around the room not certain if this was something he ought to know about or not.

"Well...what is a slash, Mr Humphrey?" he asked hesitantly. "I have never heard of it before."

112

"You know, a piss!" Humphrey announced proudly.

Tims turned an unhealthy red. Humphrey was getting to him again. "Yes, Mr. Humphrey, go ahead." Humphrey quickly left the room.

Sir Peter returned a couple of seconds after Mr. Humphrey. With routine matters having been dealt with, the meeting was coming to an end.

"Very good chaps, that is all for today." Sir Peter began to rise from his chair. "Now Parker you are quite sure you will have that freightliner in Scotland in time, are you?"

"Indeed, Sir Peter! No problem, Sir Peter!"

"Look, Parker, I have told you to stop calling me 'Sir Peter' every time you speak. It is not necessary."

"So sorry, Sir Peter!"

"Just make certain that freightliner is sent." The knight was exasperated.

"Of course, Sir Peter!" he replied again, much too loudly and much too quickly.

"Well then, that about takes care of things I guess, chaps. Thanks ever so much for your patience."

"Ya, Sir Peter, Sir Peter!" Humphrey called, arms waving madly in the air.

Sir Peter begrudgingly took notice. "Yes, Humphrey, what do you want?" he said without a trace of warmth.

"Well actually, Sir Peter, I just wanted to say that I like the new car park."

"What's that, Humphrey?"

"I just wanted to tell ya that I like the new car park that's been put in at the palace."

Sir Peter rolled his eyes towards the ceiling, and then at Mr. Humphrey. "Humphrey, we are all well aware of the parking lot, thank you."

"No, No, Sir Peter, I really mean it. No one else has mentioned it but I just wanted you to know that it makes life ever so much easier if you're comin' by car—"

"John," I edged him lightly so that no one would notice, "Sir Peter isn't interested."

Sir Peter ended the meeting and the room cleared. Humphrey still couldn't understand what he had done wrong.

"Well thanks very much Malcolm. You didn't give me a chance to tell Sir Peter about me new car."

It was Friday afternoon, and on Sunday the Queen's Court would be making its way to Holyrood Palace; once the home of Mary Queen of Scots and her husband Lord Darnley, who was supposedly murdered over 400 years ago.

PALACE OF HOLYROOD

July 1st - July 7th

1

As the British Rail train sped along on its way to Edinburgh, I was enjoying a Corvoisier in the dimly lit dining car. I was not able to board the train until an hour before midnight, and shortly I planned on retiring to my private cabin to bed. It would take roughly ten hours to complete the journey from London to Scotland and I was very tired. There is so much planning to undertake when the Court moves that the exhaustion can be very real.

Officials, such as myself, enjoyed the privilege of traveling first class when moving with the Queen's Court. Members of Staff (footmen, pages, cooks and other servants) traveled second class, the cars of which were located at the other end of the train, somewhere. If the journey was a relatively short one, to Windsor Castle for example, then I would make use of one of Her Majesty's fleet of ten Jaguars, usually the one bearing the licence plate 'BP 3'. This was the rule no matter where we went.

On trips to other countries Her Majesty is provided with her own personal British Airways L1011, which has been specially refurbished for her. Footmen and pages go ahead of her on a commercial airline, economy class. There were two notable exceptions to this rule—the Royal Chef and the Queen's Palace Steward. Although they were both members of Staff, they were granted first class status for the sole reason that they were so large neither could fit comfortably into the economy class seats.

Removing the image of the Royal Chef from my mind, I gazed out of the window at the blackened countryside. The occasional cluster of bright lights flashed by, denoting a small village or town, the only sign of life in the wilderness of dark. The soft lighting inside the railcar added a warmth to the starkness, or possibly it was the cognac, I do not know which.

Miss Victoria Martin, former chief housekeeper, came running into the dining car, hair unusually askew, looking as though she had just seen a ghost. I suggested she sit down immediately and ordered the attendant to bring her a stiff drink.

"Oh, Mr. Barker, I never thought it would happen but it has," she blurted out with shortened breath.

Several minutes passed until she was able to tell me of her fright. I couldn't imagine what she must have seen.

She now cradled a large brandy and slowly opened up.

"I have just come through the Staff car, Mr. Barker..." A dramatic swallow interrupted.

"Yes, Miss Martin, and what happened there?"

"Oh, Mr. Barker, it was dreadful. Absolutely dreadful."

"Yes, I am sure it was. Do tell me what has happened to cause you such distress. I promise you will feel better if you share it with someone."

"Well," she began ever so slowly, "I was just coming through the Staff car where I found most of them in the most frightful state of imbibement and very much out of control."

This was nothing new, I thought, but continued to offer ear to her story. "Yes, Miss Martin, yes. And then what?" It appeared she was teetering on hysteria.

"...And then, I told them to please stop...that their behavior was disgraceful."

"Yes, Miss Martin, yes." She was about to crack I could tell.

"And then one of them...one of them...one of them..."

"Yes...What? What? Miss Martin. Do tell me."

"One of them...tol...tol..."

"Yes Miss Martin, yes?"

"...told me to piss off!"

Silence. I had imagined a werewolf at the very least. I was sympathetic. Putting a trembling, kindly old hand to her chest, she continued. "It was awful, Mr. Barker, simply awful. Those young footmen were being abusive to me and their language was quite repugnant. I must tell you I am most distressed. Most distressed I am." She gulped another golden measure from her brandy glass.

Straightening her hair bun and pulling down on her dark pleated skirt, Miss Martin became engrossed in her nightmarish tale. To her, this was a major blow.

"A fight," Miss Martin continued theatrically, "has broken out further along with the senior guard and what is more painful to me, Mr. Barker, is the degree of *spirit* which I have noted to be firmly in existence. There is *spirit*, Mr. Barker, there is evil *spirit* everywhere!" Miss Martin suddenly took note of the brandy glass cupped between her own hands and self-consciously set it on the table in front of her.

"Yes, well, the footmen do like the odd drink don't they? Tell me though, I hope that you are alright?"

Miss Martin sighed heavily and placed an open hand to her heart with an extravagant display of emotion. "Oh yes...now I am. But I don't know what has happened, Mr. Barker. This never would have occurred twenty years ago, you know..."

Miss Martin carried on for a few hours. On and on, that is.

When she was finished, I willingly helped the former housekeeper to her room and she retired into her small compartment.

As I have said, Miss Martin at one time was the chief housekeeper in Buckingham Palace, but nowadays was only brought out of mothballs to help during certain busy times of the year. A strongly built lady with a purposeful face and stout black shoes to match, Miss Martin was as Edwardian as any I have seen. Having worked for King George V in the early thirties, she could not imagine that life had changed so much. But it had.

However Miss Martin was spared the worst that evening. Near riots broke out later amongst the footmen, and British Rail guards battled through most of the night and early into the next morning struggling to keep the footmen and pages under some frail thread of control. One British Rail guard was roughed up quite brutally when two footmen set about him with their fists and a sandwich tray. While some might argue that the brawl was minor, and more or less confined to one carriage of the train, the shouting, and squabbling, and the running up and down the train's corridors ultimately became a disruption to the other passengers on board. At one point somewhere near dawn, one of the guards threatened to stop the train in the middle of the countryside and put all the Queen's Staff out if they didn't simmer down.

Indeed the behavior of the footmen had been noted that night. The guard who was manhandled by the footmen complained to his area manager in Aberdeen who in turn spoke to Sir Peter Ashmore in London. The guard even wrote a letter to the Master of the Household, and in it he compared the scene on the Edinburgh-bound train with "a bunch of football hooligans returning from an away match" which he stated he had had the odd misfortune of being involved with.

Conditions had significantly changed in the Queen's Court over the past two decades. Her Majesty simply was not able to acquire the same calibre of individual she once had access to. In many cases she had to put up with what could be found, and often enough the standard was not very high. Many of the Staff positions were put into the hands of boys who had simply written to the palace asking if there were any vacancies. Parents themselves regularly wrote and asked if their "perfect little lad" could have the honor of serving the "much adored and loved Queen." To many parents, Buckingham Palace seemed to be an alternative to reform school.

Fortunately, there were one or two marvellous and devoted individuals serving Her Majesty. A gentleman by the name of John Taylor, the Queen's Page of Chambers, is a perfect example. Her Majesty confides daily in this faithful servant and he does a superb job for her. But for the most part, those in the Royal Household fall far short of the mark. As on countless other occasions when Staff were found to be abusing their position, Sir Peter gave this lot a severe reprimand for the British Rail incident, but none of them were fired. This, even though they behaved just as badly on the return trip to London! Fortunately on the train journey back though there was really only one incident involving the footmen that could be deemed serious, but as I frankly told Sir Peter later in their defence, it was basically the dog's own fault.

2

There were a number of hangovers the following morning when I disembarked from the train in Edinburgh at eight thirty. The Waverly Street station was only about a mile from Holyrood Palace but it took a great deal of effort to round the footmen and pages all up and corral them onto their bus. I followed behind in a car.

The Queen arrived at Holyrood Palace around two thirty in the afternoon, along with her Mother, Sir Peter Ashmore, the Duchess of Grafton and one or two key advisers. They had all flown up together from London in one of the Queen's long serving Andovers, and when they landed at Edinburgh Airport, about a thirty minute drive from Holyrood, her black and maroon Rolls Royce, a Silver Jubilee present from the company in 1978, was there to meet them.

As soon as Her Majesty arrived at the sprawling, turreted Palace of Holyrood she had to immediately go through the ancient ritual known as the Ceremony of the Keys. This involves the Lord Lieutenant coming to the palace and handing over the keys of the city of Edinburgh to her. It is a very old custom, and a dull one. Her Majesty detests the chore. But as with so much in her life she is obligated to perform her duty. With the visit itself, for instance, the Queen must travel to Holyrood in order to maintain her position as the Queen of Scotland. Similarly to Windsor Castle and Buckingham Palace the ancient Scottish palace is not the personal property of the Monarch. In the case of Holyrood, it is owned and run by the city of Edinburgh and it is Her Majesty's least favorite home. She dreads the obligation she must fulfil each year, even if it is only for one week.

The royal apartments in Holyrood are comfortable but even at the most sultry time of year a little heat does not go unwanted. Evenings can be bone chilling cold and the palace is invariably damp and draughty. Except for this one week period the entire palace, including the royal apartments, are open for tours to the public. The only room that outsiders do not see is the Queen's bedroom. Scarcely anyone in the Royal Family offers to accompany Her Majesty on her yearly trek to Holyrood, and those that do, do so begrudgingly. The Duke of Edinburgh is expected to be there every year, but usually he manages only one out of every two. Princess Anne and her brothers manage to put in an appearance once every few years and Princess Margaret refuses to go at all.

Shortly after arriving at Holyrood, and with the important key ceremony now taken care of, a very embarrassed Sir Peter arrived in the Queen's apartment to tell Her Majesty that there was a tiny, ever so slight problem: there was nothing to eat in the palace for her or her guests. The freightliner carrying all the vital goods needed for her one week's stay had not arrived! What was worse, it was carrying all the wine and spirits from the royal cellars in London. Despite Sir Peter's repeated reminders back in London, it was learned that Michael Parker had completely forgotten about the freightliner, and the Queen had to be told that there was not so much as a pint of milk in the palace—the cupboards were bare.

The Queen was understandably *very annoyed*, but as always, she kept her temper. It did not matter that Sir Peter had done his best to assure the freightliner arrived on time. The fact was, as far as Her Majesty was concerned, it wasn't there and what was she to do now?

Sir Peter busied himself on the telephone. Firstly to Forsythes in Edinburgh, which normally handled all the grocery requirements for the Queen's stay in the Scottish palace. Unfortunately, due to the late notice, they were only able to supply a small portion of what was needed. Nowhere near enough to fulfill all our requirements. There were banquets and garden parties planned, the daily needs of the Queen and her family, not to mention the entire Royal Household to look after as well!

Sir Peter ended up personally driving into town and dashing from shop to shop purchasing enough provisions to at least tie everyone over for the night. When he arrived back at Holyrood he found further problems: the Queen was cold, very cold. For while he was out doing the shopping, the heating system in the palace had broken down, and then an hour later, the electricity went out and there seemed to be no one around who was capable of fixing it. The city of Edinburgh was actually responsible for Holyrood's maintenance and normally service was prompt, however it employed union men, none of whom wanted to venture out to Holyrood at this time of day. After all, it was past five o'clock.

It wasn't until the following morning that the city finally sent someone in to perform the necessary repairs on the palace fuseboxes. Her Majesty was forced to spend the entire night in the isolation of Scotland, in a damp and draughty palace, with little or no food and barely a drop of good wine in the house. Her Staff found hot water bottles for her bed and dotted candles throughout the eerie rooms. Apart from Sir Peter, the Queen said not a mean word to anyone. The Duchess of Grafton on the other hand was a totally different matter.

3

I have never been one to give much credence to the ancient tales of Mary Queen of Scots' palace being haunted. Indeed, I normally laugh at anything so silly. I have never believed in ghosts, spirits, unnatural forces or any other form of communication with the dead. Not until I stayed at Holyrood Palace, that is.

At Windsor Castle, my office was the room in which George III was locked up in during his period of mental instability. At Holyrood, my accommodation was housed in part of the original castle which was begun in 1498. I felt slightly weak when I was told that my bedroom formed part of the original chambers occupied by Mary Queen of Scots herself.

It was a spacious, oak panelled room with a crimson rug covering some ancient, creaky floorboards. On the walls hung pictures of medieval Scottish noblemen, and against one wall were two heavy oak chests. The only concession to modern-day living was a washstand in one corner. Two small windows insured that the room was in semi-darkness even during daylight hours.

On my first night I was reading in bed and desperately trying to convince myself that any thoughts of haunted figures coming in to view were total nonsense. This probably would have worked well if there had been some light. In the shadowy glow of a candle, however, I was having a tough time ridding my mind of the evil images. It sounds ridiculous to one who was not there, but the mental picture of the Scottish Queen and the bloody figure of her murdered husband, Lord Darnley, became all too vivid that evening. Of course, when you happen to be actually lying in the very room where so much of the intrigue took place, it is perhaps understandable. Think about it…in the exact room, around midnight, with only candlelight!

I must have dozed off. I was asleep for two or three hours when I awoke with a start. The candle was extinguished—probably by a draught or something (it was the 'something' that I didn't like). I felt a strange presence in the room, as if I were not alone. I got out of bed, re-lit the candle, and went over to the door. It was still firmly locked. I wandered slowly over towards the windows and peered out into the night. All seemed well. Petrified, I crept back into bed.

The huge room felt oppressive and I simply couldn't shed the overwhelming feeling that someone or something was also in there with me. I spent most of the night reading in my bed; the howling of the wind and creaking of the old wooden structure was almost more then I could bare.

When I arrived downstairs for breakfast the next morning, I was noticeably pale. My condition was noted by an old porter in the hall. "Mr. Barker, what is wrong?" he asked me. "You look like you have seen a ghost."

"Well, actually I feel as though I have," and I told him of my experience. "I feel so silly though," I added when I was through with my tale. "I know it was only my imagination working in high gear."

"Mr. Barker," the long serving porter said in a quiet, serious voice. "I have been here for forty-five years and my father and grandfather before that. Let me assure you it was not your imagination. Didn't you know the ghost of Mary Queen of Scots lives on?"

I slept very little after that.

Parker arrived in Edinburgh later that morning on a train he had almost missed. Enjoying the atmosphere of his favorite London pub, he cut short his socializing only just in the nick of time.

Another minute and he would have missed the train altogether. When he arrived at Holyrood he was summoned 'on the carpet' by a frazzled Sir Peter, who looked desperately eager to throttle the man to death.

By the look on Parker's face after the meeting, he had received the full brunt of Sir Peter's rage. When asked what happened to the shipment he had so confidently assured Sir Peter was on its way, Parker said, "Yaaah. Oh dear, Sir Peter. It must have slipped my mind." He hadn't, in fact, done a bloody thing at all.

The end result was that Sir Peter angrily advised him he would no longer be handling the supply arrangements outside of Buckingham Palace. This was his punishment. The only amusing spot in the unfortunate affair was Mr. Humphrey's comment back at Buckingham Palace on hearing of Parker's foul-up. "Bloody typical of him, isn't it," he told me shamelessly over the telephone.

Now *that* was rich.

4

On the second and third day of the Court's visit, which can last anywhere from five to eight days, Her Majesty spends her time opening factories and visiting buildings which she has committed herself to prior to the visit. She will also view any worthwhile projects that are happening in the area and possibly take the opportunity to inspect any regiments of which she happens to be Colonel-in-Chief. Suffice to say, it is extremely heavy-going. A visit to a dreary, industrial factory in Edinburgh can hardly be described as glamorous. At these times she thinks fondly of her beloved Balmoral Castle, situated 150 miles to the north.

On the fourth evening of the Court's visit, Parker arrived back from a late night of drinking to find the doors to Holyrood Palace firmly locked. There was no one in sight to admit him. What was he to do? Even though it was July, it was cold outside and he was tired and wanted to go to bed. An idea struck him. He went around to the front of the palace and threw a pebble up at a third floor bedroom window.

No answer.

He decided that the pebble wasn't quite working so he picked up several little ones and threw those up at the window.

Still no one came.

He looked around the ground beneath him for something that would be a little more effective, and picked up a stone which he threw with more force. He was hoping to awaken me so that I could go downstairs and let him in. This time the stone was effective and sailed through the closed window smashing glass in a horrific explosion in the soundless night. I still didn't hear it though because Parker was aiming at the wrong window. Instead of myself, a very sleepy and bewildered Sir Peter appeared at the window and looked down at Parker standing below.

"Who the devil is that? What do you want?" Sir Peter called, understandably shaken.

"Oh...? So sorry, Sir Peter. It's you is it? Aaaah...? Awfully sorry to trouble you but, um, it seems as though I can't get into the palace. I thought it was Malcolm's window I was hitting."

"Damn it, Parker...I will call someone to let you in but I want to see you in my office at nine tomorrow morning. Do you hear me? Nine tomorrow morning. Now leave me alone."

But the following morning Sir Peter had another matter on his mind, although not immediately attributable to Parker. During the previous evening the Royal Chef had been reprimanded by Sir John Miller for using the Queen's personal door to exit the palace. A very serious offence. The Royal Chef wasn't used to obeying any rules set for the general Staff and was more than aware that his services to Her Majesty were valued by her enormously. He well knew that she wasn't about to dismiss him on as petty a matter as that.

"Go stuff yerself," he told Sir John when confronted outside the palace, and then carried on with his goal of reaching the local pub in as short a time frame as possible.

When the Royal Chef returned much later that night he and Cyril Dickman, the Queen's Palace Steward, thought it would be fun to play with the sentry boxes that were used by the Royal Scots Guards to protect the palace. They turned the boxes completely around so that they faced inward towards the palace and not outward as they were normally more effectively positioned.

When the sentry boxes remained that way the following morning we were all perplexed as to why the guards did not either prevent this, or at least return them to their proper position. The reason was discovered later in the morning when Sir Peter learned that the two guards designated to keep watch had gone to the pub and then called it a night. Holyrood was left completely unattended for the entire evening. Anyone could have entered the palace grounds.

Amazingly enough, the two guards kept their jobs.

5

On day five of the Holyrood visit, Crown Equerry Sir John Miller picked up the telephone and called for a car and driver.

"Where would you like to go, sir?" came the obedient voice at the other end."

Sir John retorted in his Etonian manner, "I want to go to the swimming pool and I want to go now."

"To the swimming pool, sir?" came the surprised voice at the other end.

"Yes, that is what I just said, isn't it?"

"Do you mind if I ask which swimming pool, sir?"

"What do you mean by 'which swimming pool,' man? I want to go to the swimming pool I always go to." Sir John was completely dumbfounded by these questions.

"Yes sir, but which swimming pool is that?" The driver was quite obviously new.

"The Royal Family's swimming pool you buffoon. Where do you think?" The old knight was not amused if this was a joke.

"Well, if you will pardon me, Sir John, might I suggest you walk there."

"WALK?" came the disbelieving reply from Sir John's office. "Why would I want to do that?"

"Because if you open your door and walk a few yards you will find the royal baths to your right." The line to Sir John went dead.

Prior to this date Sir John had never considered walking to the baths. He would order a car and when it arrived he would open the door, climb into the chauffeur driven automobile with towel and swimming trunks in hand, and then would be driven a distance that used up no more then thirty seconds. With his swim over, he would ring for a car, and climb in for the return trip.

Sir John really could not understand this modern age at all.

6

On the final day of Her Majesty's visit to Scotland there was a garden party to attend. There are a total of four garden parties held every year, and the Queen attends each of them. One of the four parties is held at Holyrood Palace in July and over four thousand invited guests will throng there together, sipping tea and chatting. Depending on the duration of the Court's visit there might be a second garden party held at the palace. Whichever, they are both identical in nature.

Scottish aristocracy is still plentiful and makes up a large percentage of the guest list. But landed gentry are not the only ones invited to these parties. Local businessmen, civic dignitaries and politicians are also very much in evidence, as are ordinary men and women from every corner of life. Perhaps one deserving citizen has risked his life to save another, or an elderly farmer's widow might be invited because of her years of devotion to some charity organization. The list of those who are considered is endless.

The guests had congregated on a large lawn at the back of Holyrood Palace and the weather was fortunately in a cooperative mood. Those in attendance were waiting happily for the entrance of the Queen. Around three o'clock Her Majesty and the Queen Mother arrived at the garden party with a small entourage, and slowly, patiently, walked their way through the crowds of appreciative guests, indulging in casual conversation with as many people as time would allow. The Queen Mother was already enjoying a conversation with a young female swimmer who had achieved a major sporting feat for her country.

Everyone was splendidly turned out for the special occasion; men in top hat and morning suits, ladies in light summer dresses and flowery hats. Even the Queen donned the simplest of attire which included only the most discreet pieces of jewelry. Whoever the Royal Family member happens to be, they know what to do. The goal is to methodically move amongst the guests in a reasonably straight path towards the other end of the marquee. Unlike the more formal gatherings at Buckingham Palace, such as State Banquets and other official obligations, the garden parties are an exercise in social equality. It does not matter whether you are a Lord or a truck driver. Her Majesty will seek you out and want to hear what you have to say.

There was a hushed excitement amongst those in attendance as the two Queens moved ever so gracefully forward. There were plenty of anxious guests waiting their turn to catch one of the

Monarch's ears. No one appeared so desperate however that they were forced to engage the Duchess of Grafton in conversation, who was following several steps behind the Queen. At one time the Duchess would have been required to take charge of all the gifts and flowers which were once offered by the guests at these gatherings. The Queen however found that this was too exhausting for everyone, especially herself, and understandably put a stop to the gift giving.

The invited were indulging and chatting happily as the orchestra played gaily into the mid-afternoon. Cyril Dickman, the Queen's page who was the centre of attention behind her at the televised Reagan banquet, was next to the pastry table laboring over a decision: should he take the Bavarian cream *à la cevenole*, or the Apricots *à l'imperatrice*? Difficult choice. He settled it by taking a generous sampling of each. Of course, in his position he should not have been making a selection at all. But three dozen trestle tables lay glistening with afternoon delights: chocolate gateaux, scones, vanilla slices, tarts (no, not Queen Charlotte, the jam version), meringues, profiteroles and the temptation of so much more.

The only distinction between these garden parties and the numerous other functions the Queen hosts each year is the absence of liquor. Nothing but a wide variety of the very finest teas and soft drinks are offered, and this regulation applies to the garden parties held at the palace in London as well. One can generally assume that the only liquor making an appearance today was in Cyril Dickman's jacket pocket.

As the royal women continued forward the Queen spotted many a well known face. Lord Home chatted with the Earl of Strathmore about his nearby estate. The Marquis of Zetland was talking in earnest to Sir Hector Monroe, a former minister of sports in the British government. Sir Peter Ashmore, still seething over the many problems the visit to Holyrood had wrought, was having a joke with the Duke of Sutherland. The Queen smiled at them and continued on.

For those who want a personal introduction with Her Majesty there is a card that must be filled out weeks before the actual day arrives. This is handed to the Lord Chamberlain, at that time, Lord Maclean, and he will see to it that the introductions are made. Most members of the public invited though are understandably too timid to make such a request. As a result, the official line of people that must be dealt with when the Queen first arrives is never very long. To some, a face to face meeting with the Monarch can be a daunting prospect and often completely overwhelming.

The Queen and visiting members of her family must usually start any conversation and they have some standard ways of going about it. Her Majesty might say to one couple, "Have you come far today to see me?" or "Have you been waiting to see me for long?" These are naturally good openers as they immediately invite conversation on ground the individual feels secure on. For the most part, Her Majesty does a lot of listening and not a great deal of talking.

Some people ask the most ludicrous questions. One lady shrieked at Her Majesty when she approached, "Oh where did you get those shoes love?" and another, "Oooooh you are such a sweet thing Queen!" and yet another addressed her as he bit into a crumbling pastry, "This is a lovely sausage roll, Yer Highness, absolutely lovely it is." Her Majesty will not correct the slip. If they prefer, she will be "Your Highness" and not "Your Majesty" for the afternoon. Being presented with such comments, Her Majesty will smile politely and move on—quickly.

This year's garden party was progressing well as Her Majesty continued to greet the crowds. Much to the Duchess of Grafton's obvious relief they were now fairly close to the end of the marquee. Here, in a few moments, the hosts would meet and at last be handed a very much welcomed cup of tea. This is normally all they will want. Even with one as experienced in these social affairs as the Queen, she does not enjoy being stared at while she consumes a scone. Who would? So she will remain with tea if anything at all.

Suddenly—to the Queen's right—a loud splitting noise was heard, as if one of the sombre Scottish Lords had tucked himself too tightly into his trousers. And then...all heads turned in Her Majesty's direction as one of the trestle tables—struggling under the burden of tons of food—gave way and came crashing down to the ground with a thunderous din!

Silence came upon the party.

Dishes, glasses and cutlery were strewn everywhere and the just replenished trays of food were scattered all over the grass and on some of the guests who had been standing in front of the collapsed table. Her Majesty instantly searched around for her footmen to help wipe them off. Out of the corner of her eye she spotted Parker peering at her from behind a pillar. "Tell that damn Parker to go away!!" she ordered to a footman now busy wiping chocolate from her shoe. It was all terribly embarrassing for her.

Still though, as I said to Sir Peter after all the guests had departed, if any of the Royal Chef's creations were going to end up on the Queen, it might as well have been the *Mousse à la Reine*!

BUCKINGHAM PALACE

July 8th - August 15th

1

We had been back at Buckingham Palace for a week and extremely occupied with the upcoming wedding of Prince Charles to Lady Diana Spencer. Preparations for this day had been going on for almost one year. It was a major undertaking and I honestly do not think it could have been accomplished without the invaluable organization and guidance of Rear Admiral Jannion, who had been specially brought in at the request of the Queen.

Days before the wedding was to take place there were numerous celebrations happening in the palace. On the eve of the royal wedding there was a great fireworks display in Hyde Park as a festive celebration for all of London. Although I maintained an apartment in London, I often stayed at the palace for several days on special occasions, and the royal wedding was certainly one of them. Some of the guests invited to the wedding by Her Majesty and the Duke were considered so important that they were staying at the palace itself. This naturally required increased supervision all round.

One of the guests was the much favored King Olaf of Norway. Shortly after dinner he left the palace to take a look at the impressive fireworks display for himself. Not being in the best of health, the King was not out long and arrived back at the palace with his footman and guards earlier then expected.

Before retiring for the evening he requested his footman, Keith Magloire, to bring him a simple ham salad sandwich and a glass of beer. Under normal circumstances this would not have presented a problem, however when the footman attempted to place the request he received no reply from the kitchens. The Royal Chef was nowhere to be found.

I happened to be in my office working alone on some minor details involving the next day's events when my telephone rang. Who could it be at this hour, I wondered, looking at my watch for confirmation of the late hour? It was nine thirty.

The King of Norway, the young footman informed me, had already called him once to see what the delay was and the footman was growing increasingly alarmed over the apparent disappearance of the Royal Chef. What should he do?

I assembled a small search party to locate the Royal Chef and despatched it to all four corners of the palace. "The King must have his sandwich!" I declared to all. Within half an hour we found the Royal Chef in a back room just off his office, slumped in an armchair and fast asleep; his snores reverberating around the tiny room like the organ in St. Paul's at Evensong. Clutched under one arm was an almost empty bottle of Scotch, hanging precariously and dripping on his already soiled and grimy trousers.

All attempts to stir the chef failed and I was forced to admit to the King's footman that I felt he was way beyond even minor repair. We returned to the kitchens, and I decided that if King Olaf was going to be provided with anything to eat that night then it was I who would have to prepare it for him. And that is exactly what I did.

A huge party was thrown following the fireworks and the invited guests were amongst the most distinguished in the country and abroad. Sir Harold Wilson, former Prime Minister of Great Britain, stepped out from his car having arrived at the Grand Entrance of the palace. As he did so he declared to the surprised footman who met him, "Here we are at B.P. That stands for British Petroleum you know, young man!"

Inside, Her Majesty was dressed splendidly in a burgundy colored evening gown and chatted amiably with guests as her husband, the Duke, occasionally checked a table or mantle for dust. This was not unusual. Checking for dust was an annoying habit that had earned him the name 'Pompous Pip' within the palace. Not very flattering, but then next to the Queen's name of 'Squeaky Liz', it could probably be tolerated.

Prince Charles had personally chosen the musicians to entertain the guests. There was Kenny Ball and his Jazzmen, Joe Loss and his Orchestra and one of the Prince's favorite rock groups, Hot Chocolate, with lead player Errol Brown. In their suite prior to the performance, the latter ten-member group ordered—and drank—two bottles of gin, two bottles of scotch, two bottles of vodka and two bottles of dark rum.

Sir Harold Wilson, who was very much liked by the Queen, and very much partaking of her refreshments, suddenly knocked a glass belonging to the Duke of Northumberland off the piano and it hit the floor of the Green Drawing Room with a loud crash. Sir Harold turned bright red as he quickly shot a glance around the room to judge if anyone had taken notice of his blunder. Much to his annoyance, former Conservative Prime Minister Mr. Edward Heath was looking his way, and his hysterical laughter nearby must have tripled his embarrassment. However, the fact that several years later it was 'Lord Wilson of Rievaulx' and still plain old 'Mr. Edward Heath', representing the inelegantly named constituency of Sidcup, should tell you something about which of the two was most admired by Her Majesty.

Princess Margaret had arrived alone and was sipping something clear over ice as she spoke disinterestedly with Lady Ashmore, the wife of Sir Peter. Unfortunately Lady Ashmore was again wearing the gaudiest of attire and this was generally considered to be the reason her husband wasn't seen with her very often. Even the French Ambassador was more popular in royal circles, and that is saying something!

Sir John Miller was laughing with a group of friends and coming to the end of a joke with what seemed like uncontrollable snorts, when the Royal Chef interjected from a food table nearby. "Havin' a good booze-up are ya, Sir John?"

The two ladies with the knight looked slightly pale with incomprehension. Obviously they did not know the Royal Chef or fully appreciate his sense of humor.

The Royal Chef had come out of the kitchens for a moment's breath of fresh air and was now helping himself to some punch in full view of the guests. Chugging it down in one effort, he called over to me, "Eeehhh, Malcolmmmmm! What do ya think of me new outfit?"

"Super, Peter, absolutely super," I replied to him quickly, thinking about the royal outfitters who had recently come to the palace to provide the chef with a new uniform. Since the previous fitting, though, it had been discovered that the Royal Chef's waist had increased somewhat to a dimension that had hitherto not been offered at their shop. Not wanting to risk any repercussions and guarding their royal warrant with great zeal, they had to have garments specially made up for him.

The Queen and the Duke retired around midnight, which was their usual style, but the party continued on festively until the wee hours of the morning.

3

On the day of the royal wedding, around eleven in the morning, Mr. Humphrey excitedly entered our office requesting that I follow him immediately. He had something very important to show me. Reluctantly I followed, growing ever more curious as we neared the apartments of the Royal Family. Looking up and down the corridor, Mr. Humphrey opened the door to Princess Anne's suite and ushered me in as he softly closed the door behind us.

"Well, what is it you want to show me here, John?" I asked still not understanding the point.

He pointed a stubby finger towards the trolley in the center of the Princess's living room. "Look Malcolm. It's that over there."

"What," I said, still not comprehending.

"The food and champagne, what do ya think I mean ya silly bugger?"

"You mean this breakfast trolley which was sent up specifically for Princess Anne and Captain Phillips?"

"Heh heh heh!" he laughed heartily. "I don't care who it were for. It's mine now!" he beamed with pleasure, selecting a ripe peach while at the same time pouring a crystal flute to the top with champagne.

"John!" I cried sternly. "These croissants and fresh fruit are meant for Princess Anne's enjoyment. I don't think she would be very pleased to know what you were up to."

"Oh sod Princess Anne. She hasn't even touched any of this," Humphrey mumbled devouring the peach while at the same time choosing another from the trolley. "Go on, Malcolm. Help yourself to some champagne."

"No I will not, thank you. I am leaving and I suggest you do the same before anyone catches you." I turned towards the door and Humphrey slurped down the last of the champagne.

As I paused, waiting for him to follow, he placed the empty glass and the discarded peach stone on top of Princess Anne's television set. A fitting monument to the man, I thought, and no doubt more than a little perplexing for the princess when she returned!

I raced back to my office, leaving Mr. Humphrey outside the Princess's suite wondering if he should go back for another peach. There seemed still to remain a thousand tasks before the wedding breakfast.

No sooner had I sat down at my desk and picked up the telephone to place a call to Lord Maclean then in burst the former Chief Housekeeper, Miss Victoria Martin. We were so occupied with the wedding, and had been for almost a year, that she had been brought in once again to assist the lady who replaced her in the post, Miss De Trey White.

"Mister Barker! I must report to you a shameful act which I have just witnessed," Miss Martin stated matter-of-factly.

"What would that be, Miss Martin?"

"It would be a distressing occurrence concerning one of your footmen."

"Well, what happened? Do tell me."

"Well Mr. Barker…I knocked on the door of one of my maids, wishing to discuss a matter of some importance with her, and when I heard some muffled noises I walked in."

"Yes, yes," I replied trying to show great concern.

"Immediately in front of me I saw a footman lying naked on her bed performing an act of…an act of…."

"Yes, yes, an act of what, Miss Martin"?

"An act of…of…"

"Of what,Miss Martin, of what?"

"An act of…fornication, Mister Barker!" she shrieked with emotion, "and I want to know what you are going to do about it?"

"Well, Miss Martin, it sounds to me as though it has already been done. What can I do?"

"Steps should be taken to prevent this sort of unnatural act in the future, Mr. Barker. I cannot have young men behaving in such a disgraceful fashion, forcing themselves upon my helpless, innocent, virtuous young ladies. It is not decent Mr. Barker, it is simply not decent!"

She stormed out of the office close to tears. Nothing like this had ever happened during her tenure in the palace many years ago. Similarly to her unsettling encounter with the riotous footmen on the train to Holyrood, she failed to appreciate that times had changed. I didn't bother to tell her that the type of activity she had just witnessed was of little concern to me. *Straight* footmen were considered a god-send. My hands were full trying to keep the footmen themselves apart!

4

The Royal Family waved from the balcony of Buckingham Palace as the crowds roared and cheered from the Mall. This was their last chance to see the newly wed Prince and Princess of Wales before they departed for their honeymoon on board the Royal Yacht *Britannia*. As I stood watching the Royal Family wave to the tens of thousands of excited spectators gathered in front of the palace I could not help but feel, as did we all, the incomparably satisfying sense of achievement, mingled with joy and great pride. The only sour spot during the whole day was when Her Majesty spotted a mistake in the itinerary of the newly wed couple's honeymoon. She noted with astonishment that Parker had spelled Britannia with two t's and one n. "He cannot even spell that properly!" Her Majesty shook her head with dismay.

The following morning, as a start to my day, I received a telephone call from Sir Peter Ashmore regarding an episode involving one of Her Majesty's footmen. Actually, I should say an ex-footman who went to work for the Duke and Duchess of

Gloucester. Arriving back from dinner and the theatre, the Duke and Duchess walked into their private sitting-room to find it in complete darkness, save the flickering of their television set. Switching on the lights in the room they found their butler and pantry footman sleeping naked on their sofa entangled in each other's arms. Running on their video machine in full glorious technicolor was a gay pornographic movie.

If nothing else, this only goes to prove that one just cannot find reliable help any more, even if your butler did once work for Buckingham Palace.

Humphrey walked into the office as another young footman went storming out past him, the two almost colliding.

"Here...watch it you!" Humphrey called threateningly after him.

"What's up with him, Malcolm?" he asked, plugging the kettle in for a cup of coffee and then stripping down to his underwear and settling into his armchair. An alarming odor drifted across the room.

"I am afraid Sir Peter has fired him. He's not been fulfilling his duties and this is the hundredth warning he has received. He wasn't very happy by the dismissal."

"Good," mumbled Humphrey, eagerly venturing into a Mars bar. "I never trusted that one anyway."

The telephone rang a few moments later. It was Sir Peter again.

"Malcolm?"

"Yes, Sir Peter, what can I do for you?"

"I'm afraid I have just been speaking with Her Majesty and there has been a spot of trouble..."

There had been trouble alright. After leaving my office, the young footman went directly up to the suite where he had previously been assigned to serve the visiting royal occupants. Once there, he went barging into the Queen of Saudi Arabia's room where she was in the process of dressing, turned his back to the

141

surprised Monarch, took down his pants and shrieked in a thick Cockney accent, "Do ya like me bum, Queeny?"

No, she certainly did not like his bum and telephoned the Queen personally about her encounter. Her Majesty was mortified but as the servant had already been fired there was nothing more to be done, except offer a sincere apology. If only the incident had happened in Saudi Arabia, we probably could have had the boy flogged or the offending parts chopped off, at the very least!

5

Mr. Humphrey left for a holiday at the end of the week and although the pace had slackened considerably now that the excitement of the wedding was over, I still had plenty to keep me occupied. Occupied in ways I had not envisaged...

An American porno queen, as she was referred to in the tabloids, had been at the palace for about a week as a guest of Prince Andrew. This was not going over well at all with the Queen. Against her better judgement, she allowed Prince Andrew to have his way, and she bravely put up with the visitor with as much tolerance as she could possibly muster. The Queen was generally extremely good-natured and not difficult to work for at all, as were practically all members of the Royal Family, but when she was crossed or unhappy it definitely showed.

The situation regarding Prince Andrew and his girlfriend had now reached a critical point, and Her Majesty had to step in and take some sort of action. The newspapers were being ruthless in their exploitation of the story, and with each new day came more public speculation, gossip, criticism, and worst of all, as far as the Queen was concerned, more photographs. I believe it was a London tabloid's front page coverage of the Prince's 'secret rendezvous' in the Caribbean that finally clinched it. Her Majesty called Prince Andrew into her sitting-room, sat him down formally, and informed him that she wanted his young friend out of the palace by the following morning.

Do the Queen's children still obey the Monarch when she speaks? The next morning at nine o'clock, a dark grey Jaguar bearing the license plate 'B P 1' pulled up at the trade entrance (appropriately enough) at the rear of the palace. In stepped Prince Andrew's girlfriend, with the aid of two footmen, a porter, and the Queen's Private Secretary, Sir Philip Moore. Her Majesty was taking no chances on this one.

As the young lady slipped into the soft beige leather interior, I bade her good morning from the other side of the car, tempted to reach in front of me and lessen the contents of the mahogany cocktail bar. No, it was a touch early, and I didn't want to risk the dreadful consequences should the young lady escape my clutches before I secured her on board the aircraft.

"Mind if I smoke, Mr. Baker?"

"Actually the name is Barker, and no, I do not mind if you smoke."

"Good."

A few moments passed in silence.

"Old Queeny certainly gave Andy a rollicking, eh? I don't know how ya put up with the old bag?" She suddenly remarked arrogantly.

I could have put her so blissfully in her place with just one sentence, but I refrained. "We manage," I said smiling demurely into her heavily made up scowl.

Ensuring that she was safely seated on board a direct British Airways flight to Chicago, I made it back to the palace in time for lunch.

It was oddly quiet without Mr. Humphrey around as I sat alone in my office following lunch. Normally one would have expected to have twice as much work to perform when a colleague leaves for a holiday, but as I have stated, I already did Mr. Humphrey's work as well so there was really no additional burden placed on my shoulders. The only nuisance of the afternoon was when Sir John Miller called requiring a delivery of the Queen's furniture.

"Yes, yes, yes...Malcolm? Good...yes. Would you have your chaps deliver up a load of furniture from Her Majesty's stores? Shotover Park is looking rather sparse," he would typically order when he telephoned. Shotover Park, of course, was his country residence, and when he tired of the surroundings there, he would return sofas, chairs, and the odd box of silver in exchange for other items in Buckingham Palace that he had not yet tried. Many members of the Queen's Household took similar liberties. With their grand mansions, castles and vast country estates one need only imagine the frantic activity taking place in the palace stores.

Sir Ralph Southward also called me frequently. He was the Queen Mother's physician, and he was regularly ordering the Queen's china and silverware. When Lady Southward wanted to have a dinner party what better than to serve her guests on china engraved with the insignia 'E II R', and so I would make the arrangements to have a selection sent over to their home in Baker Square, interestingly enough, just up from the famous Baker Street immortalized by Sir Arthur Conan Doyle in his tales of Sherlock Holmes. Although acting as the Queen Mother's personal physician, Sir Ralph also maintained a practice in the fashionable area of Harley Street where it is not uncommon to see doctors rushing off to the hospital in their Rolls Royces or Mercedes sports cars.

Sir Ralph's son, Dr.Nigel Southward, was the current Royal Physician, or 'Apothecary to the Queen' as his official and ancient title read, and although he has been in the position a much shorter period, it is he who has perhaps left a more lasting impression on the palace.

At one time, Paul Almond, the palace prankster, took his little girl, Katie, to see a palace doctor. She was only three years old and her health had been deteriorating steadily over the previous few months. She was diagnosed as having a severe case of influenza and they were sent away with various cold medications and instructions to keep her away from school for the next week or so. But the problems still persisted, and she grew more sick with each passing week. Once again, Paul took his daughter to see the physician, and once more they were sent away with the assurance that this sort of condition was common amongst children in such close contact with others in school, and that his young daughter would be fine in a matter of time.

Several months later however, convinced that something more serious was happening, Paul took his daughter to see a specialist, and after running a series of tests on her the doctor informed him that there was no doubt about it—his daughter had leukemia. The specialist went on to inquire as to why Paul hadn't brought her to a doctor sooner then this. After all, he added, the condition was so obvious that a pre-med student could have diagnosed it.

The normally quiet and likeable Paul became a highly bitter and resentful man after that, never forgiving what he considered a major defect in the doctor's credentials and dedication. Perhaps this is why he resorted to making fun of those who worked for the Queen. My own doctor told me shortly after the diagnosis that in his opinion, this particular doctor was one of the most incompetent men in his field that he had ever met. Paul considered a lawsuit, but then thought better of it, considering the additional trauma such a move would bring upon his own family.

Paul Almond had only recently come to work at the palace. He replaced an assistant to Sir John Miller in the Royal Mews named Alec Carlyle, who shortly before I arrived, met an untimely and particularly gruesome end. Alec was known within the Royal Mews as being somewhat eccentric if not more than a little odd. His wife was seen several times running out of their apartment into the courtyard between the Royal Mews and the palace screaming, "Murder...Murder...Help! I'm being murdered!" This was naturally viewed with some alarm. The incidents usually occurred between midnight and two a.m. and those who witnessed them were uncertain as to what they should do. Alec was a very Senior Official after all.

But then suddenly Alec's wife stopped running about and creating the disturbances and it was hoped that their rather extreme matrimonial difficulties had come to an end. It was generally thought that they had patched up their differences and were living in harmony once more.

About two months later, the Carlyles left for a holiday and no more was thought of them. Two weeks later when they were expected back, they did not return. Of course, everyone assumed that there had been some minor problem. Perhaps something unexpected came up. There were numerous acceptable reasons and it was thought that the Carlyles would probably be back in a day or two. But when three had passed and the Carlyles still had not made an appearance in the Royal Mews, suspicions were raised. Could the delay have been due to a change in their travel arrangements?

It was decided that someone ought to open the Carlyles' apartment and search for some clue to their disappearance. Upon entering, an Official discovered that there had indeed been a change in their travel arrangements. He was greeted by such a sickening smell that he was physically ill, and there, lying on the sitting room floor, was the body of Alec Carlyle with a bullet through his head. His body was covered in maggots.

Was he murdered?

This question was answered when detectives, arriving on the scene an hour later, discovered Mrs. Carlyle's dead body in the room as well. She was buried under the floor boards of their sitting room. Further study revealed that Mrs. Carlyle had most likely committed suicide. Alec had buried her when he found her dead, and then suffered with the secret before finally killing himself with a gun.

The detectives theorised that his own death must have taken place on the evening he and his wife supposedly departed for their holiday. They concluded that Mrs. Carlyle must have been under the floor boards of their apartment for at least two months, judging by the deterioration of her body. She was in fact riddled with maggots herself to such an extent that even several years later the odd one could still be spotted in the offices below.

Nothing of the horror story was ever revealed to the press, and to this day the secret has been kept, known only to a few.

7

The royal couple returned from their two-week honeymoon in the Mediterranean.

It has been widely speculated that in the early years of the Prince and Princess of Wales's marriage that there were considerable marital difficulties. Many people believed, unrealistically I feel, that after that glorious wedding day in July the royal couple were destined to eternal nuptial bliss. But inevitably, there were problems.

Initially, Prince Charles and his wife lived in Buckingham Palace while their two residences, Kensington Palace in London and Highgrove House in Gloucester, were being prepared for them. For the Princess, the transition from being a young working girl sharing an apartment with friends, to being a Princess living in a very traditional and sophisticated environment, was far from easy. Nor did the fact that Prince Charles left for Australia by himself, shortly afterwards, alleviate her concerns. During his absence I met her many times in the corridors and royal apartments of the palace looking very flushed and distraught, often pacing the halls wearing a walkman strapped to her shoulder listening to her favorite tapes. The reality of her life was only just sinking in.

Not being familiar with royal protocol she would frequently enter the royal kitchens and help herself to what she wanted, ignoring the services of the page and footmen assigned to personally look after her. "I just want an apple!" one would frequently hear her chime as she entered the Royal Chef's domain.

"Well if ya want an apple all ya have to do is ring yer bloody bell," he would admonish her severely. The Royal Chef did not like unannounced visitors. This often resulted in the Princess breaking into tears and running out of the kitchens like a humiliated little schoolgirl.

Diana was not the biggest fan of the Royal Chef's cuisine either. She found it all too stuffy, and just a touch "too French," as she put it. Picking at her food while in the company of her new family, she would frequently wait until the meal concluded, at which time she would send down her request to the kitchens for a cheeseburger or baked beans on toast; the latter, her all time favorite.

After numerous complaints from the Royal Chef and others close to the family, the Queen finally took Diana aside and had a chat with her regarding her actions. Her behavior had both frustrated and irritated Her Majesty and finally led to the Princess being banned from future visits to the kitchens altogether.

Exit one Princess in tears.

When Prince Charles returned from overseas, Diana became a little more relaxed, but war broke out once again when her wish to continue teaching at nursery school was squelched by the

Queen. These types of problems persisted throughout the coming weeks.

Diana took a liking to retiring to bed with a cup of herbal tea, which she insisted be prepared for her by Prince Charles—personally! She had even gone out and bought a little electric contraption for doing just that, and kept it next to the bed in their suite. The Prince, having never so much as even seen a tea maker before, let alone use one, detested having to perform the chore each evening before bed, and with great frustration he would try and explain to his wife that there were plenty of servants to perform such mundane tasks now. She didn't have to worry. Why him? But the argument never succeeded.

It was a common sight in the palace to see Prince Charles calling his footman from his bedroom door at night, "Stephen? Could you find me some water please. The Princess doesn't think you are capable of making a cup of tea for her!"

One evening the Prince arrived home later then expected from a dinner engagement at the Dorchester Hotel. It was close to midnight and Diana had expected him back by ten thirty. He had promised her after all, and this was the time she liked to be served her herbal tea. She flew into a terrible rage when the Prince finally returned and several footmen and I outside their suite could not help but hear the commotion. Lambasting the Prince for his "lack of consideration" and screeching, "Where is my cup of tea? Where is my tea?" Diana proceeded to hurl the tea-making apparatus at her husband who was standing at the door, completely bewildered by the outburst. Fortunately, the tea maker missed, but the next day when the craftsmen arrived to examine the dent in their door, I couldn't help take note of the puzzled expressions on their faces. What could have happened, they mused to themselves?

After about two weeks the Princess settled down and from that point on began to have, what I would call, a 'cordial' relationship with the Queen. But inevitably with two such determined persons from different generations and backgrounds there were many heated arguments. Diana decided at one stage that certain state rooms in the palace, such as the Green Drawing Room, needed "modernization" to bring them "up to date," as she put it to the Queen. Her Majesty was outraged that a newcomer to her Court should be so insubordinate and self-opinionated and she put the Princess firmly in her place. "How dare you be so rude. This is my home and I like it just the way it is, thank you!" The Queen was not amused.

Exit one Princess in tears again.

Diana was forever running somewhere in tears, and it became a standard joke within the palace to put one's hands over one's face and run about doing 'the Diana look.' She soon realised though that she was powerless in the Queen's home and this naturally brought about a good deal of resentment on her part.

When the Prince and Princess of Wales had at last moved into their new home, Highgrove, Diana was still very bitter. When the Queen sent a delivery of some of her finest furniture from the palace, as a special gift to help them fit out their new and sprawling home, Diana sent them back to the Queen with a note attached that read: "The furniture you have so kindly thought to send does not suit our tastes."

Once at Highgrove, Diana began to attempt to twist the Prince's attention away from some of his staff and more on to her. The Prince had developed a close relationship with his two body guards and valet; after all, they were the closest friends he had had for most of his life. But not long after their marriage, the Prince's valet, bodyguards, private secretary and chauffeur were all either moved on to other duties or fired. In the case of the valet, Stephen Barry, his ego had become so inflated since his eight years with the Prince that no one within the palace wanted him at all. What a good time for him to leave for America, everyone thought. The Prince, and even Diana, meeting him outside a fashionable London shop, wished him well in his future. Little

The Duke of Edinburgh has another disappointment at the Royal Windsor Horse Show.

"Are you trying to tell me that Margaret was actually sober…here on this planet?"

"So that's what you keep under your kilt, Charles"

Princess Margaret orders a large gin and tonic while visiting Uganda.

A rough landing at Heathrow for one of the Queen's Corgis.

Ronald Reagan's reaction on being told that he is the President of the United States.

The Royal couple in Sark, 1949. A royal welcome of an unexpected kind.

An interesting word appears to be hovering on Princess Diana's lips at the Epsom Derby.

The Queen laughs on being told her sister has given up drinking.

The Queen Mother at Heathrow Airport departing for Paris.
"And don't forget to keep those footmen out of my bed."

A helping hand for Princess Diana.

Hair Apparent!

(above) The Queen in company with the King of Tonga. *(below)* A conservative estimate of the King of Tonga's weight is displayed on the license plate of his official car.

"Oh, no, Margaret's ordered another drink."

"Oh, so you can't stand Mrs. Thatcher either!"

Prince Andrew inspecting the Royal Marines aboard HMS *Brazen*.

"Oh, look, it's raining gin!"

The Queen with the King of Morocco.
"Now it's going to be *my* turn to keep *you* waiting."

Princess Margaret launching a new British Airways aircraft.
"Can't I drink it first."

Princess Margaret thundering down the course to catch last call at the bar.

"I wonder. Do you have anything a little cheaper?"

The Queen lunching with the King of Morocco. Now doesn't that dish look tasty?

Prince Philip with an unwelcome intruder. "You try that again and I'll take you carriage driving every day for a month!"

"Oh, I hope my son makes it to the liquor store in time!"

King Khaled of Saudi Arabia with the Sovereign.
"Are you *sure* your wife didn't like the footman's buttocks?"

did they realize that some wicked and deplorable American publisher had enticed their former valet to the United States with an offer to write a book. Quite scandalous, if you ask me!

8

There was another crisis of sorts brewing within the walls of Buckingham Palace. Nothing to do with the Royal Family however. The problem was, as Sir Peter Ashmore and Sir Edward Adeane saw it, what to do with the extraordinary build up of bottles that had been amassed in the palace. There were bottles everywhere. In the Master of the Household's corridor, outside the offices of the Officials, stuffed in plastic shopping bags in the halls and bedrooms of footmen and maids, and in row upon row of overflowing boxes found in public rooms and in the kitchens.

The housekeeping department reported that it had reached a critical stage and they could no longer control it by themselves. Everyday they would cart away the empty gin, vodka, scotch, martini, brandy, beer, cider and wine bottles placed outside rooms and offices the night before, and the very next day there would come more in their place. It was truly out of hand. Such was the requirement and consumption amongst those in the Royal Household that the Prince of Wales organized a 'bottle bank' with a garbage removal company in London. A huge metallic container, similar to the ones found at football and rugby matches, was delivered to the palace and the prince himself performed the opening ceremony at the request of his private secretary, Sir Edward Adeane.

It was a big day. All available Royal Household advisers, Officials and Staff collected on the tarmac at the rear of the palace, as Prince Charles explained that from now on everyone within the palace were to put their empty bottles into this container. The

151

bottles would then be recycled and the profits given to his favorite charity.

"All brown spirit bottles are to go into the brown slot," the Prince declared, "all green bottles such as wine and sherry into the green slot, and any white spirit bottles must go into the white slot." The side door adjacent to the park opened and out strolled the Royal Chef, carrying two large and weighty green garbage bags crammed with his empties. In full view of all, including the Prince and Sir Edward Adeane, the Royal Chef went about meticulously placing each of the fifty bottles or so into their respective slots, spending the majority of his time in the area of the white bottle hole.

As the Prince continued, loud crashes were heard intermittently as the Royal Chef sent the bottles securely and squarely to their final resting. Tramping back across the square and then slamming the kitchen door shut behind him, the Royal Chef had made his point, or so he had thought.

"Well ladies and gentleman," the Prince quipped as the Royal Chef disappeared, "there is one man who certainly needs no instruction!"

The bottle bank was certainly needed and was an excellent way of dealing with the problem. However the flow of empties was so demanding that pick-up arrangements with the Greater London Council had to be amended shortly thereafter from once every month to once a week. Each Monday a huge truck would arrive to cart the empties away, and the industrial crane it carried on its back could be heard straining under the pressure of raising its Titanic load.

9

A dreadful uproar took place at the beginning of August when I had to tell Dr. Southward that his offices were going to be redecorated and he would have to relocate. I had to pay Dr. Southward a visit anyway as I had sustained a rather serious burn to my hand. When I found him not in, which was not unusual, his assistant, Sister Patricia Deakin, said she would take care of me.

After searching tirelessly through drawers and cupboards for what I considered was going to be some sort of miracle drug or treatment, she came up to me and asked me to hold out my hand. As I painfully turned my head away from what I was sure was going to be an agonizing remedy, Sister Deakin simply stuck a Band-Aid on it and that was that.

Approximately 55 years of age, Sister Deakin was what you would typically expect from someone in her matronly field. Of average height, she was most noticeable for her reedy voice and slurred speech. She would invariably appear in the palace wearing a dark blue nurse's uniform and white hat, along with the most unfeminine mud-brown shoes I have ever seen. I thought they were surely meant for a man. If one could avert one's gaze from her laddered stockings, you would find at the other end, a slim, powder white face with vibrant red lips. Another feature of Sister Deakin was that she never appeared to wash very much, and as with so many others in the palace, seemed to have a passion for that 'unkempt' look when it came to managing her hair.

Most mornings and afternoons would find Sister Deakin, or 'Dolly Daydreams' as everyone referred to her in the palace, shopping in town or perhaps continuing with her research into the London distilleries in the comfort of her beautiful palace apartment, exquisitely decorated with a gorgeous spiral staircase in the center. A few days earlier when I arrived seeking the doctor, I had surprised Sister Deakin in her office. As she sat behind her desk I glanced down at her feet and spotted a Gordons gin bottle peeking out from under her chair. Now I stood there with my aching hand, looking at her and wondering if I should comment on the lack of proper treatment or simply go elsewhere for medical relief. Just then, Dr. Southward entered.

"Ah, there you are, Nigel. I wanted to let you know that your office is up for refurbishment and I will have to relocate you for a short time."

"RELOCATE???" came the incredulous reply from the meticulously groomed doctor, as Sister Deakin rushed dramatically to his side. "I can't move. I've got everything I need here."

"I'm sorry Nigel but you don't have any choice. It has got to be done sometime."

"Well what about Sister Deakin? Where will she go?" he asked hopefully. A look of hurt crossed Sister Deakin's face.

"She can stay where she is. But I'm afraid Nigel that you and Canon Caesar will have to share an office until the painting has been completed. Shouldn't be more than a couple of weeks."

"A COUPLE OF WEEKS? I'm not sharing an office with *anyone* for a couple of weeks. I'm a doctor not a priest," he stormed, swishing out of the room, wrists limp and waving in their standard frenzy.

Mr. Humphrey entered as the doctor fled in a panic. Turning, he shouted after him, "Heh Heh Heh! The two of you will make a good pair!"

Mr. Humphrey was back from his holiday.

BALMORAL CASTLE

August 16th - October 15th

1

When the Queen and Duke of Edinburgh arrived at Balmoral it was the sixteenth of August. They passed through the simple wrought iron gates engraved with the initials "GR" and "MR", denoting King George V and Queen Mary, which marks the main entrance to the estate. Rolls Royce 1 proceeded over the River Dee on the Brunel bridge, onto the estate and up the carriage-way flanked by magnificent Silver Fir trees leading directly up to the front of the castle.

The Court would be spending eight full weeks at the castle and I thought of the prospect happily as I strolled about and admired the splendid castle grounds. The central sunken gardens at the front and in the centre of the castle were ablaze with flowers of pink, apricot, burnt reds and stony greens. The Duke, who was now responsible for their care, had improved and enlarged them over the years, the fruit, or flowers, of his labor now blossoming into life.

Looking north along the west and south borders of the castle, I indulgently absorbed the sweeping pastures of multi-colored flowers and felt a certain comfort. With their wind-swept appearance they seemed as natural as the rolling purple heathered hills themselves, creating an exquisite simplicity that suited the castle supremely.

In the expansive grounds I passed statues and monuments erected over the previous one hundred years in memory of various Monarchs. Of course there was one to Queen Victoria and the Prince Regent. Continuing along I met another with an inscription to George IV and on the cricket ground, I came across memorials to two dogs, positioned a respectable walk away from those of royal blood. One monument was dedicated to 'Noble,' the favorite and faithful dog of Queen Victoria. It passed away in 1887 after sixteen long years of devotion to her. 'Tchu' was the second much-grieved royal pet and it was brought all the way from China by the Duke and Duchess of Connaught in 1890. Unfortunately, despite all its royal care, the silly thing up and died later that same year. So distraught was its mistress, the Duchess, that on its death she had to mourn in the only manner that she was familiar with: BIG!

This, of course, is a fitting example of the carefree spending of the nobility and Royal Family of the past, quite the opposite to the almost meagre existence the present Monarch must act out. One need only imagine the uproar that would take place if the press learned that our present Queen had spent one thousand pounds on a head stone for one of her corgis!

Behind and around the castle flows the River Dee and I spent an enjoyable hour strolling the tranquil riverside path. The sun shone warm and strong. It was the best time of year. As I approached the rear of the castle, I came across a granite memorial to King George V, "erected in humble loyalty and affection by the employees and tenants on Balmoral, Birkhall and Abergeldie estates." This Monarch was as much loved as is the present one.

The rose gardens on the same side of the castle were as abundantly arrayed as the main garden in front, and they too were in full flower. A perfect harmony in all directions, everything looking at its best. In fact the gardens were originally planned with this in mind and are always at their peak when the Royal Family are in residence.

Since the Duke of Edinburgh has been overseeing the enlargements and improvements to the gardens, a peaceful water garden has been added between West Drive and Garden Cottage.

A short distance away I happened by one of the many glass conservatories that dot the grounds, and these too were overflowing, rich in their color, all around, a landscape of the deepest emerald green, the gardens and lawns luxuriant and expansive.

Balmoral is more than just a favorite vacation home to successive generations of the Royal Family. The land is held in trust for them and this is kept foremost in mind when it comes to planning and modifications on the estate. Apart from the sheer beauty of the location, Balmoral is an important area in other ways. The Ballochbuie Forest to the west of the castle for instance, contains one of the largest areas of natural pine left in Scotland. It is also the winter home for the red deer, one of only a handful of natural grazing areas that remain. The Queen, as patron of the Highland Cattle Society, also keeps a fold of twenty breeding cows, and hay is grown for the Queen's ponies and deer here as well.

As I returned to the castle and passed through the ballroom I thought of the annual Ghillies' Balls that were held there towards the beginning of autumn. Here, one finds the noblest in all of Scotland.

Although the castle is grand, it is decidedly spartan. Very much in keeping with the simple life which the original owners, Queen Victoria and Prince Albert, enjoyed so much. Ministers in their day griped that Balmoral was too simple and complained that Queen Victoria spent far too much time there—"five hundred miles out of the capital," as they put it. But the Queen paid no heed. If anything she increased her visits, and towards the end of her reign would spend the entire month of May enjoying the northern climate and as long as three months in the autumn. Those ministers that came were often less than comfortable, as Her Majesty liked the minimum of heat. They were glad to return to the 'warmer' latitudes of London. (Anyone who has been to London will agree that must have been cold!)

Balmoral is the Royal Family's principal holiday home and it is easy to understand why. Her Majesty may experience a degree of freedom here that exists for her in no other place. Like her ancestor, the present Queen loves to wander far afield. On one afternoon, Her Majesty was out walking the grounds quite a distance away from the castle when another woman out strolling came wandering up to her. She was probably from one of the nearby villages. The woman inspected Her Majesty as she passed her by. Then she turned around and took another look. Not certain whether to continue the woman hesitated for a few seconds and then proceeded slowly back towards the Queen, who was standing serenely enjoying the view. Taking a gentle hold of Her Majesty's arm the old woman peered closely at the Queen's face. Stepping back and clasping her hands she said to Her Majesty, "You know dear...you look just like the Queen!" and then continued on her way. It may not have occurred to the woman that she had truly met the Queen of England and Scotland!!

It is, of course, a rare occurrence for a commoner to be within unsupervised range of a member of the Royal Family, however the property is so vast that it simply cannot be patroled entirely. Fortunately, some of the greatest beauty is seen from the windows of the castle itself. Queen Victoria wrote in her diary in 1855: "The view from the drawing room, and our rooms just above, of the valley looking up to the Dee with the mountains, which one could never get from the old house, is quite beautiful."

When the time approached for Queen Victoria and her husband to leave the highlands for the south, she wrote: "Every year I seem to become fonder of this dear place," and then continuing without the least bit of concern for her immodesty, "still more so, now that great and excellent taste has been stamped everywhere."

2

The Queen had been in residence at Balmoral for only two days, awaiting the arrival of other members of her family. Everyone would come, for Balmoral is truly a family home. This year would bring Prince Charles, Princess Anne, Captain Mark Phillips, Prince Andrew and Prince Edward. Stretching well into the autumn, various other relatives would arrive at points throughout the enjoyable two-month stay. Even Princess Margaret, who is not seen much in public these days, commits herself every year without fail, usually timing her arrivals to coincide with one of the Ghillies' Balls that are held in the castle.

The two youngest of Her Majesty's children, Prince Edward and Prince Andrew, enjoy the happy times at Balmoral as much as their older siblings and indeed older generations. As a child, Prince Edward loved to try and catch the brightly-colored butterflies that are so plentiful about the castle grounds. When he was unsuccessful or too many escaped his net, he was known to throw bad temper tantrums and to storm around in the castle, fuming. Some of the Staff would attempt to appease him and he would turn his foul mood onto them. He could be "a difficult blighter," as one of the old pages to Her Majesty enlightened me on one of the many occasions when he cornered me in the palace bar.

When I began at the palace, Prince Edward was already coming out of his rebellious stage, blossoming into the kind, sensitive person that he is now. These days the Prince does a bit of shooting and riding and the occasional bit of fishing. He usually brings friends from college and makes use of the private golf course on the estate. Out of all the Queen's children, he seems to like Balmoral the most.

Prince Andrew was a different matter. A long time servant to Her Majesty named Fred Whiting, who acted in the capacity of her Yeoman of the Royal Wine Cellar, told me about the time he had had to go and see the Queen over a problem he was having with her son. The Prince was just a lad of about eleven years old at the time, but even at this stage he was already attempting to throw his weight around. Knocking bravely on the door to Her Majesty's sitting room the Yeoman entered, bowed, and said to the Queen, "I'm afraid, Ma'am, that I have had to lock young master Andrew in the wine cellar."

Unalarmed, Her Majesty replied, "What has he done this time, Fred?"

"Well, Ma'am, he has been extremely rude to me, ordering me about and tying my shoe laces together. Just a few moments ago I caught him mixing up the bottles of wine I had selected for next week's dinner engagements."

"Well then," Her Majesty said calmly, "I should make sure you leave him there until he calms down. All afternoon if necessary!"

Rudeness is not tolerated by Her Majesty within her own family or to a member of Staff.

But like Her Majesty's Staff, Prince Andrew used the informality and relaxed atmosphere of Balmoral as a platform for his very worst behavior. He was forever dragging the worst bunch of tarts up to dine with his mother, each seeming to compete with the previous for lack of brains. The one characteristic his girlfriends did not lack though was ample breasts. Her Majesty took such a strong dislike to one girl Prince Andrew brought to the castle for a weekend that she seated her at the far end of the table, away from both herself and her son. Normally, any friends of the royal offspring invited to Her Majesty's homes are seated near the head of the table opposite their partner, so this was quite a rebuff.

Princess Anne puts in an appearance usually without her husband but never stays more than a few days. She is so busy with her charity work that she has little free time. While the Queen and the Duke are naturally sorry she cannot spend more time with the family, they do not feel the same of their son-in-law, Captain Phillips. He is a constant source of embarrassment to them and more than a tiny mystery as to why their daughter chose him in the first place.

Captain Phillips has always been uncomfortable in the company of his wife's family. He feels as though he does not fit in. Frequently stopped by police for speeding or other motorcar infractions, he is indeed considered a major nuisance by the Royal Family. During a television interview with Princess Anne and her husband once, the interviewer asked Captain Phillips, "Are you overawed by your wife at times, Captain Phillips?" The Princess's husband thought about the question, remained speechless, continued to remain speechless, and then apparently not knowing what answer to give the interviewer, who was still waiting patiently for his reply, gave up entirely. The silence increased until finally, and mercifully, Princess Anne said, "Come on Mark, surely you can answer that?" But he still did not speak. With a heavy sigh the Princess undertook it for him. "No, my husband is not overawed by me," she said almost fiercely to the camera.

Responding to a question from a British journalist on one occasion, Captain Phillips declared, "My wife and I are just an average couple living on a mortgage." Now the Royal Family do not want to flaunt their wealth, but there are limits! Considering Her Majesty bought Gatcombe Park for them for approximately five hundred thousand pounds sterling it was an odd remark. Does he really believe the average member of the public is that naive? Apparently so.

Princess Anne's husband is very much in the same category as Lady Maclean, the wife of Her Majesty's Lord Chamberlain. Neither seem to appear terribly much with their better known spouses and for similar reasons. While Captain Phillips and Princess Anne married quite early in life, it is fascinating to note how much more mature and responsible Her Royal Highness has become compared to her husband.

Princess Margaret, as I have said, is very much in evidence during the summer season at Balmoral and will divide her time between the castle and staying with her mother at Birkhall. She also has plenty of friends in the area and will often make the rounds during her stay. On one visit, Princess Margaret brought along her only son, Lord Linley. A keen cyclist, Lord Linley loved to spend many happy hours exploring mountain roads and country lanes around the estate. One afternoon he was out with friends on a bicycle trip, and they had stayed out late to enjoy a barbecue. However the rain started to come down heavily and he raced back to the castle. Whilst speeding up the driveway the bicycle ran over a large stone, puncturing a tire and buckling the back wheel. This did not impress his Lordship, who was already soaked and looking forward to another excursion the following day.

He put the bicycle away and wrote a curt note to Prince Edward's footman telling him to have the machine repaired, cleaned, and ready for his use at nine o'clock sharp the next morning. As it was after midnight and the footman's light was out, he slipped the note underneath his bedroom door and went to bed himself. He reasoned that as he had no footman directly assigned to himself he would procure someone else's to carry out his orders.

The footman was furious when he read the peremptory note the following morning and complained to Prince Edward when he went to awaken him at eight o'clock. It wasn't that he objected to orders, he pointed out, it was the impolite way he was told to do it, and the expectation that he—who knew nothing about bicycles—could perform a major repair job in two or three hours.

Prince Edward fully agreed with his footman and told him to leave the matter and he would speak with his cousin later on. By this time, however, Lord Linley was up and wanting to know what was being done about his bicycle. He caught up with the footman and demanded to know what was happening. The footman replied, "Sir, on the instructions of Prince Edward I am unable to assist you."

163

The result was deafening. Princess Margaret's son was livid and called the footman every conceivable name in his vocabulary. He tore up one side of him and down the other and then equally gave Prince Edward more of the same. He was absolutely wild. Finally, having complained of his ill treatment to anyone in the Royal Family who would lend their ear, he was summoned by the Queen herself and told by her to grow up and stop acting like the spoiled brat everyone knew he was. After this meeting, his protests ceased and he was instructed by Her Majesty to offer his apologies to the young footman to whom he had been so cruel.

A member of the Royal Family who does not frequent Balmoral if it can be avoided is Princess Diana. She detests the castle completely. There is nothing she finds attractive about the place. She does not like riding, nor fishing, nor shooting, and she detests the remote country life. As far as she is concerned, there are no redeeming qualities to Balmoral and she prefers to stay at home.

The Queen Mother spends a good deal of time at Balmoral herself, living in her own residence called Birkhall, a mile or so away. She often spends the day walking the grounds or fishing for salmon on the River Dee, and in the privacy of her home, she freely admits to having no aversion whatsoever to the odd gin martini now and again. I would often come across her sitting all alone on the river bank, smiling and as gracious as ever. Occasionally she would engage me in conversation, but more often than not, preferred just to be by herself and enjoy the beauty of the estate.

Most of the Queen Mother's staff are gay, both at her Clarence House residence in London, and also at Birkhall. She has always preferred gay young men to straight, primarily because she feels they are much neater in appearance and are likely to stay in service to her for much longer. Footmen who look after her tell of how kind and considerate she is to them, almost as attentive as a mother.

The Queen Mother has had the occasional difficulty with Staff, however, as do other members of her family, and has returned unexpectedly to find her young footmen casually stretched out on her sitting room sofa watching her television and eating her food. But she will only reprimand them, again in a maternal way, and send them off with a good stern lecture.

One weekend every year the Royal Family attend the Braemar Highland Games, which have been going on for over 170 years. There they enjoy some of the ancient and primitive sporting events, such as tossing the caber, throwing the haggis and the Scottish dancing. The atmosphere is very much like that of a country fair. Spectators and competitors come from all over the world for the events and even Prince Andrew has competed in several, in particular, the haggis throwing. Haggis is a famous Scottish treat that is more commonly eaten then thrown, and to most people outside the Highlands unappetisingly consists of lungs and heart of sheep or calf, mixed with suet, onion, seasoning and oatmeal, and all encased in the stomach of the animal and boiled.

The Duke is fond of taking his family out for barbecues on the estate. He prides himself on "getting down to the basics" and really "slumming it" by doing all his own cooking. This is rather amusing to everyone else because what actually happens is that all the food the Royal Family will need is prepared earlier in the day by the kitchens. Then, when the Royal Family is ready to leave for their 'barbecue' a small trailer which keeps the food warm is connected up to a Land Rover and off they all go.

There is an old tradition at Balmoral of having the Prime Minister stay for one weekend during the summer. In earlier times, the late Sir Winston Churchill was a charming three-day guest. More recently, James Callaghan and Harold Wilson have been in attendance.

Mr. Callaghan had the misfortune of tripping on the stairs when he arrived one summer. The Queen laughed good-naturedly and asked him, "May I help you up?" Of course these small accidents occur to everyone at one time or another, even if you do happen to be the prime minister of Great Britain. It must have been terribly embarrassing for him though the following year, when he tripped in the exact same place once again! This time it was Her Majesty's Page of Chambers who aided Mr. Callaghan to his feet.

Prime Minister Margaret Thatcher is not quite such a regular guest as some of her predecessors. When she does stay, it is purely out of obligation to the ancient tradition and apart from dinner she sees very little of the Queen. To be totally frank, Her Majesty cannot bear the sight of her. That is a fact.

Balmoral is appealing to those who work for the Royal Family as well. The tranquility and relaxed atmosphere is not lost on them. Officials will go to a nearby lodge for dinner and drinks several times a week, and there are one or two favorite pubs in the area to fight off boredom when it sets in. Staff are not allowed to mix socially with the Officials or the Queen's senior advisers, so it is fortunate that there is an abundance of recreation spots for all.

On days off, it is permissible for members of the Royal Household to take picnics out to the grounds and there is practically unlimited land to explore. One of the attractions of Balmoral to the Royal Chef, however, has little to do with the natural beauty of the castle itself, although it could be considered natural. Here the Royal Chef is able to unwind in the company of his assistants and attempt to set that new Highland record he has been hoping for. This feat could never be accomplished in London or Windsor and the mornings are far too cold at Holyrood Palace for it to work. I am speaking, of course, of the Royal Chef's farting competitions which take place in the kitchens of Balmoral every year. Under direct tutelage of the most imperial master himself, there is much heated competition for the title. (Balmoral is *extremely* informal.)

Participating in these rituals are the two pastry chefs, several sous chefs, and the holder of the current farting title, the Royal Chef himself. (It has never been confirmed but it is rumored that the title has never 'passed' from his hands.) The rules are simple and go as follows: the loudest and the longest fart wins. Mornings are the preferred time for these sessions, usually following the Staff breakfast which conveniently usually consists of baked beans.

While I enjoyed my time at Balmoral immensely, I was always glad to return to London at the end of the summer. Although the pace was less hectic than in London, the responsibility was somewhat increased. Sir Peter Ashmore spent only five or six days out of sixty with the Royal Family and that meant that I was fully in charge of the castle. In this situation I was directly answerable to the Queen and no stay was entirely peaceful or without event.

My office was far less comfortable than the one I shared back at Buckingham Palace and it could be called a boiler room compared to the one at Windsor Castle. It was extremely simple, as was the entire dwelling. Even Sir Peter Ashmore's office and indeed the royal apartments themselves could be considered stark and simple. There is none of the opulence and richness of the Queen's other homes. Charles Grenville wrote about life at Balmoral in 1849 when the Royal Family were still living in the old castle: "They live there without any state whatever...not merely like private gentlefolks, but like very small gentlefolk, small house, small rooms, small establishment...they live with the greatest simplicity and ease." Little has changed.

My castle office was notable for one reason though and it had nothing to do with its decor. It was directly opposite the Royal Chef's, and throughout the morning and sometimes into the afternoon, I would not only hear the 'royal flatulaters' when they moved from the kitchens into the chef's office for the final rounds, but occasionally I would even have the opportunity to savor the aroma of the Royal Chef's own unique spicing.

"You try and beat that!" the Royal Chef bellowed, following an unusually lengthy and particularly odoriferous break of wind even for him. "Two quid says ya can't!!" he beamed with pride as a young pastry chef braced himself against a counter about to attempt to match the Royal Chef's offer.

Out for her usual morning walk, the Queen, having exercised her two favorite corgis in the grounds of the castle, decided to pay an impromptu visit to the royal kitchens. The royal flatulaters had completed round one and were busy attending to the Staff lunch which would be required shortly. I was discussing an important matter with the Royal Chef when Her Majesty made her entrance, royal corgis rushing in behind her taking the liberty of snapping at the ankles of any servant they deemed deserving.

Glancing around the kitchen to see that all was well, the chefs all gave her an obedient "Good morning, Your Majesty" and then set vigorously into their tasks. Wrinkling her nose slightly, no doubt at the mysterious odor, her eyes alighted upon a young apprentice chef whom she had not met before. The boy was about seventeen years old and had joined the Royal Household only two months earlier. Her Majesty decided to engage the latest recruit in a brief conversation.

"Good morning, young man," said Her Majesty in friendly tones.

"'Allo yer Highness," he replied as though addressing a drinking buddy in a pub, "an' how are you today?"

"I am not Your Highness, I am Your Majesty," the Queen pointed out to the young boy, naturally displeased.

The boy, apparently totally disinterested in the proper decorum used when addressing the Monarch, responded with an extremely gruff, "Yeah? O.K. then."

The Queen, not to be deterred, and probably assuming the boy was nervous, noted that he was in the process of filleting a large tray of what were obviously freshly caught trout. "Now that looks lovely," she said to the boy with enthusiasm. "What are you cutting up there?"

"Fish!" he said without a moment's hesitation, looking directly up at the Queen.

There was an embarrassing, interminable ten-second silence during which one could sense Her Majesty's utter disbelief that anyone could give such an imbecilic reply. Suddenly, everyone appeared to be far busier in the kitchen than before, and doubting my own ability to control the desperate urge to roar with laughter, I disappeared behind a large refrigerator and viewed the proceedings in relative safety. The Queen considered the situation for a moment and in due course recovered her power of speech.

"Yes," she commented impatiently, "I can see that it is fish. But what *kind* of fish is it?"

"Ugh...don't ask me. A fish is a fish" he said unapologetically.

This offensive reply was too much for the Queen. "Oh, I have had enough of you," she stormed with frustration, and with that swept regally through the kitchen door, her two corgis racing out after her in a fret, suddenly losing all interest in the delicious ankles around them.

The young lad stayed in service for another six weeks after which it was reluctantly decided that working in the Royal Household was not his metier.

3

If the royal apartments at Balmoral were spartan, then the Staff's quarters were down right dumpy. The footmen, located in what I can only describe as a shack on the estate, had to endure much less comfort then they were used to at the palace. Constructed entirely of wood, their run down quarters were freezing cold especially during the month of September. But this did not seem to matter a great deal to them. As I have said, the boys were all young and looked forward to a highly slack time at the castle.

There was one footman however who could not handle the living quarters and went completely mad one year. Tormented by the other boys he could not take any more and in frustration started throwing the furniture around and smashing tables. Eventually he was subdued and given a train ticket home. Fortunately most others seemed to manage and the cold of the autumn night didn't stop the footmen from dancing in and out of each other's rooms—and beds—until the wee hours of the morning.

There was one senior page aged about forty who had a strong streak of sadomasochism in him. He liked to have some of the younger footmen beat and whip him with a horse whip. He was frequently seen about the castle with bruises on his arms and face, but this did not matter. He adored the treatment he received at the hands of the young footmen and often paid them for their valued services. A heavy drinker, he had frequent accidents and was always falling down the stairs. One evening he made advances to one of the few straight footmen and was given a bad beating for his efforts, out of which he sustained a broken leg. This was one beating he seemed not to like.

I came into the Officials' dining-room early one morning for a cup of coffee and found him with a bottle of Scotch to his lips. Despite his mental problems, he was not such a bad chap and I didn't want to be cross with him. When I asked him what he was doing, drinking Scotch in a room that was out of bounds, he replied, "I am sorry, Mr. Barker, but I wasn't able to get any supplies of my own this morning. If you expect me to get through the day then please leave me in peace."

Another footman at the castle, who later went to work for Princess Anne at Gatcombe Park, liked to dress up in women's clothes. He would attend the Friday night discos held at Balmoral decked out in a full length dress, heels and tiara, and would set about teasing the other boys with his feminine movements. He was one of the most delicate men I have met. Although in his late thirties, he possessed a child-like face, and was always complaining that the trays he had to carry in the castle were too heavy for him to manage. It was not uncommon to see him running about the corridors yelling, "I need a man! I need a man!"

A porter who later became a footman in the Royal Household seemed to require the same. His name was Patrick Kelly and when on duty at a banquet or dinner party he was fond of making suggestive gestures and eyes at the other guests, for instance to school friends of Prince Edward, or to young barons who happened to be in attendance with their parents. But his remarks were not reserved just for the young men. Senior dukes and knights were also fair game. On one occasion Sir Keith Joseph arrived for a party at the castle. Sir Keith at the time was Minister of Trade and Industry in the government and was considered a *very* serious man. Upon handing Kelly his name card at the door for a formal introduction to those gathered, Kelly said to him, "Ooooh, you are looking awfully sweet tonight, Sir Keith."

As Kelly served drinks and carried trays of food around the party he would whisper in the ear of complete strangers, no matter what their rank, something along the lines of, "I'm looking for a sweet young man tonight so if you know any, send them my way."

While serving the Royal Family back at the palace in London Kelly made a little extra pocket money as a male prostitute. His base of operations was in the public washrooms at Buckingham Palace Gate and he was proud of all the contacts that he made there. It was well known around the palace that he was available to anybody and *I mean anybody*. Kelly also had a boyfriend named, believe it or not, Dennis Pickup who worked in the palace as a porter. They purchased a tiny flat together in London and it was for this reason that Kelly claimed he resorted to prostitution: his paltry palace salary was not enough to cover his mortgage.

Once he announced to me that he and his boyfriend Dennis were going to Spain for their holiday, and mentioned they had found a small apartment to rent for the duration of their stay. "Well at least Spain is nice and cheap for you," I said to Kelly realising his tight budget.

"Yes, that's for sure," he replied. "Of course it's meant an awful lot of extra work for me trying to earn the money me and Dennis are going to need, you know."

"Oh really?" I said rather surprised. "I haven't noticed your name on the overtime chart lately, Patrick. You won't make much that way."

"I don't mean here at the palace, ya silly bugger," he answered. "I mean I've had to take on a few more tricks in the lavs than usual!"

Needless to say, there was an element of perversion to the young man's life and this was most realized when we discovered that Kelly was the culprit who was spreading Joyjell, anal lubrication jelly, all over Buckingham Palace. For weeks the stuff was mysteriously appearing on desks and doorknobs on cutlery and chairs, even for some bizarre reason on the tops of vases. There was a variety of colors too. Lemon and lime, strawberry, raspberry, and apparently his all time favorite, peach. We presume the peach flavor was in his good books because one morning it was discovered spread all over the Royal Family's umbrella stand!

Kelly was an odd one alright. An epileptic, he once had a fit at Windsor Castle in front of the Queen and twenty dinner guests. But still he was kept on, even though he was frequently seen streaking through the Queen's homes. But Her Majesty felt sorry for him and as with others who were slightly unbalanced, it was thought to be safer to put up with them rather than risk the repercussions of terminating their employment.

The decision was finally made to demote him back to the position of porter a few months later when Sir Geoffrey De-Bellaigue came to stay. Sir Geoffrey was Surveyor of the Queen's

Works of Art, and had been invited for the weekend as a guest of the Queen. About midnight Sir Geoffrey rang for a footman to bring him a nightcap before he retired to bed. When no one came to his room to attend to him he opened the door and peered out into the corridor. At that moment Patrick Kelly came through the hallway and Sir Geoffrey said to him, "You there! There doesn't appear to be anyone around and I need a footman." To which Kelly replied, "Oooh do ya now, Sir Geoffrey? Well ya can't have me, ducky!"

The knight unfortunately did not find this amusing, and it was decided, reluctantly, to assign Kelly to duties where he could do less harm to the guests!

Apart from the constant amusement of the Staff's antics (if one can call them that), Balmoral was a very slack time indeed. I would spend a couple of hours a day in my office talking on the telephone. As an Official I had unlimited use of it and would spend a good deal of time connected with friends in Canada, the United States and Bermuda. Because there was only a skeleton of a Staff maintained at the castle, I did a little bit of everything. I would order food for the Royal Family every day from a shop called Strachans in the town of Aboyne, about a mile away from the principal centre in the area of Ballater. The Royal Chef would try and sneak spirits onto his list of requirements under the guise of needing it for cooking. This became clear the morning he handed me a list that included Glenlivet twelve-year-old Scotch. For cooking I asked?

The town of Ballater was more important to the Royal Family than the much smaller Aboyne. A small shop there by the name of Murdochs baked all the Royal Family's bread and cakes, and every day a Staff member was sent in to collect the trays of freshly baked goods. The shop is a very well-established, family-run business which supplied the castle in Queen Victoria's time. While Murdochs sells to those living in the surrounding area as well as the Royal Family, there are certain breads that are made specially for the latter which are not sold to the general public at all. Of course, no matter what is sold and to whom, you can be fairly certain of a unique experience should one chose to sample their 100-year-old recipes. Everything that comes from Murdochs kitchens is indescribably delicious.

At points throughout the day I dispatched important documents to London, and was in close communication with the palace there. It was being operated on a much smaller scale while the Court was away. This was about all that was required of me during most of the summer. After this, luncheons with my mother or friends featured on a regular basis, as did a little shopping in town, and a lot of walking.

One afternoon while strolling around the castle grounds I came across Princess Margaret hard at work, performing one of her favorite tasks, pruning roses.

"Hello Malcolm. Are you enjoying the fine weather?"

"Yes, Your Highness, I certainly am. I see you are doing well with those roses this year." (It was always well advised to be as obsequious as possible to any member of the Royal Family.)

The Princess stood up and brushed her clothes. "Oh they are not difficult to tend to up here. And of course, the care they receive from the gardeners does something for them I am certain." She smiled.

"May I be of any assistance, Your Highness?"

"Yes, Malcolm, as a matter of fact you can. Here, take this," she said thrusting her trowel in my hand. "It's cocktail hour!"

Discarding the gardening instrument as rapidly as I could I headed back to my room in the castle. Across the quadrangle from the Royal Family I had a lovely spot with a view overlooking the River Dee. One could count on reading many a good book there during the long summer afternoons.

In the evenings I would occasionally go out to dinner at one of the favored establishments close by. The most popular was Tulloch Lodge, a delightful Victorian mansion set on a wooded hill in picturesque grounds, also overlooking the River Dee. Inside the lodge, fine food, a healthy French wine list, and handsome antiques complemented the civilized and relaxed atmosphere.

Tulloch Lodge was owned by two charming and considerate hosts named Hamish and Hector. They both loved to entertain and made no secret of their long-lasting relationship. Palace employees were always welcome, and some were old friends. If a member of the Royal Household was to return two or three times to the lodge then he was sure to receive a large kiss and a prolonged hug from at least one, more probably both, of them. While most of us enjoyed our friendship with Hamish and Hector, their friendliness came as somewhat of a shock to the head of the food branch, Michael Parker. He was not quite as appreciative of Hamish and Hector's affectionate approach to the restaurant business and became most upset when the two lovers cornered him in the bric-a-brac cocktail lounge shortly after he arrived for his first visit. Their friendliness towards him stopped that same evening, however, when later that night they asked him how he had enjoyed his meal. Parker replied, "Yaaah, quite well, but it's not as good as the castle's I can tell you." Parker was unable to compute that this was not the way to make friends with Hamish and Hector.

4

As one would expect, Scotland is a place where clans display their loyalty to their ancient family name by wearing a kilt. Famous clans such as Macdonalds, Stuarts and Campbells all take great pride in wearing the colored tartan appropriate to their respective families, and take great offence if anyone from outside should presume to sport their colors.

However, one afternoon while I was leaving the castle for a walk, the Queen spotted Parker walking proudly around in a kilt of red, grey and black. Strange? thought Her Majesty. What possible connection to Scotland could a man bearing the name 'Parker' have?

"Mr. Parker?" Her Majesty called politely.

"Yaaah, Ma'am?" Parker shouted out much too quickly and much too loudly.

"I see that you are wearing the kilt of Balmoral tartan."

"Yaaah, Ma'am, that is correct."

"Well, if you will forgive me for asking, but I did not realize that you were either Scottish or a member of the Royal Family."

"No, Ma'am, I'm not. But I thought I would just get in the mood of the country. Everyone else seems to be wearing them."

The Queen was utterly baffled.

"Well, everyone else is wearing them, Mr. Parker, because they have the right to. Only members of the Royal Family may wear the Balmoral tartan. Only Scottish people belonging to a clan may wear other tartans. You belong to neither category."

"Sorry, Ma'am, but I was in Forsythes some time ago and I came across this kilt and I thought to myself, now that looks smart. Just the sort of thing I want."

"Yes, but Mr. Parker, you have nothing at all to do with the colors you are wearing. You are not a member of the Royal Family!"

"No, Ma'am, that is correct. But it's nice to pretend I am, don't you think?"

Her Majesty shook her head in disbelief and continued on her way.

Towards the end of September I was returning with Parker from another late night at Tulloch Lodge. Hamish and Hector could be enormously flexible with their bar hours if they chose to. On arrival back at the castle, one of the Queen's footmen came rushing up to us in the main entrance and excitedly told us about a terrible fight going on in the servants' bar.

When we arrived on the scene two footmen were beating the hell out of each other. Apparently they had discovered that they had both been sleeping with the same housemaid for a full month, the girl having told each that he was "the only one." Her secret web came undone that night and she was calmly sitting on a stool, watching the débâcle in front of her and cheering along with hordes of others who had raced to the bar for a ringside seat. Footmen and maids, porters and pages were all screaming with delight at the entertainment, not one of them attempting to help quieten the two boys down.

"This is my girlfriend, not yours," one footman shrieked, and then, "She's anybody's girlfriend round here," the other replied insultingly, resulting in still further blows. With great effort we were at last able to make them all calm down, and, as usual, relationships healed over night and the matter was forgotten.

Balmoral could be very much like a summer boarding camp when the footmen became involved; a summer camp with a heavy dose of teenage love drama once they broke into their stride.

Now as I have said, on Fridays the footmen all went to the disco' and it was usually after these sessions of impressive indulgence that they showed their worst colors. They loved to play tricks at Balmoral and were constantly dreaming up new atrocities. One Friday they rounded up all the sheets, pillow cases and towels in the castle and stealthily carried them out onto the estate where they deposited them in a cowshed.

The next morning the chief housekeeper, Miss De Trey White, was wild about the situation. There were no fresh sheets for the Royal Family's beds! Realising it was most likely a prank, the chief housekeeper mounted a massive search. (The thought that a robber would break into Balmoral Castle and steal Her Majesty's linen just did not make any sense to her.) Several hours later, after the entire castle had been searched—even Sir Peter's office—the baskets were found.

It was for these reasons that many of the Queen's Household did not visit the castle more often. They were aware of the lenient and lax rules governing the footmen in this particular royal residence, and to be honest, they really did get way out of control at times.

It was not unheard of for them to grab one of Her Majesty's senior advisers while they leisurely strolled along the peaceful riverside walkway late at night, strip them naked and then hurl them ceremoniously into the River Dee. Incredibly enough, they got away with this sort of behavior because Her Majesty wanted them to have fun, and as she was fond of taking a stroll before retiring to bed herself, she could hardly have missed their antics. In fact, she was very fortunate not to experience the temperature of her beloved River Dee personally!

Being aware of the Staff's free rein myself, I made it a habit to keep well away from the riverside walkway late at night. I have never been terribly partial to taking a ball-freezing dip in northern Scottish rivers at any time of year, let alone at midnight in the middle of fall!

One evening when Her Majesty was out for a late night stroll, she came across a member of Staff whose behavior she did not fully appreciate. It was a little before midnight, and Her Majesty had just come out of the castle when she heard a strange noise close by. It was coming from her right. Eyes not quite focused to the dark she slipped behind a bush. The noise grew louder and then she heard a man's voice moaning. As her eyes adjusted she became aware that the bushes immediately beside her were moving. What could it be? This was her own private garden and she was the only member of the family in residence at the time.

Then, another noise. Sounded like water, and lots of it. In fact it was a torrent of water. Her Majesty peered from behind a tree limb and then realised the cause of the disturbance—one of her old porters was pissing on her rose bushes. Her Majesty did not confront the man. She went back to her apartments and went to bed.

The next morning I was told about the incident but fortunately Sir Peter was there to deal with it. Her Majesty was most annoyed and did not appreciate her Staff taking short cuts through her garden and then relieving themselves on her bushes. The Queen recognised the offender and was able to identify him for Sir Peter. The porter received a stern lecture and was presented with the horrific punishment of being told not to do it again.

6

It was near the middle of October and at this time every year the Queen gives a ball for some five hundred of her Scottish friends and visiting English aristocracy. Known as the Ghillies' Ball, the occasion is one of two that are held at the castle while the Queen is in residence. I was privileged enough to be invited to these glittering and unique occasions. The dancing, in the huge and ancient Grand Hall, is strictly traditional Scottish and is always a merry and exuberant evening, quite different from any ball held at Buckingham Palace. It is the only time when a member of the Royal Family may be asked for the pleasure of a dance by a 'commoner.'

On this particular Ghillies' Ball, the evening commenced at eight o'clock and the Royal Family had made their entrance in a leisurely fashion. The invited guests were dancing to the music of the Royal Highland Fusiliers and the Queen appeared to be thoroughly enjoying herself, mingling with the guests and wearing an exquisite pale silk evening gown with a diamond tiara. The Queen Mother, who has been coming to Balmoral since 1921, also looked relaxed and radiant and as usual was dressed in her favorite color of pale blue. She was dancing with Prince Charles and seemed to be more than capable of matching his energy. In fact she moved around a great deal more spryly than the Prince himself.

I had just finished an enjoyable conversation over a glass of sherry with the Duke of Argyll, and was helping myself to the lobster mousse at the buffet when Princess Margaret appeared. She had apparently just arrived from London on one of the Queen's private planes. As usual, she was late, having been up late the night before at another party.

Her Royal Highness is renowned for her late evenings and will frequently keep her personal staff up until four in the morning, talking and drinking the night away. In fact, one footman in her home complained to Sir Peter that Princess Margaret's Household was not allowed to even think about retiring until she had gone to bed herself. The Queen instructed Sir Peter to inform them all that, regardless of her sister's wishes, they should take it upon themselves to go to bed at midnight. But Princess Margaret would not hear of this and so continued to keep her staff up, fully expecting them to be back on the job the following morning at six a.m.

This evening the Princess looked tired but was dressed beautifully in a peach satin gown. Noticing me close by, her eyes mischievously lit up and she proceeded to move briskly towards me calling "Malcolm! Malcolm!" Grabbing me by the hand she literally pulled me onto the dance floor and soon after began gyrating her hips as though she were at one of her favorite west-end London discotheques. The Duke of Edinburgh was looking most displeased as he trod on everyone's feet.

It is well known in royal circles that Princess Margaret enjoys the company of young men (many of whom are gay) as often as possible. Being such a young member of the Royal Household myself, the Princess was naturally attracted to me from the beginning. We danced for a few more minutes during which time she threw a reassuring smile to the Queen who was dancing with the Marquis of Bath. Spotting her sister through the corner of her eye, Her Majesty then gave me what I can only describe as her 'ugly look.' In other words, do something!

The Princess suddenly excused herself and quickly headed for the staircase at the end of the hall leading to the royal apartments. I had noticed a strong smell of gin on her breath while we were dancing, which surprised me as only sherry and wine were being served on the occasion. In due course, the Princess returned, but made many more trips to her suite that night.

At eleven thirty she showed obvious signs of flagging, looking very unsteady on her feet. I quickly moved forward and inquired if she needed some assistance.

"Oh, thank you Malcolm," she gasped.

I took hold of her by the left arm and her page took her by the other. Together we managed to help her up the long staircase to her suite, and ensured that she was comfortably settled. "Good night, Your Highness," I whispered, and softly closed the door. I mentioned to her page outside the suite that the Princess appeared to have been drinking excessively.

"You know she's always like that," he chuckled. "Wine and sherry aren't strong enough, so she comes up here for her gin, and there was plenty of that with her on the plane I can tell you, Mr. Barker." I made no comment. It was no secret amongst those close to the Royal Family that Her Royal Highness "made love" (as she was so fond of putting it) to at least two bottles of Mr. Beefeater a day.

When I returned from the royal apartments the ball was coming to a close in the Grand Hall. It was now growing late and the Queen still had another duty to perform before she could retire for the evening.

At the same time as the ball, those members of Staff not on duty hold their own party in another building on the estate. At the end of the evening Her Majesty always judges their fancy-dress competition, an occasion which she scarcely relishes. Accordingly, the Queen and her entourage, of which I was one for the evening, left the Grand Hall for the Staff quarters. We found the party there still in full swing, though thankfully the rowdy noise abated upon our appearance. The fancy-dress competitors immediately began lining up in front of the Queen, who went through the motions of acting extremely interested in the whole procedure.

There was a wide variety of enterprising costumes, including a pig, a penguin, Santa Claus, Julius Caesar, Count Dracula, Mrs. Margaret Thatcher, and a character who was dressed remarkably well to resemble the Royal Chef. All in all there must have been about twenty hopefuls, including a large and ferocious looking gorilla, who began really playing the part by frantically waving his arms in front of the Queen and making some terribly rude noises. Initially, Her Majesty responded with smiles and laughter, but when this act continued the smiles quickly turned to an annoyed and dark glare.

Anxious to conclude this event Her Majesty decided upon the three winners, which did not include the gorilla incidentally, and then handed out the prizes. She then left abruptly with her entourage. I decided to stay behind, for earlier in the evening I had observed a certain member of the Royal Family slip furtively away from the Ghillies' Ball and that individual had not returned.

The Staff clapped and sang loudly again once Her Majesty retired, and as everyone danced wildly amongst each other they persuaded the gorilla to remove his head. When he complied he revealed, as I suspected, none other then Prince Andrew! Later on I asked the Prince about his surprise appearance at the Staff party and he told me how they had invited him to join in their fun. Far preferring a boisterous evening of drink and laughter to what he considered the stuffiness of a royal ball, the Prince had gleefully accepted.

I departed for my own quarters and kept very quiet about the incident. Relations between the Queen and her second eldest son were frequently strained and I felt a family dispute during their vacation should be avoided if possible. Certainly the Queen would not have been amused, especially considering she was still perturbed about the modern decor the Prince had chosen for his Buckingham Palace suite. Purple, orange and green, she felt, did not suit the palace at all.

I must admit I had to agree with her.

7

My feelings were mixed as I seated myself comfortably in the Daimler limousine at Balmoral Castle en route for the airport. On the one hand, my eight weeks in the Scottish countryside was at an end, and the formality of London and the palace beckoning, but I was returning in the best possible fashion. An Andover aircraft of the Queen's Fleet awaited me at Aberdeen airport, and the Duke of Edinburgh and Prince Edward were among my traveling companions.

The hour-long car journey passed quickly. The Duke appeared preoccupied, probably going over the speech he would be giving to the World Wildlife conference the following day. Prince Edward seemed sad to be leaving Scotland as he sat beside me gazing wistfully out at the rolling Scottish hills carpeted in purple heather.

Arriving at the airport I took my seat opposite the Prince whilst his page and detective were placed in the rear cabin of the plane. The interior was extremely spacious despite the small size of the aircraft. The seats compared favorably with most First Class sections on a commercial flight, and there were beautiful glass cocktail tables positioned about the roomy cabin. The deep royal blue of the interior added an extra measure of elegance. The Duke was nowhere to be seen, so I assumed he was taking a keen interest in the pilot's flying skills in the cockpit.

"Would you care for a drink, Your Highness?" inquired the attentive steward a few moments after we were seated.

"Gin and tonic, please," the Prince requested.

"And for you, Mr. Barker?"

"Oh I think I will have the same, thank you."

"And make those stiff ones," instructed an amused Prince.

"Thank you, sir," I said appreciatively.

"That's alright. You'll be glad of it when my father takes over the controls."

"Oh really?" I returned, trying to hide my concern. I hadn't realised that the Duke would be flying the plane, and I had heard several reports of his erratic flying.

Shortly after leveling off at twenty five thousand feet the Prince's prediction proved correct, for while enjoying my smoked salmon hors d'oeuvre the aircraft took an unexpected and terrifying lurch forward. Prince Edward grinned at me. "See what I mean?"

I smiled weakly. "Just an airpocket, sir."

As the Prince did not seem unduly concerned about his father's turbulent flying, I resolved not to worry and to enjoy my lunch. The noisettes d'agneau were delicious and perfectly complemented by the fine claret. My company was also equally enjoyable and the Prince and I carried on a delightful conversation.

184

"It's just not the same away from Balmoral," sighed the Prince. "I hate having to leave the excellent salmon fishing."

All thought of fishing and Scotland were soon forgotten however as we made our approach into Heathrow. The Prince and I had been discussing the boarding schools we had both attended when he suddenly stiffened and tightened his seat belt. "Get ready for father's landing," he advised.

I soon understood what he meant.

The whine of the throbbing turboprop dropped alarmingly as we made an uneven final approach. As the aircraft attempted to correct its course and line up with the runway ahead, it rocked, shook, and heaved to the point where I seriously began to wonder if we were going to come out of this alive. Finally the 1960 vintage Andover bounced down onto the runway and shook unnervingly, before straightening out and gradually coming to a grinding halt.

Although I consider myself to be an experienced flyer, and have many times braved the fog-shrouded runways of Halifax, Nova Scotia, it was truly the roughest landing I had ever experienced in my entire life. I was thinking that a dry martini would go down extremely well.

Prince Edward took it all in his stride.

"Relax Malcolm," he smiled at me as the car drew alongside the plane to take us back to Buckingham Palace, "that was one of father's better landings!"

BUCKINGHAM PALACE

October 16th - January 1st

1

The Court was back in residence at Buckingham Palace but the royal standard was not flying. Her Majesty had indeed returned from Scotland but left shortly thereafter for a tour of India. She would be gone for two weeks. I bade the policeman at the palace gate "Good morning," and walked the lengthy stretch to the Grand Entrance. Although it was only eight thirty, there were, as usual, hundreds of people clinging to the wrought iron gates, hoping, against hope, to snatch a quick look at the Queen, or maybe if they are unbelievably fortunate, Princess Diana peeking from a bedroom curtain.

One can visualize Princess Anne contemplating, perhaps in an insecure mood, what the commoners were thinking of her family at that precise moment. The Princess might draw back the curtains on the middle window of the centre room, fling open the French doors that overlook the Mall, note the enthusiasm of the masses gathered in utter acclamation at the front, and then summate to her parents sitting at the breakfast table, "It's alright Mother. They still love us!"

But the sad point is that the people who stand there all day are rarely going to catch a glimpse of anyone in the Royal Family, simply because they have wisely chosen to live on the other side of the palace. Who on earth would want to be stared at all day by strange tourists? I took a sharp left inside the marble foyer and glided down the silent Master of the Household's corridor.

Naturally, Humphrey was not in evidence. With my portion of his work, plus my own, I found it necessary to come to work at least an hour early and leave more then two hours late at the end of the day. But I was beginning to accept this and almost did not mind. Sir Peter knew what was going on, but in accepting that there would be no change in my colleague—now or ever—he made it clear from the start that it was me he would be relying on to fulfill our commitments to the Royal Household; both my commitments, and Mr. Humphrey's.

One of Mr. Humphrey's recent omissions involved a senior employee in the deputy press secretary's office, Mrs. Anne Neal. She had left with Her Majesty on the tour of India. But months before leaving, and in preparation for the long journey, she brought in a black suitcase asking that Mr. Humphrey have the zipper repaired for her. This was a simple request, and all Mr. Humphrey had to do was telephone Mayfair Trunks who handled all the palace's work and it would be picked up that same afternoon. It was a full two months before the Queen and her entourage were to depart and there seemed, to Anne, plenty of time to have the broken zipper repaired.

"Oh ya, ya, Anne, I'll have this seen to right away," Mr. Humphrey confidently told her when she brought it to his attention.

"Well, see that you do, please, because I am going to need it for the trip," the elegant silver-haired lady instructed.

"Ya, Anne, no need to worry. I'll take care of it right away." She handed him the black leather case, thanked him, and left. After she had gone Humphrey telephoned a porter and instructed him to come to his office and see him right away. When the porter arrived, Humphrey handed the case to him and said, "Here, Bill. Take this case and stick it in one of the storage rooms in the basement." As instructed, the porter left with the case.

"John, what are you doing? Anne needs that case for the trip with the Queen." I felt he had gone too far this time. "You are supposed to send it out to the shop, not fling it in the basement."

"It's only a bloody case," he waved his hands in the air not bothered by what he had done. "She has lots more of them. I can't be wastin' my valuable time on somethin' silly like that."

"Well then I am going to call Mayfair Trunks and see to the case myself." I picked up the telephone, irritated.

"Listen you," Humphrey warned, "just leave it alone. That case is stayin' put where it is." Reluctantly I replaced the telephone receiver. When Humphrey was angry I did not argue with him.

A few weeks later Anne called to check on the state of the case she assumed was away being repaired.

"Ya, ya, Anne," Humphrey said matter of factly into the receiver. "It's away bein' repaired now so don't you worry. It'll be back in plenty of time."

Meanwhile the case was reposing where it had been placed; in the basement of the palace.

Two weeks before departure Anne again called regarding the case, and was once more assured that it was being taken care of at the repair shop. "Ya, Anne, they've had some trouble findin' a matchin' zipper," Humphrey said to her authoritatively. "I've been onto them several times and they're doin' their best for ya. But you'll have it back in time. Don't worry."

"Yes, well just as long as it *is* back in time, Mr. Humphrey. I do need that case you know, and I will be leaving with the Queen soon, you realise."

"Ya, ya, Anne, I fully understand and promise to have it back before you go to India."

One week before departure, Anne came into the office.

"Mr. Humphrey? Where is my case?"

Mr. Humphrey looked shocked. "What do ya mean, Anne? I told ya it's away bein' fixed."

"Where is it being fixed, Mr. Humphrey?"

"I told ya, Anne, at Mayfair Trunks."

"Well, that is most odd, Mr. Humphrey, because I have just rung Mayfair Trunks and they tell me that they do not know a thing about my case. They haven't seen any case belonging to Buckingham Palace and they say they do not recall speaking to you about one either."

"Now that's absolutely crap, Anne." Humphrey was roaring into gear. "I've been onto them almost every day about that case. You didn't speak to the right person, probably someone new or junior. It needed special attention ya know."

Anne looked drawn. "Mr. Humphrey, I spoke to the head man who looks after all the palace's repairs. He knows nothing about any case."

"Now Anne, I give you my personal assurance that I have been onto them about that case every week. Now I'm goin' to call them up an give them a piece of my mind I am."

"Never mind, Mr. Humphrey. It is too late now," and she headed out the door totally crestfallen and naturally confused.

Humphrey called out after her, "I'll let ya know, Anne, what they have to say about that case."

To my knowledge, the suitcase is still laying in the storeroom in the bowels of Buckingham Palace, untouched for almost a decade.

Now you know where your case went to Anne!

2

At ten forty-five a.m. Mr. Humphrey declared his presence for the day. "Mornin' Malcolm," he said congenially and then stripped to his underwear and sat himself comfortably in his red leather chair.

I was encouraged to press a question.

"John?" I asked carefully, "Victor Fletcher has been onto me about some wheels for the Queen's cocktail trolley."

Mr. Humphrey said hesitantly, "Ya? What about them?"

"Well, he says he asked you to order them back in 1977."

"Oh bloody hell, I've got more important things than them trolley wheels to look after," he said defensively, and plunged into his Daily Express. "God, would ya look at them thighs, Malcolm! I wouldn't mind a night with her, eh?"

"I haven't got time for the sunshine girl today, John. The Sultan of Oman is arriving in two weeks or have you forgotten?

"Sod the Sultan."

"Oh yes, I know what else I had to tell you, John. Tims has been looking for you again." "Oh bugger him," he rebuked scornfully, giving his arse a healthy scratch.

The door opened and in walked Victor Fletcher.

Victor was about sixty years old. Balding, with a red florid face, he was noticeable for his afflicting gout which forced upon him a terrible limp. As the Queen's Yeoman of the Silver Pantry, Victor's responsibilities were to four underbutlers aged between seventeen and twenty. Victor preferred his boys young—*very young*, and if at all possible, *very* shy! He was required to train the underbutlers to wait on tables at banquets and on family occasions. Devoted as he was, he offered to give them private lessons in his room above the pantry. I used to marvel at his dedication when I saw one of his flock leaving his room well after midnight.

As I have said, Victor was roughly sixty and he looked every day of it. Tragically, he found it increasingly difficult to get the desired responses from his division. More often than not, he had to make do with just looking, and aaaaah...how delightful they looked too!

Victor stood firmly just inside the door.

"Mr. Humphrey?" the Yeoman tried to sound firm through his effeminate lisp. "I have come to see whether you have ordered those trolley wheels I need for my cart."

"What do ya mean *order*, Victor?"

"You know exactly what I mean, Mr. Humphrey. Have you ordered my wheels yet?"

"'Course I have."

"Well, where are they?"

"They haven't arrived yet," Humphrey said giving his arse another scratch.

"How can they not have arrived yet, Mr. Humphrey?" Victor was annoyed and as always when pushed to his limits moved his pliable wrists into action.

"Don't ask me. I don't know, do I?"

"Mr. Humphrey, you have been telling me the same story every time I come in here. Now what is going on?" Victor held his limp wrists tightly to his chest.

"Look, Victor. I've been onto them again at Harrods but I still haven't received any word on when they'll be arrivin'."

"But Mr. Humphrey, I need to have them now," Victor cried with a note of desperation.

"I know, Victor, but there really isn't anythin' I can do."

Victor's scarlet face flushed with pent-up rage.

"Mr. Humphrey, I have been after you to get those wheels since Mr Callaghan was Prime Minister and I still haven't had any luck. Surely it isn't that difficult to replace some damaged trolley wheels?"

"No, no, ordinarily it isn't a problem, Victor, but these are very special parts and I know Harrods have been doin' their best for me."

"Mr. Humphrey, I want my wheels!" the Yeoman's wrists were now waving frantically again.

"Ya, I know that, Victor, but I'm honestly tellin' ya that I've been doin' my best. Honest I am."

Victor relented a little and almost seemed to relax. With a heavy sigh he continued, "Mr. Humphrey, all I want are my wheels. What do I have to do to make you see that? The Queen has been asking me about them again, you know. She is not blind, Mr. Humphrey, our Monarch is not blind!"

"'Course she isn't. What makes ya think that? Heh Heh Heh!" Mr. Humphrey was pleased with his jest.

Victor continued undaunted. "For several years, Mr. Humphrey, Her Majesty has commented on her cocktail trolley and posed the natural question as to why it is taking so long to repair it. The wheels vibrate so badly that the trolley cannot be moved at all. I cannot push it up to the table, Mr. Humphrey. Do you understand me? I must serve the drinks from the side." The wrists were moving into third gear. "Now Her Majesty will be back from India soon and I assured her I would attend to the matter. What am I to tell her, Mr. Humphrey? The Queen wants her trolley wheels. I want my trolley wheels!"

Victor was working himself into a panic.

"Well, Victor, it's like this: you will just have to tell her that this sort of thing can't be handled overnight."

"Overnight, Mr. Humphrey? It's been years!"

"Look. You will get your wheels as soon as they arrive. I'm tellin' ya, I'm doin' my best for ya, now that's that."

Victor shook his head miserably and held his hands out for Humphrey to stop. He wanted to hear no more.

"Mister Humphrey..." He paused, and placed his fingers to his temple. "Just order the wheels for me, Mr. Humphrey, please!" Fatigue lined his face as he quietly departed.

Mr. Humphrey opened the closet and took out his brown wrinkled suit. The suit he wore every day. Placing it in a pile on his desk he reached into a drawer and took out a sampling of socks. Sniffing them each in turn he made his choice.

"John, have you ordered those wheels for Victor yet, or not?" I asked apprehensively as Mr. Humphrey pulled on the first sock.

I wondered if today's selection could possibly be less palatable than the last.

"Heh heh heh…'Course I haven't!"

"Why not, John? He does need them you know."

"Look, Malcolm, so what? I'm looking after it, not you."

"But, John, the Queen wants her trolley wheels fixed. You can't keep her waiting forever. Why don't I take care of it and that way it will be done?"

"Look, you," Humphrey pointed a finger aggressively, dropping sock in hand, "just you leave well enough alone. He's not gettin' those wheels and that's that! Bloody poofter always wettin' his knickers…"

Humphrey picked the cheap, long-since dead jacket off his desk and simultaneously gave his yellowed crotch an open-handed scratch. "Hmmmmmm," he ruminated slowly to himself, and the thought of déjà vu flashed through my brain. "Think it's time to change me undies!"

3

The Queen and the Duke returned from their overseas tour in mid-November. Paul Almond came excitedly into my office shortly after my hour-long lunch. Mr. Humphrey still had another hour and a half to go. Seating himself on the corner of my large walnut desk, Paul exclaimed high-spiritedly that he had come across a wonderful new toy. From behind his back he produced a large ragged doll and proudly held it up for inspection.

"What about it?" I asked him. "Can't do much with a doll in the palace can you Paul?" He gleefully pulled a string in its back and the doll's voice filled the room with surprisingly realistic animal noises.

"Sit there Malcolm and listen," he instructed and then picked up the telephone and dialed the Assistant Master of the Household, Mr. Tims.

Over the speaker phone Tims answered. Paul held the doll close to the receiver and pulled the string. The doll moved into action. "This is what the piggy says...OINK! OINK! OINK!"

Tims was furious. "Who is this? How dare you—"

Paul hung up.

Next, Paul dialled the Duchess of Grafton's exchange. I knew she had only arrived in the palace an hour ago and was aware that she had left instructions with the switchboard operator that she required a nap and did not want to be disturbed.

The Duchess answered her ringing telephone wearily. "Hello? I told you I am not receiving any calls at the—"

"This is what the sheep says...BHHHAAA! BHHAAA! BHHHHAAAA!" the child-like voice simulated with striking accuracy.

"Look, who is this?" the Queen's Mistress of the Robes ordered in outraged tones.

Paul pulled the string a second time and the doll roared to life. "This is what the hen says...CLUCK! CLUCK! ClUCK!"

"Now I want to know who this is," the Duchess wailed emotionally. "I happen to be taking a nap and do not find this the least bit amusing. Who are—"

Paul disconnected the call.

For a finale to the session, Paul dialled the Duke's private apartment and sure enough the Queen's husband took the call.

"Yes? Hello?" he asked, as usual in a terrible mood.

"This is what the cow says... MOOOOooo! MOOOoo! MOOOooo!"

"Who the devil is that? I am very busy..." the Duke retorted.

Paul pulled the string again. "This is what the doggy says...RUFF RUFF!—RUFF RUFF!—RUFF RUFF!"

Paul unceremoniously cut the Duke off. The novelty of the toy waning, he thought he should get back to the Royal Mews and perhaps do some work.

No more than a minute after he had gone, Tims burst into my office and stood in the entrance looking around suspiciously.

"Are you alone in here, Malcolm?" he asked after a lengthy pause.

"Yes, of course I am, Mr. Tims. Why do you ask?"

Tims scrutinized my face with care, as if searching it for some revelation of the truth he thought he knew.

"Quite alone?" he again inquired, this time with eyebrows raised.

"Quite alone, I assure you, Mr. Tims. As you can see, Mr. Humphrey is out."

"I am not interested in Mr. Humphrey, Malcolm. I should be surprised if I were to find him in." He paused again, and was obviously making efforts to keep his temper in check. His doctor had been quite pointed on that. "You haven't heard of anyone making rude noises over the internal telephone have you?"

"Rude noises over the telephone, Mr. Tims?" I said with astonishment.

"Yes, that's right. Someone in the palace has been making lewd telephone calls. The Duchess of Grafton was awakened from her nap by one. I myself, Malcolm, had the misfortune of being ridiculed in this most affrontive manner."

"Oh dear, Mr. Tims. Isn't that dreadful? If I hear anything of it at all I will most certainly let you know."

Mr. Tims left reluctantly, a destroyed man once again. Paul Almond was the second most wanted man on his list and he thought he had caught him in action. Once more he had missed his triumphant moment of glory by only a hair's breadth.

Oh well, there is always next time isn't there?

One week later it was decided that Mr. Tims should take a short break. He was not relaxed at all, poor man. Mr. Humphrey

197

was put in charge of the Household and he was quite under-standably in heaven over it. He now commanded full authority over the Queen's entire Staff.

Today, in Tims's absence, he would be interviewing a young boy for the position of underbutler. The duties would involve basically standing at attention by the buffet while the Royal Family had lunch and dinner. If this was managed successfully for one year the boy would stand a chance of being promoted to a footman, which brought on the additional financial worry of having an extra three pounds per week to manage.

At eleven that morning, a meek seventeen-year-old boy knocked ever so gently on the open office door.

"Now then, Jeremy", Humphrey said in a friendly manner when he had seated the boy in a chair, "Why do you want to work here at Buckingham Palace?" A straightforward question, and a good start I thought to myself. Perhaps Mr. Humphrey was learning after all.

The boy was obviously nervous. "Well..." he thought to himself carefully before replying, "I love the Queen, and...and...and if I got the job I would work harder than anyone to please her." (That was all he could come up with?)

"Right then!" Humphrey bellowed happily as though the inexperienced boy had just won on a game show. "You've got the job! Report back to me in one week and you can start then."

The boy was thrilled. "Wow! Thank you, Sir Humphrey."

Mr. Humphrey was noticeably pleased with the boy's mistake. "Off ya go then ya cheeky thing, ya, and congratulations." The ecstatic lad virtually ran from the office beaming in disbelief at his good fortune.

"John? Don't you think you should have asked some more questions? You don't know anything about him and you've just offered him a place here in the palace."

"Malcolm, I could tell more then I needed just from looking into that boy's sweet, innocent young face. Believe me, he's just the sort a person we want here at the palace."

I was not so sure.

Two days after Tims returned from his holiday he came screaming into our office looking for Humphrey.

"Where is that man, Malcolm? Where is he? I want to see him immediately!"

"He's still out to lunch," I replied covering for the fact that he hadn't even been in that day. "Why? What has happened?" Mr. Humphrey was always doing something.

"Did you meet that boy Humphrey hired while I was away?"

"Just when he came in for an interview. Humphrey seemed to think he was ideal for the palace."

"Humphrey would wouldn't he. The police have just rung me. After completing their vetting of him it has been discovered that the boy has a criminal record." Tims temper was boiling.

"Oh no," I said alarmed, "What has he done?"

Tims was distraught.

"He has been convicted three times in Liverpool for having sexual relations with the dead! Apparently he even prefers to dig them up! Oh where is that man? Just wait until I get my hands on him." At this rate Tims would be in need of another break soon. He flew out of the office ranting, "Tell that man to ring me the very instant he arrives."

John was sitting in his armchair when I returned from lunch. "Oh there you are, John. Tims is looking for you. He has been calling all morning."

"What's he want now?"

"Apparently that underbutler you hired a couple of weeks ago has been convicted for necrophilia—having sex with dead people in Liverpool. What do you say to that?" I stood looking seriously at him.

"Oh well, I suppose if that sort of thing is goin' to happen it might as well be in Liverpool as anywhere, heh heh heh!"

"John, it isn't funny. You should have waited till the police vetted him before offering him a job at the palace. There is no telling what he might have done."

Mr. Humphrey looked with mock confusion. "Why? No one dead around here is there? Except maybe the Duchess of Grafton. Heh heh heh!"

"I'm serious, John. The boy is a real luney. Not only is he into sex with the dead, but it seems he prefers to dig them up himself out of their graves. Now what do you think about your choice? I warned you to look into him before giving him a job."

"Oh well," he said, opening the Daily Express and biting into a family size chocolate bar, "you win some, you lose some."

Tims and Sir Peter, however, were not in the mood for Mr. Humphrey's jokes. He was given one of his biggest lambasts to date, and sulked for two days. Then, with the matter forgotten, he got on with his usual routine.

4

It was near the end of November and abnormally cold as I made my way to my office. I had just come from the Grand Entrance where I had witnessed an incident that had been unsettling to say the very least.

A drunken punk rocker, dressed resplendently in black leather and chains and sporting a cockatoo hairstyle, casually walked into the main lobby of Buckingham Palace and began satisfying his bestial character by hurling some of Her Majesty's furniture around. Chairs, mahogany tables, lamps and flowers from the magnificent vases were strewn all about the red carpeted foyer.

The police were notified by the guard stationed just inside the doorway. He had been busy with his lunch when the punk rocker arrived and didn't notice him until he was well into his third chair. When the two palace policemen arrived, it took both of them to drag the aggressive youth out of the main entrance. Kicking and swearing at them as they did so, they deposited him outside the gates on Buckingham Palace Road. The punk rocker was not arrested or questioned or investigated. He was simply removed from the premises and allowed to wander away free.

It had been a bad period for the security forces in operation around the palace, if one could call it 'security'. Beams were found to be totally without effect; guards supposed to be on duty were nowhere to be found; windows and doors weren't checked for weeks at a time; police would admit practically anyone with two legs. In short, the entire protection of the Royal Family of Great Britain was in hopeless chaos.

Prior to the punk rocker affair, two teenage girls on holiday from Sweden climbed over the gates at the rear of the palace, set up two twin hunting-orange tents on the lawn, cooked themselves a little supper over a spit, said goodnight to each other, and then promptly went to bed. The two young girls spent the entire night camping on the lawn, directly behind the royal apartments of Buckingham Palace, and were not discovered until the following morning around ten thirty! They were not noticed until one of the guards happened by them on a route that should have been patroled on an hourly basis.

The two Swedish girls, who were no more than twenty years of age, were brought to the police station for questioning. "Vell," one of the girls began in broken English, "it vas like this: first ve see tha lovely green lawns of Buckingham Palace in a book. Ve think how beautiful they are to our eyes. So, ve decide...on our first trip to London, ve go to Queen's garden and camp out and see for ourselves. Ve come to palace. See the valls so easy to climb over that ve simply give each other boost. No one come to tell us different so ve think, Queen don't mind if ve use her beautiful gardens. She nice your Queen, no?"

The girls convinced the investigators that they had meant no harm. They didn't even realize it was illegal, they claimed. Satisfying the police, they were simply escorted outside the station and were allowed to go happily on their way.

But a much more serious event was to happen soon after which caused a major reshuffle in the ranks of those who protected the Queen.

It started one evening just after midnight when a housemaid gave a sharp screech and shot up erect in her bed. She called a palace detective and told him that she had seen a figure in her bedroom window. She was sure it was the face of a man.

"No, young lady," the detective assured her when he arrived in her room. "You haven't seen a man in your window. You must have been dreaming."

The housemaid was certain she had seen him, but it did seem highly unlikely so she gave him the benefit of the doubt and went back to sleep; much to the relief of the detective who didn't want to have to launch a pointless investigation at this late hour anyway.

At seven the next morning the Queen's bedroom door opened slightly. The Queen was not quite up yet and her private lights were extinguished. As the door quietly pushed open, light filtered in from the illuminated hall outside.

"Who is that?" Her Majesty asked as the door softly closed behind the unknown figure. "Who is there, please?"

The figure was now by her bed and the Queen snapped on a light at the head of her bed. "Who are you?" the Queen demanded again of the strange man she could now see in front of her, dressed in faded jeans and wrinkled shirt. "What do you want?"

"I've come to talk to you Queen Elizabeth. That's what I'm here for. I just want to talk." The intruder smiled sinisterly, staring continually at her as though half mad.

The Queen did not panic as most would have done. When the door to her private bedroom opened she had pressed the security button hidden at the side of her bed. She knew it might only be one of her drunken Staff, but it was safer to be cautious. In this case her decision had paid off. Or so she thought.

Her Majesty knew that the red emergency button was supposed to alert her detectives and armed help would appear any second now. She would just stall him until they arrived. The man was still staring at her vaguely.

"What would you like to talk about?" the Queen asked him, waiting for the entrance that would save her from this danger.

"I just want to talk," came the emotionless reply.

The Queen patiently indulged him.

Five minutes had elapsed since she had first pressed her emergency button and still no one had arrived. Perhaps it was faulty she thought. She would wait a little longer.

But no one came.

Her only way of coming through this danger was to remain calm, she was well aware of that. She must not panic. She must assure the intruder that there was nothing to worry about. But she was going to need help soon. There was no telling how demented he might be.

"What is your name?" Her Majesty inquired as controlled as possible."

"My name is Michael Fagin."

"Well, what would you like to talk with me about, Michael?" The man began willingly telling the Queen about his life and that truly seemed to be the only purpose of his visit.

The Queen thought quickly. "Can I offer you some refreshment? A cigarette perhaps?"

"Yes that would be nice," the man replied in a childlike manner. "I would like a cigarette."

The Queen now saw an opening. If she could just persuade him to allow her to call one of her footmen then help could still be summoned. Obviously something was wrong with her alarm. Calmly Her Majesty told the man that she was just going to push a small button and ring for a footman who would bring her some cigarettes. That was all. "Now it is quite alright," she continued. "He will just be bringing us some cigarettes and then you and I will have a nice long talk. Alright?"

"Alright then," he answered obligingly.

The Queen slowly reached towards her bedside table and pushed the bell that would summon her personal footman. That morning Keith Magloire was on duty. When he arrived in the Queen's bedroom he was immediately aware that all was not right.

"Ah, yes, Keith," the Queen said with continued calmness, "my friend Mr. Fagin here would like some cigarettes and so would I. Would you please bring us some immediately?"

Fortunately for the Queen, Keith was a little more responsible then her detectives. Even if Her Majesty had for some bizarre reason invited the strange man into her bedchamber, and that was unlikely, Keith knew that Her Majesty did *not* smoke.

When he returned with the cigarettes, he persuaded the intruder to leave the Queen's bedroom and come and have a talk with him. The man complied with the suggestion. Keith sat him down in the Queen's pantry just outside her room. There, he gave him a cigarette and chatted to him while he waited for the policeman whom he had summoned moments earlier. Fagin was easily taken into custody that morning.

Throughout the following days, it was discovered that Fagin had climbed over the palace wall that night, crawled up an outside drainpipe, and gained entrance into the Queen's home through an unlocked window in Sir Peter Ashmore's office. Pacing the palace corridors and rooms for over seven hours he was able at last, with the use of a map, to gain access to the Queen's bedroom.

It was discovered in the course of the investigation that the security beams placed to detect such intruders along the palace walls were faulty and the windows which were supposed to be checked nightly by a guard had been overlooked; but even worse was the confession of the two armed detectives assigned to stand outside Her Majesty's bedroom while she slept. They admitted that they were fast asleep further down the hall in one of the sitting rooms. The sergeant, who heard the Queen's urgent plea for help when she pressed her buzzer, said that he considered it to be another false alarm (it was always going off) and continued eating his bacon and eggs in the police security area on the ground level of the palace. Everyone, including Michael Greene, Chief of the Royalty Protection Group at the palace, was fired.

About three months later, the Queen's private police officer, Commander Michael Trestrail, was also given notice for a far more minor breach of duties when a young boy revealed in a London tabloid that he was having a homosexual affair with him. Although the Queen specifically asked the Home Secretary not to publish the reason for his dismissal, he refused, and the details were made public. Even though this was of significantly less importance than the aforementioned negligence, Commander Trestrail was considered to be a major security risk and his employment was duly terminated. It did not make sense. But then not a great deal did at the palace.

The London newspapers were so appalled at the lack of security that in some editorials they called for the resignation of Sir Peter Ashmore. Officials in the Master of the Household's department, including myself, all signed a letter of support for him which was given to the Queen. Every Official signed, that is, except for Mr. John Humphrey who said, "Why the bloody hell should I sign that? He's a bloody piss artist anyway. Heh heh heh!"

In my time as an Official to the Queen, I felt the security afforded her and the rest of the Royal Family was in a general state of apathy. It consisted of retired policemen and old watchmen, with no more ability or interest in safeguarding the Monarch than a two-year-old child.

5

The banquet for the Sultan of Oman was proceeding nicely. The dinner guests were just being served their main course, and the Queen and Queen Mother, situated on each side of the Sultan, chatted pleasantly with those around. The Queen Mother smiled sweetly at the Archbishop of Canterbury to her right who was saying something serious to Princess Anne on his other side. The Queen Mother was dressed splendidly in a pale blue evening gown and was now feeling quite pleasant as the gin martini cocktail she had consumed was really clicking in. Across the table, Prince Charles seemed only vaguely to be listening to His Highness Sayyid Fahad Bin Mahmood Al Said, the supreme Arabian monarch whose name took up more space on the menu than the entrée, which tonight was 'Duchesse de Barbue Florentine'.

Behind the scenes all was progressing smoothly as the liveried footmen and pages scurried around the crimson, white and gold ballroom, ensuring that service to the important and honored guests was as smooth as the polished brass candelabras that adorned the long horseshoe table.

Humphrey peered into the banquet room from behind heavy ornate doors which led to the East Gallery. The red carpeted corridor along the west side of the Grand Hall gleamed with its white and gold ceiling and coupled columns of pale grey Carrara marble. Mr. Humphrey noted that the meal was well under way, and made a mental note of what was presently available for consumption in the kitchens.

"Mr. Humphrey?" said a woman's voice from behind.

206

Startled, Mr. Humphrey came away from his peep hole. "Hello there Miss Colebrook? Not goin' out on the town tonight, are ya?" It was the deputy chief housekeeper with whom he was totally infatuated.

"No, Mr. Humphrey, I rarely go out on the town nowadays."

Humphrey remembered to ask her something. "Oh ya. I been meanin' to ask ya somethin', Miss Colebrook. What's this I here then about you sayin' I'm all talk, anyway?"

"Well, Mr. Humphrey," the deputy housekeeper answered, primly patting the tight bun at the top of her matronly head, "I have heard that you have been making comments about me behind my back, calling me the 'palace bicycle' and saying that anyone can ride me. That's not very nice now is it, Mr. Humphrey?"

Mr. Humphrey's heavy brown eyes twinkled with delight. He felt lucky this evening. A good roll in the sack, and then a delicious meal from the royal kitchens, and he would be all set. "Ya, well it's true, isn't it, Miss Colebrook?" His heart began to race.

"What is true, Mr. Humphrey?" she replied, not removing the eye contact she was determined to maintain. The deputy housekeeper decided that she wouldn't mind a good roll in the sack either. It had been far too long.

"You know, that anyone can ride ya. Heh heh heh!"

The deputy housekeeper smiled slyly. "Mr. Humphrey it doesn't matter if it is true or not," she began to move slowly away from him, "because you will never know. But if you ask me...I really do think you are all talk, Mr. Humphrey. Yes, that is exactly what I think." She was almost out of sight.

Humphrey considered this parting taunt for a few seconds and then realizing its implication raced after her. "Bloody hell. I'll show her if I'm all talk or not!"

Miss Colebrook was 'taken' as it were from behind. He caught up with her and willingly she allowed herself to be 'forced' into an unmarked door, only yards down the hall from where the banquet was busily taking place.

"Mr. Humphrey!...Mr. Humphrey!...No...No! What are you doing Mr. Humphrey?" The door closed and the deputy housekeeper's protesting ceased.

Back in the Grand Ball Room everything was moving along as planned. As soon as dinner concluded, the speeches would begin. The Queen Mother sat back in her chair and looked behind the Sultan of Oman over at the Queen on his other side. She tried to attract her daughter's attention. Out of the corner of her eye, the Queen spotted her mother. It seemed she was waving frantically at her. Her Majesty politely broke off conversation with the Sultan and as subtly as possible she too leaned fully back in her deep upholstered chair and as gracefully as she could, whispered to her mother, "Yes? What is wrong?"

Archbishop Runcie spoke to the Queen Mother as she was about to answer her daughter. A moment later she again looked across at the Queen to catch her eye. She was very upset.

The Queen was distracted once more by her mother waving at her madly with an expression of the utmost urgency. When she could, she leaned back, and out of the corner of her lips whispered, "What is wrong, Mother?"

The Queen Mother self-consciously mouthed, "MY FOOTSTOOL!"

The Queen thought hard for a moment, and before having an opportunity to answer was again engaged in conversation with the Sultan, who was now aware himself that something was wrong. He hoped it had nothing to do with him. But now to his right, the Queen Mother was waving at her daughter again, and it was beginning to annoy her. What could possibly be so important about her Mother's footstool, she thought—if she had heard correctly!

When she could, the Queen reclined fully in her chair and ever so slightly turned to her right. The Queen Mother broke off conversation with the Archbishop and did the same.

"What about your footstool?" the Queen whispered.

The Queen Mother was having difficulty hearing with all the chatter. "What did you say?" she grimaced with frustration.

The Queen rolled her eyes slightly and then as loudly as she dare whispered, "I said...what about your footstool?"

The Sultan of Oman turned and looked at them both. If something was wrong then why didn't they just tell him? He was positive now that they were whispering about him.

Both Queens flushed a little at their discovery, and immediately sat straight up. The Queen Mother smiled warmly at the perplexed Sultan who really did want to know what was going on.

As the Sultan stood up and his speech got underway the Queen simply could not believe it but her Mother was once more waving at her! They at last had a chance to talk.

"What is wrong, Mother?"

The Queen Mother pointed under the table and cried, "It's my footstool."

"What about it?" Her Majesty still did not understand.

"I cannot find it!" she wrinkled her expression with true grief.

Now the Queen knew the situation was serious. Her mother suffered from poor circulation and for the past five years had taken to installing a permanent red velvet footstool under the table so that she might rest her feet while the often dull and lengthy speeches were given. Everyone in the palace knew that was her footstool and realized its importance. The Queen Mother had even gone to the trouble of bringing it from her own home herself. It was not to be moved.

The Queen Mother looked at her daughter accusingly, more than a little hurt. She was beginning to sulk, and when she sulked the Queen knew that she would hear all about it from her mother the following day. Although very much loved by the Queen, she could be more then a touch interfering in her two daughters' lives, and actually, when she wanted to be, a bit of a royal pain. The Queen knew that the footstool had to be found—and soon!

The Queen's page was summoned to the table and informed of the emergency. He was instructed to organize an immediate search for the prized footstool and employ anyone who could be spared, the Queen whispered clandestinely in his ear.

The Duke had been aware that his wife's attention was not fully on the Sultan's speech. He wasn't certain as to what was happening, but he did not like it. With crossed arms he shot her a stern glare. Her Majesty mouthed, "Footstool!" which only perplexed him more. She would tell him of it later, she decided. Just at that moment the Queen spotted someone peering in through the closed ballroom doors. She could not quite make out the face...but then...yes she could: it was Michael Parker staring at her again!

Fifteen minutes later the Queen's page returned with bad news: the footstool was nowhere to be found, anywhere. First, the Queen told him, "Tell that damn Parker man to go away. I have had enough of him!" Then she told him to look again for her mother's footstool, and begrudgingly he complied, although he saw little point.

There were only so many places to put a footstool and who would knowingly remove it when they must have realized that it would be missed? He too considered the trouble that was in store for them all if the Queen Mother's footstool was not returned. Probably worse than the time he went to pour her another glass of wine at a banquet and half of it ended up on her lap. Oh yes...it most certainly had to be found!

But the footstool was not found, and there was nothing that could be done to appease the Queen Mother that evening. The Queen tried to be helpful and suggested that a small box or makeshift rest be brought from the kitchens. But the first improvisation was found to be so wholly inadequate by the Queen Mother that no one dared offer another. She spent the next forty-five minutes sitting stationary and glaring straight ahead. She was in the most atrocious discomfort and quite as she had predicted, her ankles were swelling.

When her page helped her up from the table at the end of the evening, she was one very unhappy Queen Mother. "I am going home now. You will have to forgive me, but I am in such pain!" She still did not know the whereabouts of her cherished footstool, but she felt that the least her daughter could do if she was to continue attending these long-winded banquets was to ensure that such a simple request as a footstool be in place when it was required. "Take me home!" the Queen Mother ordered petulantly to her page. "I will not be staying for an after-dinner drink tonight."

The footstool remained a mystery until two months later when it was found by accident behind a painting in one of the storage rooms in the basement. It most definitely did not move there on its own.

But there was a greater significance to the evening than the Sultan of Oman's presence, Michael Parker causing annoyance to the Queen, and the disappearance of the Queen Mother's footstool. No, it had nothing whatsoever to do with any of these events, important as they were in their own right. Of historical significance, for the first time ever recorded, there were three 'Addresses' given at Buckingham Palace instead of two: the Queen's to the Sultan of Oman, the Sultan's to the Queen and Mr. Humphrey's to the deputy housekeeper of Buckingham Palace.

6

It was early December and the King of Tonga was arriving in three days for a private audience with the Queen. He had visited her many times before. More commonly, their discussions hovered around the topic of the natural disasters that so frequently seemed to affect his tiny South Pacific island. On occasion, he was invited as a personal guest of the Queen, as for instance was the case when the Prince and Princess of Wales were married.

Now, as most people are aware, the King is a large man...a very large man. Taller than Mr. Humphrey and broader than the Royal Chef, he weighed in at more than 400 pounds and because of his size, there were no chairs in the palace that could sustain his ample frame. Aware that the King of Tonga had a specially made chair for his use on visits to the Tongan High Commission, we called over and asked if it could be sent for his use while in audience with the Queen. They sent it over the following morning.

The sturdy, throne-like chair was placed in Her Majesty's private sitting room next to the one she would be occupying during their meeting. No more was thought of it until the King arrived as planned and was greeted by the Queen. All went well for the thirty-minute meeting, and Her Majesty and the King chatted warmly about the many problems facing his people on the impoverished island.

The meeting went well, and Her Majesty seemed to truly enjoy his company. When Her Majesty stood up to bid the King of Tonga goodbye, a footman appeared to escort him down to the Grand Entrance where there was a car waiting to return him to his High Commission. The King went to stand up, but found he could not move. He held his huge hands on the arms of the chair and attempted to force himself out of his confinement. Still he could not budge. The footman waiting to lead him out of the Queen's sitting room was instructed to help him. Still, the King could not get up out of his chair. Her Majesty stood by watching.

Helpfully, she suggested to the King that he try two footmen. A few moments later there were three gathered around him and his chair, and then a fourth was called in by the Queen. Looking on, she watched as the boys tugged and pulled at the King's arms, but still they were unable to free him from his seat. Her Majesty instructed her older page to assist. Now there were two boys spreading the arms of the wooden chair while the other two, along with the Queen's page, braced their legs against the wooden chair to achieve maximum leverage. The five of them pulled at the King with all their strength. With great effort and much cracking of wood the King came flying forward and landed heavily on the carpet in front of Her Majesty, along with two of the footmen.

The King was assisted to his feet and dusted off. Without a word of the affair to Her Majesty, he smiled, bade her farewell and was led safely away to his car. The chair, I am sorry to say, did not have the same good fortune and we regretfully had to inform the Tongan High Commission that it was in several pieces. "That is alright," an aide informed me when I delivered the bad news, "Since the King's last visit to London, he has added an additional eighty pounds. We thought we might have some trouble!"

While the footmen maintained that all during the struggle to free the King, Her Majesty never once showed even a hint of a smile, although it must have been tempting; later on, in the privacy of her apartment, she did manage a damn good roar in the company of her family.

Apparently, her footmen have never seen her 'squeak' so heartily!

7

It was only a few days before Christmas, and Tims called ahead to say that he was on his way down to retrieve a piece of jewelry that had been handed in to Mr. Humphrey the previous day. Apparently the Duchess of Welsham had been in touch to claim a diamond brooch, which was found following a private dinner party with the Queen. When he arrived in the office, we both went over to the safe and I chatted pleasantly with him as I went through the combination. As I turned the handle and swung back the door to reveal its contents, there—laying at the very front of the cavern—was a pair of large, soiled underpants, the ownership of which there could be no doubt. Tims turned bright red as I sifted through the articles looking for the brooch; but it was not to be found. Tims left the office without saying a word.

Sometime later, Mr. Humphrey arrived from Windsor Castle and I approached the two subjects which had been the source of great speculation and mystery to me all day. The first was the matter of what his underpants—dirty ones at that!—were doing in the Queen's safe; the second, the whereabouts of the Duchess of Welsham's diamond brooch.

Humphrey entered the office with Freddie Gentle in tow, beaming up at him as though he were her dream come true.

"Ya, course they're my underpants," he proclaimed unashamedly to me. "I always keep a spare pair on hand."

"Well John, is the safe really the place to keep them? Tims wasn't very pleased when he saw them."

"What was he doin' messin' around with my underpants?" he asked suspiciously. Freddie giggled as she sat herself at Mr. Humphrey's desk.

"He was looking for that diamond brooch which was turned into you after Her Majesty's dinner party last night. Apparently it belongs to the Duchess of Welsham and she wants it back."

"Oh does she now? Well I don't remember any brooch bein' turned into me. Anyway, it's too late now. I gave it to my wife as an anniversary present last night. If she can afford to lose nice jewelry like that then she doesn't deserve to have it back now."

Freddie jumped up from the chair and glared at Mr. Humphrey with hurt. Tears were brewing in her turquoise eyes and she began to sob. Mr. Humphrey realized he had made a slip and made an attempt to console her. But she was having none of it. Grabbing her imitation leopard skin coat she ran for the door, screaming, "How could you do this to me, John? How could you?" she cried.

"Oh my little red rose, my little red rose," he called after her. "It's only an anniversary present. I told ya, she means nothin' to me. Honest she doesn't." But his words were of little consolation as she tore out of the office and ran down the Master of the Household's corridor blubbering with tears.

"Look what you've done now, Malcolm. You've made Freddie cry!" Mr. Humphrey picked up his own jacket and raced out the door after her.

Around ten thirty that evening I glanced out of my office window as I prepared to go home. It was beginning to snow and appeared as though London might see a white Christmas after all. The Queen and the Duke would be leaving for Windsor Castle on December 23rd. Christmas gift-giving for the Staff had taken place a few days earlier. This annual event was highlighted by an elderly porter, merry with the Christmas spirit, tripping on the carpet in the Orleans Room as he made his way to the front where Her Majesty was standing. When she handed him a gift certificate for eight pounds, the Queen inquired politely as to what he intended to buy with it. "A bottle of Scotch," was his reply.

Her Majesty asked him why he didn't chose something more lasting by which to remember her. "Oh this will last me forever, Your Majesty," he replied unconvincingly, breathing the fumes of fire all over her.

In the New Year the Court would again move to Sandringham House in Norfolk, where the Royal Family would remain until next February, and then the Court's year would begin all over again.

The hour was growing late as I made my way down the marble staircase, through the Grand Entrance and said "Good night" to the palace policeman, already sound asleep. Out of the palace grounds I proceeded and as I walked across the dimly lit

Mall, I turned and looked back at Buckingham Palace and the imposing illuminated gold statue commemorating Queen Victoria.

Tomorrow is another day, I thought, and I wondered what excuse Mr. Humphrey would invent concerning the Duchess of Welsham's diamond brooch.

Oh dear, I do hope he remembers to change his underwear before coming in…

RECOLLECTIONS FROM ENSUING YEARS

IN VARIOUS ROYAL RESIDENCES

1

Early Monday morning, Mr. Tims showed up in our office looking for Humphrey. "Malcolm, would you kindly inform Mr. Humphrey that I wish to see him the moment he arrives? The Duchess of Welsham's personal secretary has been on the telephone again concerning her missing diamond brooch. Has Mr. Humphrey mentioned anything to you?" He stood in the doorway with anguish written all over his face.

"No, I am afraid not, Mr. Tims. I am rather anxious to find out what happened to it myself. I know it was turned in by one of the footmen after the dinner party she attended."

"Do you have any idea when he might be making an appearance? It is well past nine." He tapped the gold-and-white timepiece on his left wrist.

I smiled, attempting to be humorous without offence. "Well, you know Mr. Humphrey, sir."

"Yes. Unfortunately, I do," he said derisively before departing.

At 10:40 a.m. John made his entrance known. I could hear him jovially whistling at the end of the Master of the Household's corridor and when the office door swung open he gave a cheery "Mornin' Malcolm," then set about making a cup of coffee. While the kettle was boiling, he disappeared into the washroom *en suite*, emerging to wear, as usual, a tattered pair of underwear. Today's selection was a dark shade of red which should have been disposed of years ago. "What do ya think?" he asked parading himself in front of my desk.

"Of what, John?"

"Me undies, what do ya think?"

Suppressing my laughter, I said, "What's so different, John?"

"The color, dummy. Red! I've been wearing this pair for five days and you can't even tell."

Recoiling inwardly, I said, "Oh really?"

"I told Freddie to go out and buy me a dozen pair." Happily, he walked over to the corner and unplugged the steaming kettle. "Would you like a cup, Malcolm?"

"Ah, no thank you, John." I'd suddenly lost my appetite. "Incidentally, Tims was in earlier and is very stroppy."

John scratched himself. "Why? What have I done now?"

"You know. That diamond brooch the footman turned in to you. I'm afraid the Duchess of Welsham is not giving up on it. She wants it back and Tims is aware that it has been found."

"I don't know nothin' about that brooch," he said sullenly and sat himself down with the *Daily Express*.

"John! That brooch is not your property. You are not going to get away so easily this time."

"But I already gave it to my wife for her anniversary. I can't ask her to give it me back now."

"You are going to have to. Now I know you do not appreciate me lecturing you but—"

"You got that right, haaaaaahaaaa."

"Seriously John. This time you have been caught and believe me Tims will use it against you if he can."

"Oh bloody hell," he angrily folded the paper. "It's not fair."

The door opened and Tims walked in. Humphrey had forgotten to lock it. Tims was momentarily speechless at the sight of his senior official clad only in his underwear. "So, you have finally arrived, Mr. Humphrey, have you?" he said, carefully averting his eyes while his brain tried to work out the vision.

"Ya, Mr. Tims, I was just about to come and see you."

"I assume you were going to put some clothing on first, Mr. Humphrey. What is the meaning of your apparel?"

"Oh, ya, me undies you mean, Mr. Tims, sir?"

"Of course, that is what I mean, Mr. Humphrey."

"Ya, well, I'm glad you asked me that question 'cause—"

"Just answer my question, Mr. Humphrey. Otherwise you will be explaining this...this sordid scene to the Lord Chamberlain."

"Oh, no need for the Lord Chamberlain, Mr. Tims. One of the valets just took my suit to be cleaned. I slipped in the corridor on some mud. You wouldn't want me walking round the palace with a dirty suit, would you?"

Tims' cold, beady eyes raged with typical anger. "As soon as your suit is returned to you I would like to see you in my office. Is that clear?"

"Absolutely, Mr. Tims, absolutely."

Tims closed the office door.

"That was close John. Very quick thinking. You know, you really shouldn't walk around in your underwear in the palace. It is not appropriate."

"Why? Been doin' it long before you came."

221

"But what would you have done if that was the Queen's secretary who had come in and not Tims?"

"Haaahaaaa. From what I hear the Queen's secretary would probably get a thrill." He entered the washroom to dress.

2

I could sense that something was seriously wrong as I walked along the Master of the Household's corridor to my office one morning. Secretaries not known for haste other than rushing off for lengthy shopping sprees were darting furtively in and out of offices. The footmens' restroom, normally alive with gay laughter, was silent and, even more ominously, Colonel Stewart-Wilson, Deputy Master of the Household, was almost unprecedentedly in his office before 10:30 a.m. Upon opening the door to my own office, I was amazed to find Mr. Humphrey already present and for once looking serious and preoccupied. Without wasting time on pleasantries he said, "Sir Peter wants to see all his Officials at eleven o'clock."

By noon the meeting was over and the shocking nature of the developments had been disclosed. We were informed that a senior page and one of the Queen's personal footmen had been involved in a homosexual vice-ring operating aboard the Royal Yacht *Britannia*, which docks in Portsmouth. Apparently a gang of naval ratings (non-officers working aboard the yacht), accompanied by members of the palace staff, had been terrorizing the Portsmouth male civilian population. Staff had been picking up single men late at night, blindfolding them, and taking them back to the yacht and subjecting them to brutal gang rape.

The naval ratings were permanently assigned to *Britannia* and palace staff would assist them in their vicious attacks when joining the yacht prior to sailing. Furthermore, it was established that some of the junior ratings not involved in this vice-ring had been subjected to the same treatment while the yacht was at sea with the Queen aboard! Indeed, it was these young men rather than the civilians who had finally come forward and told the truth. They identified the people involved, including several members of the Queen's staff.

Such was the seriousness of the offences and the appalling scandal associated with the Royal Family that the facts were hushed up at the time, although the police were horrified and launched a complete investigation. With the exception of several tiny items in British newspapers stating that some naval ratings had been "charged with offences" and "faced court martialling," the entire nightmare was shielded from the press. This was terribly ironic considering the gang that set out at night in search of prey was known as "The Press Gang" in court circles because of the way it pressed men into subservience.

The Navy held its own enquiry into the goings-on and the appropriate action in the form of court martial was indeed taken. It was learned that some victims had either been bribed to keep quiet or were threatened with their lives. At the palace, one high-placed employee was dismissed, while a footman received a reprimand after it was established that he had played a minor part in the sordid affair.

In the aftermath of the Royal Yacht *Britannia* scandal Sir Peter addressed the entire Royal Household with a general lecture reminding everyone of the need to uphold moral standards and to remember their responsibilities to the Crown.

The Queen gives frequent private luncheons when in residence at the palace. These events are notorious in royal circles for the acute embarrassment, discomfort and, in some cases, dread they afford her guests. The luncheon guests are taken from all walks of life and usually number about twelve. In contrast, therefore, to a royal garden party, where the Queen merely has to acknowledge the multitudes with indulgent smiles and the occasional mundane question, these luncheons are an opportunity for Her Majesty really to become acquainted with her visitors and are a supposedly useful way for her to find out what is going on outside her court.

I recall one such luncheon shortly before the Prince and Princess of Wales were married. The guests included a president of a major company, a soccer player, a medical surgeon, a trade-union leader, a gardening expert, a merchant banker and the winner of a popular game show, among others. These privileged people were asked to gather for cocktails in the Orleans Room at 12:30 p.m., with lunch served at one o'clock sharp in the Bow Room.

Over cocktails, the visitors had a wonderful opportunity to allow their imaginations to run into overtime as they struggled valiantly to find something in common with each other. The royal hosts were the Queen and Prince Charles, and both were desperately trying to put some of their overawed guests at ease during pre-lunch drinks. Her Majesty was speaking to the well-known soccer player.

"So, do you think that Manchester United are going to win the championship this year?" she inquired with superbly feigned curiosity.

"Err...yeh...if we can stick the ball in the net enough," came the reply from as rough a sports rogue as I had ever seen.

"I see," enthused the Queen.

Meanwhile, Prince Charles was struggling with the game-show winner. "Now, do tell me. Did you have to answer some frightfully difficult questions to win your prize?"

"Oh yes," the willowy woman responded as she sipped her drink. "I won the tie breaker question. It was very tense."

"And what was that?"

"In what city would you find the Eiffel Tower? And I knew the answer right off," she boasted.

"I see. How very intriguing," was the best the Prince could manage. He probably knew the answer to that one by the age of twenty-four months.

Elsewhere in the Orleans Room, conversation was equally fitful and strained. The surgeon, for example, was being forced to listen to a torrent of complaints from the trade-union leader, who had not been slow to take advantage of the trays of cocktails being handed round the room: "If it wasn't for that bloody Conservative government we'd 'ave full employment for all the working class," he bellowed, drawing a "we-don't-talk-about-that-sort-of-thing-here" look from the Queen standing nearby.

"Don't you think it would be more productive if we rejoiced at the marriage engagement of our future Monarch?" responded the placid doctor, drawing upon his full range of diplomatic powers.

"Why? Do you know who's going to pay for the wedding? The working class, that's who."

With a glance and a nod at a nearby footman, the Queen intervened. "Let's all go in for lunch, shall we?"

225

As the assembled party glided through to the ornate pink, white and gold Bow Room there appeared to be a matter concerning the royal hosts. It transpired that the final guest, Earl Spencer, Diana's father and Prince Charles' future father-in-law, was still not amongst those present.

"Where the devil is he? It is damn well not good enough," muttered the Prince. The Queen's face remained devoid of expression.

Just as everyone was settling down in their pre-designated seats, with Her Majesty and her son at opposite ends of the silver-and-crystal-laden table, and just as the president of Imperial Chemicals was wondering what on earth he was going to say to the game-show winner, a diversion occurred. The double doors swung open, smashing back against the cabinets filled with magnificent porcelain and sending the two footmen diving for cover. Framed in the entrance was a staggering, scarlet-faced apparition of whose identity there was no doubt. Earl Spencer, who had clearly preferred and enjoyed a much longer and more concentrated pre-lunch libation session than that offered by the palace, had finally managed to complete the guest list.

An alarmed Prince of Wales, who was scheduled to have the earl sitting on his right, swiftly arose and went to assist the unbalanced peer to his seat. This manoeuvre was achieved with some difficulty for the legs of the 110-kg earl appeared to have developed a mind of their own. Finally, however, with a rattling of glass and silverware, he was safely installed.

"So sorry I am late everybody," he wheezed. "Terrible traffic in London at this time of day, you know."

"Well," commented the Queen. "Let's all enjoy our lunch now, shall we?"

4

I remember an amusing incident that happened shortly after Prince Charles and Princess Diana returned from their Mediterranean honeymoon in 1981. Diana, doubtless thinking that now that she was in the Royal Family she might as well try to appreciate horses, expressed a wish to inspect the Royal Mews. A tour was hastily arranged, and on a sunny fall morning, the Royal party was greeted by Sir John Miller for an escorted tour of the premises.

Diana's entertainment began with a visit to the famous carriages used for important state occasions. These included the Irish State Coach, the Glass Coach, and the most famous of all, the Gold State Coach, used for coronations. The princess, still very much a newcomer at this stage, was unable to display the well-rehearsed enthusiasm which more senior members of the family are able to show despite the fact that they are bored stiff.

The tour continued. Sir John, thoroughly enjoying himself, guided Diana and her entourage through the stables where the famous Windsor grey horses, the pride of Her Majesty's equine stock, are housed. Again, the princess failed to be enthused, and as she headed across the quadrangle towards the royal limousine garages, it was apparent that in future her tours of inspection would be restricted to Harrod's, not the Royal Mews.

It was at this point that the morning's events took an unexpected change of course. From across the quadrangle, over by the harnessing rooms, there came a loud, piercing wolf whistle, which could only have been directed at the princess. The royal party froze. Ann Beckwith-Smith, private secretary to Diana, turned an unhealthy shade of crimson and looked sharply at Sir John, who was himself doing a very fair impersonation of the color of vintage port.

Miss Beckwith-Smith was the first to recover. Turning to the Princess of Wales, she was about to take firm hold of her arm and guide her rapidly in the opposite direction when she froze, dumbstruck. Far from looking embarrassed, Diana was responding to the whistle by waving madly towards the culprits, two young grooms, and giggling with delight.

Miss Beckwith-Smith was determined that dignity and decorum should prevail. "I really am most awfully sorry for this inexcusable behavior..." she began, but got no further. The two grooms produced an even louder whistle in unison and grinned from across the square.

This time Sir John intervened. "I shall see that these men are held responsible for their actions, Your Highness," he spluttered, "and may I personally express my profound regrets at this unfortunate occurrence which has—" Diana stopped him in mid sentence by leaving her entourage in her wake and charging across towards the two horsemen. She was soon chatting happily with them and indulging in innuendos with undisguised glee. Clearly the tour of the Queen's Rolls Royces and Daimlers would have to wait for another time.

When Diana's elderly and utterly bewildered protectors finally managed to catch up with her they were just in time to hear her declaring, "Thank you so much for making my visit to the Royal Mews so worthwhile. I shall definitely come back again!"

5

The birth of Prince William to the Prince and Princess of Wales had been greeted with great joy and celebration by the nation in 1982. He will, of course, be the next King of England following his father, and thus the future of the House of Windsor is assured. The Queen and her family were understandably delighted and eagerly looking forward to the formal christening which was to take place several months later.

The christening was scheduled to take place in the Music Room of the Palace; the traditional location for the baptism of royal additions. Naturally, it was very much a private affair, with only the immediate family members present.

At eleven o'clock in the morning on the appointed day the Queen and Prince Philip entered the Music Room and assembled with the others. Prince Philip looked irritable, his frugal mind perhaps reflecting former socialist MP Willie Hamilton's comment in the press that day, "Another bloody royal mouth to feed." The Queen was followed by the Archbishop of Canterbury, Dr. Runcie, and Canon Anthony Caesar, who had, for a short period, nobly put aside the other priorities in his life.

The ceremony itself was brief. Prince William behaved impeccably, sleeping peacefully in his mother's arms. He was wrapped in the traditional Honiton lace-and-cream silk robe used by the Royal Family since the birth of Queen Victoria's children. Immediately after, there were to be photographs taken by Lord Snowdon, the former husband of Princess Margaret, who was still very much in the Queen's good books despite his divorce many years ago. Unfortunately, this procedure had to be deferred. As Diana proudly held her baby up for inspection, and then handed him over to his grandmother, the gentle solemnity of the occasion was dramatically disturbed.

Princess Margaret had arrived, chattering incoherently,

then stood before the christening font where the Archbishop was supposed to officiate. Smiling indulgently, Dr. Runcie guided the bemused Princess back to her proper place.

Margaret was not to be appeased this time, though, and brushing past the Queen Mother she rushed forward gushing, "Oh my baby, my baby, look at my sweet little baby!" She made a grab for Prince William from his startled and bewildered grandmother, the Queen. Her Majesty did not want to relinquish him and turned a few degrees to avoid her sister's intentions. Margaret was not about to give up, however, and a tugging match began. The Queen hid her displeasure well but in the end gave in. Clutching the little fellow like a cherished trophy, Margaret proceeded to cavort around the room, holding the baby aloft as if he were the next lot up for auction at Sotheby's and bubbling, "Oh, isn't he gorgeous? Oh he's mine, he's mine!"

The little Prince's tranquil repose came to an abrupt halt. The contrast between the euphoric Princess Margaret and the terrified howling infant could not have been more pronounced. Prince Charles, who had been observing the proceedings in annoyed silence, took charge. He moved purposefully forward. "Come along now, auntie, let me have him back."

Prince William's incessant din seemed to rankle Princess Margaret. "Oh very well," she snapped, then glared at Diana. She abruptly handed the baby to Prince Charles.

Fortunately, Diana's expert maternal touch enabled the young Prince to quickly recover from his turbulent airborne ordeal, and the photographic session was able to go ahead without delay. Quipped one of the prelates later: "I usually enjoy christening ceremonies, but I do hope that those two are not planning on a *large* family before I retire."

6

All preparations for the state banquet in honor of the King of Nepal appeared to be complete. The dinner was scheduled as usual to begin at 8 p.m. in the Grand Ball Room and would include many members of the Royal Family, as well as the Archbishop of Canterbury, the Prime Minister and other eminent politicians, together with distinguished people in British industry and the arts.

At 7:15 p.m. I was walking through the state apartments, checking that all was in order and nothing had been forgotten. I was relieved to observe that the staff were obviously making use of the previously mentioned bottle bank, as I failed to find a single empty liquor bottle tucked behind a cushion or china cabinet or anywhere else. Most unusual.

As I passed through the Green Drawing Room into the East Gallery, I found Sir Peter Ashmore walking up and down restlessly and clicking his tongue with impatience. He looked up as I approached.

"Ah, Malcolm, just the man. Look. There are three bulbs which need replacing in the picture lamps. I sent for the electrician in the department of the environment twenty minutes ago but the blasted man hasn't appeared."

I followed his gaze. Sure enough there were lights missing above two Renoirs and a Van Dyck. The East Gallery leads into the Grand Ball Room and as the royal procession would be passing through shortly, urgent action was required.

"Alright, Sir Peter, leave it with me." The incident was scarcely unusual. The department of the environment, a separate unit in the royal palaces responsible for the maintenance of the building, was renowned for its devotion to inefficiency, sloppiness and distaste for work in general.

I moved swiftly to an internal telephone and dialled 501. I tapped my foot impatiently as the telephone rang and rang. Finally, after precisely twenty-nine rings, a gruff voice answered. "Yeh?" Mr. John Foster, district works officer, had at last stirred himself.

"Look, John, what is going on down there? I'm in the East Gallery where Sir Peter requested an electrician to replace some bulbs almost half an hour ago."

"Why? I didn't know Sir Peter was into gardening!" the slurred voice chuckled down the phone.

"Oh, for God's sake don't be such an idiot," I shot back, surprised at my uncharacteristic temper. "The state banquet will be starting shortly and you can be sure that you will be held responsible for this. You have been lucky to keep your job this long."

"Alright, alright, keep yer hair on. I'll send someone to 'ave a look." The matter still seemed to rank very low in Mr. Foster's list of priorities.

"Right then, John, and make sure he brings the correct bulbs. It's the two Renoirs and the Van Dyck. You know which ones I am talking about?" I slammed down the phone and waited.

Ten minutes passed. By now it was 7:40 p.m. and I had ten minutes to solve what should have been a perfectly straightforward problem. I was mindful that my anger was nothing to what the Queen's would be when she spotted the oversight. I therefore charged down the grand staircase three at a time, rushed through the marble hall, past the silver pantry and into the offices of the environment department. One quick glance told me all I needed to know.

Mr. Foster and his associates were enjoying a banquet of their own. The bill of fare for the twenty or so "guests" was, however, somewhat different to what was about to be sam-

232

pled upstairs. Empty whisky bottles and beer cans complemented by exhausted potato-chip packets were strewn about. Nestling among the debris were slovenly bodies in various states of intoxification, some snoring, some belching, but the majority were performing the clearly well-practised art of raising bottles and cans to their lips.

At the centre of this delightful little scene, slumped behind his desk and barely visible behind the sea of bottles and smoke haze, was Mr. John Foster.

"Where are those bloody light bulbs?" I roared, long since forgetting the niceties of phraseology.

"Look 'ere. What does it matter? The King of Nepal is only a stupid, yellow nip."

I spied an electrician joining in the drunken chorus of "Rule Britannia." Any further efforts were pointless. I opened every cupboard in Foster's office until I came across the bulb supply. Grabbing a handful of them I flew back to the East Gallery and quickly had the picture lights working in record time. Two minutes later the Queen and the King of Nepal came into sight and from a hidden vantage point I watched as the King stopped to point at a painting which had taken his interest. It was Van Dyck's famous portraits of King Charles I. Her Majesty smiled and readily explained the history of the picture.

I slipped quietly away. I had seen the paintings many times before and right now all I wanted to see was a very stiff drink in my hand.

7

One of the privileges of being an Official in the Royal Household is that one is permitted to use the Royal Box at the

Royal Albert Concert Hall. This, of course, is provided Her Majesty does not require the box herself. I frequently took advantage of this facility and enjoyed many memorable evenings there.

There was one particular Sunday evening in the Royal Box which I shall never forget, but this had little to do with the quality of the orchestra, rather a distraction which occurred whilst the concert was in progress. I had decided to attend a performance given by the London Symphony Orchestra.

I arrived at the hall at 7:15 and, after a quick drink with my guests in the bar, I entered the Royal Box and settled into one of the comfortably upholstered red-velvet chairs. To my disappointment, the front row was already fully occupied, but disappointment turned to amazement when I saw that three of those seats were taken by Mr. Humphrey, his wife and daughter. Bearing in mind that Mr. Humphrey was not one to associate with the arts, the only logical conclusion to be drawn was that there had been a major disagreement in the Humphrey household, and their appearance tonight was clearly Mr. Humphrey's idea of a peace offering. I couldn't resist having a quick word with him.

"John. I didn't expect to see you here this evening. Do I take it that you are a recent convert to Handel and the classics?"

"No, you bloody well don't. I'm here under protest. And I don't know how I'm going to get through the night."

"Now, John, I told you I don't want one word of complaint out of you. Just sit there and don't say anything," said Mrs. Humphrey. She was an aggressive woman with a protruding chin and beady eyes. While "only" two-thirds the size of her husband, she was still a figure of considerable substance, and I had the difficult task of deciding which of

234

the two women in Humphrey's life—his wife or Freddie Gentle—were the least attractive in terms of appearance and character. At least you couldn't be flattened by Freddie, I thought favorably.

I returned to my seat just behind the Humphreys. I knew already that my musical appreciation was going to be somewhat diminished, for I had spotted a large carrier bag stuffed with an assortment of snacks stationed conveniently by Mr. Humphrey's right boot. The contents had already been broached, for my corpulent colleague was holding an enormous pack of chocolate eclair toffees in his paws, and the only question was whether or not any would survive into the beginning of the concert.

The orchestra, when it commenced, was excellent as usual and the central location of the Royal Box combined with superb acoustics were most gratifying. The only drawback was, of course, the continuous munching in front of me, ranging from the aforementioned chocolate eclairs to popcorn and potato chips. Each time a bag was finished it was noisily screwed up and dropped on the floor of the plush box. Behind me I could hear the Duchess of Grafton and Captain Alistair Aird, Comptroller of the Queen Mother's Household, voicing their disapproval in muted whispers.

"I shall be complaining to Mr. Tims about this," said the Duchess, who had come to hear the divine music, not the din of food making contact with Humphrey's molars.

After Mozart's *Symphony No. 13*, the orchestra moved on to Handel's *Music for the Royal Fireworks*. It was during the immediate aftermath of the ending of the first movement that the evening reached its nadir. In the deafening silence following the last note, Mr. Humphrey let out a loud sigh, scrunched up the latest empty bag of chips, and flung it over the side of the box onto the masses below.

All heads turned towards the Royal Box, clearly identified by the letters E II R and the Royal Crest above it. I still
vividly recall the almost unbearable feeling of mortification,
coupled with Mr. Humphrey's inexcusable disrespect for his
position and the sovereign.

Fortunately, the second movement got quickly underway and attention was, to an extent, diverted from us. But I,
along with virtually everyone else in the box, had had
enough, and we quietly withdrew through the back
entrance. The last I heard of the animated conversation
going on in front between husband and wife was Mr.
Humphrey defensively pointing out, "All you said was 'don't
say anything' and I didn't. So what are you looking at me like
that for?"

8

One of the supposedly less bizarre functions at the palace is
the biannual meeting of the food and welfare committee.
This institution is the brainchild of Deputy Master of the
Household, Col. Stewart Wilson, in whose debt the Royal
Household will doubtless forever be. In short, it is totally
useless, achieving nothing except to waste everyone's time.
In the eyes of the omniscient colonel, however, it provides
the framework in which household members can debate and
discuss important issues of the day before deciding to do
nothing about them.

Each personnel department within the Royal Household
has a representative on the committee, and I, much against
my better judgment, was persuaded to become the delegate
representing the Master of the Household's Officials. As the

youngest Official, I suppose it was inevitable that I should draw the short straw. With a meeting coming up shortly, I determined to canvass my colleagues to ascertain whether there was anything they wanted raised with the committee.

Humphrey's reply to this was, "Yeh...I can think of something. How about your dick?" Otherwise, I was met with silence and apathy.

My first food and welfare meeting held the promise of a special visitor—Prince Charles. He had requested to sit in on one of these meetings for a change. The colonel was beside himself with delight at this royal recognition.

And so, one Thursday morning, I found myself sitting in the Billiards Room around a table which did indeed represent every facet of life within Buckingham Palace. Derek Waters, Chief Clerk of the Privy Purse, was grinning from ear to ear, wearing a hideous scarlet sweater to complement his faded olive-green suit. At his right hand was the Bible. A footman, who was shortly to be dismissed for displaying his anal rather then verbal talents, sat feet up wearing a sardonic expression and looking bored.

Ted Cotton, manager of the Palace bar and treasurer of the Royal Household Soccer Club, was sprawled across the table, head in hands, eyes bloodshot.

"I suppose bar profits are down and he is worried," I mused to the gentleman seated next to me. (You may recall one of Cotton's predecessors had been fired for embezzling funds.)

At the head of the table, looking suitably pompous, peering over his half-moon glasses, the Deputy Master of the Household glanced at the Prince of Wales sitting to his left and inquired politely, "Are you ready to begin, Your Highness?"

The prince, it seemed, was in poor humor. "Well, of course, I am ready to begin. I was just wondering why you were taking so bloody long!"

Comptroller of Supply George Jenkins whispered loudly to me, "He's had another row with Diana." I discreetly avoided the prince's glare down the table.

The colonel sensed Prince Charles' twitchy mood. "Yes, of course, sir. . .Now before we get underway, are there any comments arising out of the previous meeting?"

"Yes, sir," someone replied. "I'd like to say that as a result of the last meeting absolutely nothing has been done about the food in the staff dining room. It has gotten worse, not better. The heating on the footmens' floor still doesn't work. The sheets on the beds at Balmoral still have holes in them. Mr. Humphrey hasn't ordered any—"

"Yes, well I think that is quite enough to start with," intervened the colonel. "I really do feel that—"

"Just a minute, sir. I haven't finished. I'm not the only one that thinks like this." Murmurs of assent arose around the table. "It seems to me that this committee is wholly pointless. We just sit around with important matters to correct which are forgotten by the powers that be as soon as the meeting is over. If you ask me, it's just an excuse to talk about nothing, do nothing, and then pretend we are all being useful."

"Sounds like the House of Lords to me!" Prince Charles quipped, his disconsolate mood visibly improving as he beamed around the room. Laughter ranging from polite chuckles to bovine roars quickly ensued.

"Eh, that is a good one, that is, Yer Highness," said the royal chef.

"Now as regards what that footman said about the

food," another voice rose from the room, "he was talking a load of crap."

"Like the food," piped up Mr. Jenkins.

The colonel rapped the table and looked horrified. "Gentlemen, please! May I remind you that we are in the presence of the Prince of Wales who has so kindly agreed to join us today."

"Oh, are we?" the Prince spoke. "Where? Where?"

Laughter again broke out. When it settled down, Prince Charles took control. "Now look, chaps. Let us try and get somewhere with this. What is wrong with the food you are being served? What *would* you like?"

"I'd like proper food like filet mignon and roast duck," said a footman who seemed to fancy himself sitting with the Queen on the top table at a state banquet.

"Yeh, and that costs eight pounds!" the Royal Chef snapped. "You'd have to double the civil list payment to pay for that!"

"Eight pounds?" The Prince was astonished. "To feed the entire staff filet mignon? That sounds quite reasonable to me, occasionally." He seemed hopeful now for a rapid compromise.

"Not to feed the entire staff, yer silly bugger. Eight pounds per person! Where have you been for the past hundred years?"

It took a moment for Prince Charles to recover his power of speech. "Well, actually, amazingly as it may seem I have not been around that long," he said. "But I must say that sounds frightfully expensive. Five pounds used to go such a long way. I remember when I was a boy..."

Again, the colonel deemed it necessary to intervene. "Quite, sir. Now, if you will forgive my interruption, I should just like to say something on this point. I personally find the food served here to be more than adequate and perfectly satisfactory. As a matter of fact, I would compare it to the Savoy Hotel. So I really do not think. . ."

"That's because you eat in the bloody Household dinin' room so you get the same food as the Queen. Yer just as much out of touch with reality as the Prince here." This interjection came from Norman Tomlinson, leading porter. "I've been sitting here listenin' to the biggest load of shit that's ever been spoken here and that's sayin' something. It's always the same: one rule for the snobs in the suits and one rule for the peasants in the overalls. It will always be like that, so let's not kid ourselves."

The meeting was now completely out of hand. There was certainly an amusing element to it, as I watched the prince squirm and flounder, hopelessly out of his depth and clearly anxious to leave. Few expected anything constructive to be forthcoming. The colonel made one last appeal for moderation.

"Well," he said apprehensively, "I suppose I would be prepared to set up a 'committee sub-committee' to investigate these allegations about the food."

Pandemonium broke loose. Derisive laughter filled the room and some representatives even started to clap hands. The prince and the colonel beat a hasty retreat, as there was nothing left to say. I thought of the respect and admiration the rest of the world afforded the Royal Family—and what the public's reaction might be if it ever learned of the way their staff really treated them.

Above the uproar could clearly be heard the shrill bird-like tones of the chief housekeeper. "And I would like to refute those accusations about holes in the linen at Balmoral. . .!"

I made my way back to the less turbulent waters of my office and Mr. Humphrey, wondering if I would be selected for the food or housekeeping sub-committees.

9

One March I was sent on a training course at the ministry of defence in London. The purpose of the course was to help expand my administrative and organizational abilities as well as to apprise me of the very individual requirements of a position within the elevated echelons of the Royal Palaces.

I was delighted to be offered this opportunity and looked forward to a welcome four-week break away from the idiosyncrasies of Messrs. Humphrey and Tims. In addition, coming so soon after my nocturnal encounters with Canon Caesar, it seemed to be an excellent chance to put the randy reverend firmly in the past tense.

It therefore came as somewhat of a shock one lunchtime as I was leaving the ministry building to find the Queen's chaplain waiting outside for me. Once again, I had underestimated his tenacity, and my initial politeness and patience with him were now fast disappearing.

"Malcolm, darling, how are you?"

"Well I'm just fine thank you, Canon. I, ah, didn't expect to find you in these parts. What brings you here?"

"I came here to find a very naughty young man who's been avoiding me."

"Oh?"

"Yes. Very naughty indeed. You're a cheeky little monkey, Malcolm, and you deserve to be punished very severely."

"Now look here, Canon. I have not been avoiding you. I

241

was sent here on a course which has been taking up all my time. Do you have to indulge in these puerile games?"

"Oh I do like a man with a bit of spirit. Now tomorrow you are coming with me to lunch and then we're going to an organ recital together."

"A what?"

"An organ reci...Oooh! I know what you were thinking you dirty little thing!" he cooed. "But no, it is genuine. Lunch first, though. One o'clock tomorrow at Friends Restaurant. And then you're taking the afternoon off with me. See you then."

I smiled to myself. I actually quite liked the man. At least he was amusing and he certainly had nerve. Besides, it would make a change from the tediously stuffy approach of the ministry of defence officials. But one matter was certain: there would be no repeat of the Canon's nefarious antics.

The following afternoon saw me comfortably settled in Friends Restaurant, which at the time was owned by Elton John. I was sipping a Perrier when there was a sudden commotion at the door, followed by a grunt and then, "Ooh...thank you sweetie. I'll have to trip on the stairs more often, won't I?" The Queen's chaplain flounced into the room wearing skin-tight white trousers, pink shirt and matching aquamarine cravat and shoes. A small purse complemented his adornment. He minced his way towards the table, gave me a quick peck on the cheek and a rub on the buttocks before placing himself on a chair next to me. "Well, gorgeous, it's fun time for us again!"

"Good heavens, Reverend. I have never seen you looking so..."

"Gay? That's the right word, isn't it? Well, that's how I feel today." And he placed both his hands on my waist, which I then hastily removed. He looked more like something dragged out of the flower-power sixties and that, far from taking years off him, he was adding to the already heavy burden. I observed that it would be interesting to see Her Majesty's reaction to his garb.

"Yes, wouldn't it be a crease? And Philip, too!" he giggled.

"But tell me, Canon, why are you in such fine spirits today?" I fervently hoped he would tell me that he had found a new lover.

"Well, isn't it obvious? Today's the day we're going to cement our relationship properly. I want you to come and live with me!"

So that was it. Why else would he have shown up at the Ministry of Defence completely out of the blue?

I managed to withhold uttering the first words that occurred to me, and composed myself for thirty seconds. This had gone far enough. I did not want to hurt his feelings but if bluntness was the only way to get the message across, then that is what I would have to do. I said simply, "Anthony, there is not the slightest chance of us living together. I do not find you attractive and nor do I wish to become involved in a scandal. [Years later that statement would scream with irony.] There is absolutely no prospect of our compatibility. I sincerely hope you find someone soon, but it will certainly not be me!" I signalled the waiter for a different drink. This was no time for Perrier.

To my surprise, this was accepted without protest and he then embarked upon a lengthy account of all the problems he had encountered in the past over his sexuality. In fact, he painted such a sad picture of a lonely old man that I became quite sorry for him. Clearly he had a very large Achilles' heel.

After an enjoyable but unusually serious meal, the canon

and I were savoring some delicious Kona coffee (in his case, supplemented by a large cognac) when, to my astonishment, he started to caress my thigh. At the same time, he moved his foot up and down my ankle.

I put my cup down with a crash. "Look! Didn't you get the message? I am *not* interested in you at all and never will be!"

"Now Malcolm, darling, you didn't think I'd give up that easily did you?"

As I stormed out of the restaurant, he called out to me: "I'll see you tomorrow outside the ministry of defence as usual!" The waiters were much amused.

I felt powerless to do anything about his persistence. But then I had a thought. Perhaps there was something I could do to distract him from his pursuit. Returning to Buckingham Palace at the end of my course, I resolved to ensure that a very young and inexperienced footman was appointed to the staff, even if it *was* like throwing him to the lions. . . .

10

One of my arch-nemeses in the household was Mr. Tims' assistant, Susan Derry. She had been at the palace for more than ten years when I arrived, and, primarily because of her glaring deficiencies, she had failed to make any headway in terms of promotion to a more prestigious position. Her character had all the glamour of a bag of fertilizer spread over the garden.

Miss Derry's worst trait, in my judgment, was her incomparable ability to complain. Yes, even worse than the Duchess of Grafton, if you can believe that. All her time was spent in attempting to perfect the art of making everyone's life utterly miserable. By the time I left, she was getting close. To be fair, Mr. Tims suffered more then anyone from her moaning, and he was usually at his worst to everyone after he had suffered an earful from Miss Derry.

One morning, Susan, or "Sexy Susie" as she was most inappropriately known, arrived in her office, late as usual, at 11:00 a.m. Her eyes were puffier and more red than normal, her hair even more like a marshy swamp, and her clothes even more violently clashing then I had seen before.

"Morning, Susan," I breezed as I strolled into her office. "Anything interesting in the mail for me?"

"I won't have a chance to look until you stop disturbing me," she snapped. She started to rustle papers in a feeble attempt to hide the womens' magazine she was reading.

"Okay then. I'll send John Humphrey along a little later just to brighten the start to your day even more," I suggested before disappearing with a high-pitched "How dare you!" ringing in my ears. The woman didn't have a humorous fibre in her bones.

Ten minutes later my telephone rang. It was Mr. Tims. "Malcolm, why have you been upsetting Susan?" he enquired frostily.

"Is that what she told you, the sneaky little thing? I'd be grateful if I could see you right away, please." I slammed the phone down and headed towards Tims' office. En route, I encountered Susie, wearing an overcoat and moth-eaten scarf, scurrying out towards the Privy Purse Door. "Where are you off to? The cat sick again, I suppose?" There was no love lost between us.

"Just you wait until you see Mr. Timmmmms" she snarled. "And, for your information, I'm going on holiday."

"Too bad," I said. "It'll seem strange having some work

done around here for a change." I ignored her screech of protest and knocked on Tims' door.

Mr. Tims gazed at me over the top of his tortoise-shell glasses. "Now, Malcolm, it is very important that we all try to work in harmony here. It really is no good..."

"Just a minute Mr. Tims..." and I related what had taken place in Susie's office, explaining that it was very much par for the course. "And, furthermore, even though it is only July, Susan Derry has already exceeded her vacation limit. She's had five and a half weeks and if she's now planning on two weeks more, you should inform her that it is unpaid leave. She also needs a doctor's sick note to justify it."

"Well," pondered Tims. "This does rather put the matter in a different light, doesn't it? But you must understand, Malcolm, that Susan has a number of problems of a personal nature."

"We all have those, Mr. Tims. But there is a difference between being an employee and a hotel resident! If Miss Derry showed more grace and application, she might find people responding to her better."

"Very well, Malcolm. Leave it with me. I will talk to her."

Next morning, I was stunned to find the sex goddess at her desk at 9:30. However, it was evident that her apparent change of attitude had not stretched to her personal attire. I was rendered momentarily breathless at the sight of her green-and-orange dress, which was evidently on a day's outing after spending twenty years at the bottom of a trunk.

"Good morning, Susan. Hope you enjoyed your holiday."

"Enjoyed my holiday?" she screeched. "How dare you ask that, you horrid, horrid man! I work sooooo hard all the time and then you have to prevent me from having a nice

246

rest. I'll tell you what you are—you're a typical male bastard and a nasty spoilsport and I hate you." A well-rehearsed flood of tears followed which, if collected, would have gone a long way to solving California's water shortage. All the time her fists banged angrily on the desk.

Tims came scampering into the office. "What in heaven's name is going on here? We really cannot have disturbance of this nature in the Master of the—"

"GET OUT, GET OUT!" screamed Susan, "And don't ever, ever come back, you awful, wicked man! You are always against me and it's so unfair! Ooooh I wish you were both DEAD!!" With this she rushed at us with her claws extended.

Once Tims and I were safely installed in his office, we looked at each other with newfound mutual sympathy. It was to be the first (and last) time we were on the same side sharing a common problem. As Susie's frantic cries continued unabated, further down the corridor, Tims made an observation. "Hmmm. . .I think perhaps we had better wait for Susan to calm down, don't you?"

I nodded. "Perhaps it would be advisable for me to put a call through to Regent's Park Zoo?"

Tims smiled. "An excellent idea, Malcolm. Which department?"

"Poisonous reptiles," I said trenchantly.

11

Sir John Miller was in good humor. It was the middle of March, which is the time of year when many important equine events get underway. This afternoon one of the biggest horse races of the year, the Cheltenham Gold Cup, was to be run and Sir John had decided to leave the office for the afternoon to watch the race on television in the comfort of his well-appointed residence.

The race was due to start at 3:30 p.m. At 2:45 the Crown Equerry switched on his television to enjoy the pre-race atmosphere. Nothing happened.

Frowning, he switched the "on" button off and then on again. Still no picture. Damn these modern contraptions. Why won't the bloody thing work, seethed the frustrated knight. When he had checked cords and buttons and satisfied himself that all was in place, he moved across the room to press a bell several times to summon his housekeeper. No one appeared. Blast the stupid woman. How dare she vacate my home just when I want her, he lamented.

Then he remembered it was Thursday. Thursday was Miss Pope's afternoon off. Clicking his teeth with impatience, he resolved to find a TV repair man, and called up his chief clerk, Paul Almond, the infamous raspberry blower, on the intercom.

"Get Bradbury over here at once, do you here me? At once, man!"

"Certainly, Sir John. What seems to be the problem?" Paul wanted to be sure of his facts.

"Problem? Problem? You do not imagine I want him to come and cook me bacon and eggs, do you? My television won't work, you fool. And I've put good money on Comedy of Errors to win the Gold Cup. I want to watch him do it on my television set so get Bradbury over here at once."

"No problem, sir."

Ten minutes passed during which Sir John's complexion passed into its usual pink shade of claret. He rapped his gold-topped cane against the side of his television set in the hope of jolting it into life. He glanced at his watch: 3:15 and still no sign of the repairman.

Once again, Almond was summoned on the intercom. "Now look here, I want to watch this year's race, not next year's. Never in all my time here have I encountered such wilful disobedience of my instructions. Where's that infernal Bradbury?"

"He is on his way, Sir John. Should be with you in five minutes."

"Do you realize I have not even seen Comedy of Errors yet? (I'd have to disagree with him on that.) You had better phone up Cheltenham racetrack and tell them to delay the start. Tell them I cannot get my television to work."

This time Paul could not hide his incredulity. "I cannot do that, Sir John! There are at least 50,000 people at that race today and about twenty million television viewers. There would be a national outcry if they were to delay the start of the event just for one person."

"Yes, well it is all right for them, isn't it? They can actually *watch* the race. I cannot."

A loud banging could be heard at the front door. Sir John belied his years and skipped to the entrance where he flung open the door to greet the diminutive repair man. "Where have you been, you oaf? I need my television set fixed this instant, do you hear me? The race starts in two minutes."

"All in good time, Sir John," Bradbury muttered in his cockney accent. "You'll give yerself a stroke if you carry on like this."

"How dare you, you impudent man. I shall speak to the Queen. Just fix my television at once!"

Opening his tool bag, Bradbury went to the set to examine it, wearing a look of incomprehension. With a quick movement and a sharp "click," the television picture appeared clearly and crisply.

"And about time, too," grumbled the knight. "The race is about to start."

"Bloody hell, Sir John. 'ave yer never switched on a television before?"

"What do you mean? Of course, I have. If this is another example of your rudeness. . ."

"Now look 'ere. In order to make it work you have to press this plug here into the socket in the wall," explained Bradbury, with the patience needed for a four-year-old child. "Now, a television operates on electricity, and unless you 'ave it plugged into the electrical current it won't function. Just wait till I tell the blokes back in the office about this one."

Sir John remained unrepentant. "Yes, yes, well my housekeeper looks after that. That is what she is paid for."

"She must be a saint or insane," Bradbury chuckled as he packed his gear. "What a comedy of errors."

"Comedy of Errors!" Sir John's mind returned to the race. Waving to Bradbury dismissively, he settled down to watch.

It was a good race, and won not by Comedy of Errors as hoped, but by a horse called Sea Pigeon. But this was not the only event to incur his wrath. Throughout the race there had not even been a *mention* of his own favorite to win. When the result was being announced, it was revealed that Comedy had pulled a muscle and been withdrawn.

Sir John was beside himself with anger. Once more he picked up the intercom and spoke to Paul Almond. "This is an outrage! A disgrace! Now you telephone Cheltenham and tell them I have cancelled the race. I want a rerun when Comedy of Errors is fit. Is that clear?"

You would had to have known the knight personally to have believed he was capable of such high-handed thinking. He most definitely was. But Paul knew all about the race he was referring to and savored the moment. "I will do so, Sir, if you insist. But I should tell you that there is no chance of the race being declared void. And in any case, you may wish to know that the Queen Mother put a substantial sum on a horse called Sea Pigeon. Do you still wish me to call the racecourse for you?"

Sir John's misery was complete.

12

"It's the department of the environment's annual party this afternoon, Malcolm," declared Mr. Humphrey enthusiastically when I entered the office one morning.

"I know. And you had better behave this year." I added cautiously, "I happen to know that Sir Peter Ashmore, Canon Caesar and Tims are all planning to attend."

"Trust Ashmore and Tims to try and ruin the one free afternoon we get all year," he moaned. "But at least you'll get some sex out of the Reverend! Heh heh heh."

At three o'clock we made our way into the department offices. It was immediately evident that, for some, the party had got off to an earlier, unofficial start. The Royal Chef and Major Nash of the Royal Mews had earmarked a corner of the room to themselves where they could pursue their private competition of who could drink a bottle of whisky first.

Elsewhere, George Jenkins, who had spewed a sandwich all over a duchess's dress at Royal Ascot, was boasting about something to Michael Parker, who was getting in lots of rapid-fire "Oh good gosh yesses" and "Absolutely indeeds."

Humphrey and I found ourselves a drink and were soon chatting with Paul Almond and Steward Cyril Dickman.

"Ooh, I don't half feel like getting pissed today," observed Dickman.

"When were you last sober?" enquired Paul.

"When I was fifteen," Dickman replied with a guffaw.

As this was a communal party, there were many members of very poorly paid, and graded, staff present, including porters, cleaners and stable personnel. It transpired that many had come direct from a lunchtime drinking session in the local bar, called The Bag of Nails. Many were singing or slapping each other heartily on the back and punctuating these activities with loud belches.

There was a large buffet table laden with food and Mr. Humphrey decided to do the polite thing and reward his hosts by sampling some of it. However, his methods were somewhat unconventional. Having piled his plate high with sandwiches, sausage rolls, vol-au-vents and cream cakes, he then produced a large carrier bag and proceeded to stuff it with more of the same fare. "Just in case I need a quick snack later on," he explained to me.

This action did not go unnoticed. From another part of the room, Sir Peter Ashmore and Mr. Tims moved swiftly forward. Said Sir Peter: "I say now, Humphrey, can't you manage to act with a modicum of decency just this once?" Simultaneously, one of the group of increasingly inebriated workmen fresh from The Bag of Nails let out a shout and pointed at Humphrey. Memories of the Royal Ascot ticket fiasco were possibly fresh in his mind. "Hey...look! He's pinching all the grub!"

All heads turned and, standing next to me, Canon Caesar squeezed my hand and whispered happily, "Oooh, I do love to watch men fight!"

All hell broke loose. The angry workmen converged on the buffet table, and Coachman Arthur Showell grabbed the bag from Humphrey's clutches, thundering, "As if you needed any more fuckin' food, yer fat stinkin' slob!"

Humphrey was naturally incensed. "Here you...give that back, do ya hear me?"

It was at this point that the first missile was thrown. Ged Powers, who had gotten into trouble over his mishandling of the Queen's Rembrandt, picked up a shrimp vol-au-vent and hurled it across the room. Unfortunately for Mr. Tims it hit the mirror he was seated alongside and the mess splattered down his nose and onto his silk tie. "This is an outrage..." he began. Laughter followed.

This was the signal for the real battle to begin. Humphrey's stealing of the food was forgotten as officials and staff alike joined in the fun. "I have always wanted to do this," enthused George Jenkins, as he selected a chocolate eclair and sent it crashing into Sir Peter, whose suit jacket was transformed into a sea of cream. Crimson with fury he beat a retreat from the scene. Canon Caesar was giggling hysterically until an errant sausage roll caught him smartly on his right ear. The Canon winced and exclaimed loudly, "Ooh, you bullies," and followed in Ashmore's footsteps. At least I would be off the hook for his post-party plans.

There was food flying everywhere and all we needed was Prince Andrew's adept skills in the art of a first-class food fight. Alas, he was away. I dived behind an armchair, thus avoiding the fracas. However, I was none too pleased when a scoop of strawberry ice cream landed on my left shoulder. Peeking around the chair, I was amazed to see the chef and Major Nash still engaged in their competition. The fact that both were plastered in various sandwich fillings and squishy desserts appeared to be of no consequence.

At the end of the fight food was smeared all over the walls, the furniture and the carpet. Ice cream streams dribbled over the impasto of paintings. As I closed the door, I heard Mr. Foster announce: "Right then, lads, now that we've got that out of our system we can get on with the serious drinking."

I made my way to my office. Mr. Humphrey had vanished some time ago and I was curious to see where he was taking refuge. Sure enough, he was there, slumped in his red leather chair with a familiar carrier bag strategically placed by his right foot. It was empty, and my rotund colleague had a satisfied grin on his face.

"So this is where you finished up, John. How did you manage to retrieve that bag of food they took from you?"

"Simple," he said, patting his stomach contentedly. "I reminded Arthur Showell that I was twelve inches taller and one hundred and fifty pounds heavier then he was."

"John! Do you realize that you caused a major food riot down there? The room is practically destroyed and there will have to be an enquiry into this. Just look at my suit...and your own!"

"Oh well, Malcolm. It was worth it. I'm takin' Freddie out for a meal tonight and I couldn't get a table until 9:30 so I needed a little snack to see me through. Plug the kettle in, will you?"

Goodbye to All That

I remained at the palace for approximately four years. It was truly an honor and a thrill which I shall never forget. After all, how many individuals in the world have the opportunity to work for a King or a Queen of England? Millions, of course, dream of doing so.

Unfortunately, however, the games and shenanigans of the Royal Household, which I initially found so entertaining and enthralling, eventually began to wear me down once I realized that I was helpless to bring about even minor changes. Mr. Tims was also a major reason for my decision to leave. He was a significant obstacle in my path for promotion and I had to ask myself if I really wanted to battle the man for the next fifty years. I did not.

A number of people have suggested to me that it has been a long time since I left the palace at the end of 1983. "Surely your book must be somewhat out of date by now," they say. Not so. Although I left eight years ago, the book was begun less then twenty-four months after my departure and remarkably few of the Royal Household members who served the Queen while I was there have changed.

In fact, a recent check of Whitaker's Almanack indicates that roughly ninety percent of the characters mentioned in my book are still employed in the palace. A couple of notable exceptions are Sir Peter Ashmore, who has been replaced; Sir

John Miller, who has retired; and, sadly, John Humphrey, who left a few years after myself following a diving accident that paralyzed his son. Humphrey resigned to assist his wife in caring for their son at home. It was for this reason that I altered his name, in the hope of minimizing his anguish. You do not need to be a scholar to work out who must have been jubilant when he left.

Do I regret writing the book? Yes and no. I am glad the truth about the place is finally out, despite the many skeptics who maintain the contents couldn't possibly be true. To them I say, "I lived and worked there, you did not!" On the other hand, I am sorry that it will never be read in Britain where it could do the most good.

And for myself? What am I up to now that I am *persona non grata* at Court? As with so many people in the world I am doing a great deal of soul-searching. For one who, for a time, had one of the best job references in the world, I am now no longer able to use it. Mind you, with all the air travel I have done on Air Canada, British Airways, Delta and countless other airlines of the world during the past five years, I could practically write a book on the commercial aviation business.

Now wait a minute. There's an idea. . .I could call it *Courting Dissent*.

Perfect.

AFTERWORD

The Oddyssey of Courting Disaster*

By T.C. Sobey

*Living with the Queen was originally published in Canada
as *Courting Disaster*.

1

It seemed simple enough back in September of 1985 when, while staying in Litchfield, Ct., we decided to pen a book about Malcolm's four years at Buckingham Palace. I had known Malcolm since the mid seventies when we had been boarders at an English public school in Lancashire. We stayed in touch over the years and, after Malcolm's stint with the royals, we thought the world needed a book that exposed the buffoonery and scandal surrounding the Queen and her family. As with most aspiring authors, I suppose, we first scouted the book stores for other books on the subject, namely, Stephen Barry's two books covering his years as valet to Prince Charles. We found them easily enough, still in paperback long after the author himself had perished.

We eagerly digested Barry's memoirs, firstly to ensure that Malcolm's revelations had not been disclosed before (they plainly had not) and secondly to discover the names of his publishers so we could tell them we had something even better to offer. In fact, we were astonished to learn just how humdrum and picayune Stephen Barry's books really were. For the most part, they concentrated on such riveting subjects as Barry running Prince Charles' bath, Barry taking the

Queen's dogs for walks around the palace grounds, Barry picking up Charles' soiled socks. Truly spellbinding material.

It was at this point, when we tried to connect with the powers within Barry's publishers, that we ought to have taken the frosty reception as an ominous sign of things to come. But we chose to forge ahead, fools that we were. You see, communicating directly with "the powers" proved as insurmountable a task as, I imagine, persuading the Archbishop of Canterbury to join one in a game of strip poker.

Suffice to say, not one of Barry's publishers would speak with us or, indeed, be courteous enough to return our calls (surprise, surprise). Evidently this was not going to be as easy as we had anticipated but we were still convinced we had in our hands a multi-million dollar property, albeit one that still had to be written, and that sooner or later a savvy editor would be handing over a six-figure advance for the privilege of publishing it. After all, with the knowledge Malcolm possessed, who in their right mind would turn us down?

If Barry's publishers were going to be uncooperative we would simply find another who was not. For this information we once again headed into the trusty bookstore to purchase—what else—a how-to book.

Step one in "How to get your book published" was to write a proposal, which, it explained, was the norm for a book of non-fiction. This we undertook, spending a full month painstakingly outlining a ten-chapter book on aspects of the Royal Family and its close staff that had never been discussed publicly; what *really* goes on behind closed doors (not what tabloid rumormongers who've never set one foot inside a royal residence serve up as the truth). Surely this breath of fresh air on a universally popular subject

260

would rock the New York houses into swift action. How could it not?

Upon completion of our proposal, we sent it to a number of the major houses in New York and awaited what we presumed would be a quick response. When the instantaneous response turned into several weeks of unqualified silence we began to telephone the publishing houses to inquire if they had received our couriered packages. By the end of November, we had talked to scores of apathetic secretaries and junior assistants in New York but had nothing to show for our efforts.

As naive as we were, it soon dawned on us we were not the only ones sending manuscripts to publishers in the belief that we had something unique.

When we explained our purpose for calling, we were repeatedly brushed off with, "Mr. So and So is in a meeting and will have to call you back."

"But I'm sure he'll talk to us if you will just explain why we're calling!" we would plead, to no effect. Indeed, it would seem that every editor in the entire city of New York was involved in one interminable meeting, if one was to believe their assistants. We came to realize our messages were being sent in one direction: the waste-paper basket! The rare editor we did get through to either could not understand the concept or told us simply that "it will not work" or "no one is buying that stuff anymore" and rudely hung up.

In short, we were given the impression that writing Malcolm's memoirs was one of the worst ideas for a book since Geraldine Ferraro's spectacular disaster in the bookstores, and that was pretty bad. But we honestly felt they were all wrong and were not so easily discouraged. We knew our book idea had merit. Even if it *was* true that the market for books about the Royal Family was saturated (and that seemed highly improbable), our book was not *about* the Royal Family. It was essentially a book about the people who *surround* them.

When we had analyzed every possible reason as to why publishers were not somersaulting to sign us up, we turned for help to our trusty how-to book again. The next step, it advised, was to locate a literary agent to represent us. Okay, we said confidently, that's the trick. We'll just write to a big New York agent, apprise them of our activity, he or she will be hopping up and down with euphoria, and we'll be in every bookstore across the United States within weeks.

We sprinted to the library in search of a listing of New York literary agents and photocopied the pertinent pages. To our astonishment there were hundreds of them to choose from.

Finding an agent who would speak to us or return our calls or answer our letters, however, proved as onerous a task as locating a publisher. Much to our consternation, a contract was not forthcoming nor any hint of interest in the project. We wrote to about twenty of the largest agencies in New York and each one fell through. But there were hundreds more on our list and we certainly were not going to take twenty negative reactions as the sign to throw in the towel. So, closing our eyes and pointing at the catalogue of agents before us, we randomly chose someone, a woman, and made a call. Our hopes soared when she actually expressed some enthusiasm for the project and set an appointment to see us.

Following the call, Malcolm and I both assessed the degree of fervor in the agent's voice. Malcolm thought it a $500,000 conversation; I, somewhat more optimistic, placed the excitement factor at about $750,000. Yes, we congratulated ourselves after the call, it was now only a matter of days until dollars would be cascading down a South-Pacific-sized waterfall into our personal bank accounts.

On Monday morning we set off from my Connecticut home en route to New York for our appointment with the agent. It was a bright, cheery winter day and the snow, glistening in the sunlight, matched our mood and high hopes.

Neither of us was terribly familiar with the geography of New York City so it came as somewhat of a surprise when we arrived outside a decidedly shabby apartment building in one of the less affluent areas of Manhattan. Our estimation of the cherished advance suddenly plummeted by a few hundred thousand in just seconds. But still, $200,000 or thereabouts was not all that bad a day's work, we agreed, and it was with this precarious morsel of hope that we pushed the agent's buzzer and rode the grimy elevator up to her place of residence.

Inside, her apartment lived up to the exterior of the edifice. She appeared to have what we both thought *resembled* an apartment but we could not quite figure out room definition. Everything was the dullest shade of grey, as if Emily Brontë's decorator had a hand in the interiors. Heathcliff would have felt very much at home. A very snotty cat occupied the only semi-comfortable chair and did not seem keen to relinquish it to strangers. We were invited into the dining room where an unnamed editor from an unnamed publishing house presided over the dining room table as though she were Queen Mary. Was this the way all successful literary agents lived? we mused silently.

The agent and "Queen Mary" read our substantial proposal in record time while we sipped tea out of cups that begged another scouring from the dishwasher. They

263

devoured some ten thousand words in a matter of minutes and, when through, announced that it was "all wrong," and would have to be completely "rethought."

"What do you mean 'all wrong?' " I asked.

"Well it just won't sell," she told us.

"Why not?"

"Because it isn't what people want."

"It isn't?"

"No," she told us authoritatively. "You haven't told us anything about what the Royals do each day; what they eat, what their favorite colors are. That's what women want to read."

"But," replied Malcolm, "don't you feel there has been enough written about that? I mean, there are countless books and magazine articles turned out weekly on those very topics. Our book is more to do with those people who *surround* the Royal Family rather than about the Royal Family themselves. We think it's time for something different. Look at this." He pointed out some of the truly shocking new material we had included in the proposal. "Personally, I think people would rather hear about the horrific state of her staff and the dangerous chaos it is in than what time Her Majesty is served her breakfast."

This was taken as an affront by the two women, who apparently considered themselves infallible experts when it came to the British Royal Household. We were instructed to go away, write them new material along the frivolous lines they had recommended, and then "we would talk."

Crestfallen, we emerged from the apartment building and headed to the Waldorf for drinks and dinner before driving back to Connecticut.

"Well," I said to Malcolm on the way home, summoning up a tiny particle of optimism, "at least she is *interested*. If we come up with a more expanded proposal I'm sure she will find a publisher for us soon."

We worked for another week incorporating the agent's recommendations into our proposal. When we called to say we were ready to meet again, she told us not to bother coming into New York but to send it to her in the mail. Two weeks later she still had not telephoned to report a deal had been cut with Random House so we placed a call to her. She was extremely rude about our augmented proposal and once again dashed our hopes by saying that it just "would not work" and that we had not "followed her orders." Heil Hitler!

At that point, we did the only thing two intelligent writers with a wonderful idea could do: we told her to get stuffed! Our search for a suitable agent would continue.

Accordingly, by the end of 1985 we were still no nearer to a book contract then we had been four months earlier. Malcolm returned to England for Christmas and to attend to business and personal matters. Although he did not say as much, I think he was convinced that our creative book would never come to pass.

In retrospect, I wish we *had* dropped the whole project. Had we known just how long it was going to take, there is no question we would not have proceeded. But I am a determined man and I could not accept that Malcolm's truly compelling and fascinating experiences at the palace would not be received by the reading public with enthusiasm. After all, I reasoned, if his tales fascinated *me*, who had never had any interest in the lives of the Royal Family, then how were their millions of devoted fans going to react to our startling revelations?

In late January, 1986, Malcolm flew back to Connecticut and we once again closed our eyes and randomly selected another name from the list of New York agents. This time, we chose one of the biggest and best known in the business, the grand master himself, Sterling Lord of Sterling Lord Literistic on Madison Avenue. Visions of dollar signs were truly dancing in our heads when the venerable man himself responded to our special delivery letter and called me at home to discuss the project. Shortly, we were en route to the city with a copy of our much improved proposal in hand.

Unfortunately, the ink was barely dry and we were an hour late for the appointment with Sterling because we could not find a photocopy machine to hide the white-out that swamped the last few pages. With embarrassment written on our faces, we finally arrived at his office and handed the slipshod proposal to him with apologies. We hoped we had not blown it.

Sterling was an elegant man in his early to mid-sixties, with grey hair and a cordial but jaded smile that clearly conveyed he'd been around the block. Thankfully, he did not seem to be put off by the state of our proposal and by the end of our meeting he was more than eager to sign us on as clients. To our utter astonishment and delight a contract was prepared there and then and, as you would expect from our story so far, we signed on the dotted line with barely a glance at the terms. I will never forget Sterling's parting words as he bid us farewell in the lobby of One Madison Avenue. Shaking our hands, he said, "We are all going to make a great deal of money out of this. A great deal of money."

With the events of the day and a propitious farewell from one of the biggest agents, there was no question that it was dinner at the Pierre. We drank two bottles of the very best champagne as we celebrated our all-but-guaranteed new wealth and careers. Finally, we had done it! We were going to be authors!

But things did not fall into place quite so smoothly. After one month of waiting for—and not receiving—a call, a letter, *any* sign that progress was being made on our behalf, we finally telephoned the Sterling Lord Agency ourselves. We were connected with Sterling instantly who calmed our concerns by saying that matters were in hand and he would be in touch soon. Thus began a debate between Malcolm and myself as to the precise definition of the word "soon." I said no more than another month. Malcolm agreed.

When four weeks had elapsed and the snow was melting in the pleasant New England spring air, we called Sterling again. He pacified us once more saying that "these things take time" and "not to worry." He knew a number of senior editors personally, he said, who would "lap this stuff up."

So we waited as patiently as we could.

In May, we called again but this time we were not put through quite so easily. Instead, we were connected with one of Sterling's assistants, who casually informed us that she would be handling the "redevelopment" and "rewriting" of our proposal in readiness for its submission to potential publishers.

This was news to us. Nothing had ever been mentioned about reworking the proposal and we explained this to her. But she was adamant that changes were necessary and a meeting was scheduled with her for the following week at which point we would be advised on the alterations she felt were required to make it "saleable."

It seemed so bizarre. We had a unique concept that was all but sure to sell. The material we promised made all previous books look like child's play. (Years later a London periodical would write, "Mr. Barker's book will make [Stephen] Barry's efforts look like Enid Blyton!") We obviously could write intelligently and in an amusing fashion; women insatiably lapped up the latest gossip on the Royal Family; Malcolm was the most senior person in the Royal Household ever to write a book; a top agent had told us we were going to make a lot of money. Now, suddenly, without any plausible explanation, we were notified we would have to completely overhaul our proposal!

Well, we did it, albeit begrudgingly, and about two weeks later, after Sterling's assistant had time to review it, we received a gushing ovation from her over the telephone. "Congratulations, guys, you've done it!" She seemed truly thrilled with our revised proposal and indicated Sterling would be sending it out immediately on our behalf. After the call, Malcolm and I embraced, believing our tortuous plight to be over and a publishing deal all but cemented. We happily dressed in all our finery and made reservations at Litchfield's premier inn, the TollGate Hill, for a lavish dinner.

My broken tooth over the main course should have been recognized as a harbinger: we were never to hear from our agent or from any of the fine staff at the Lord agency again. Our calls went unanswered. By the first week in June we were steaming mad and I hopped in my car and drove to New York without an appointment and announced myself to the receptionist, insisting on a meeting with Mr. Lord. I was told he was unavailable and it was not known when he might consent to an audience. That afternoon we sent him a registered letter indicating their services were rescinded forthwith.

This brutal action did not shock them into calling us as we had expected. Years later, we would privately thank Lord for some profound advice he had given us during that introductory meeting, but at the time we could only feel contempt.

It was now approaching the end of June of 1986 and we found ourselves no further ahead than we had been in September of the previous year. We could not understand it: no one, it seemed, wanted to hear about our funny book. Malcolm once again flew off into the distance, leaving me to work out our next move.

Did I finally dream up a brilliant and decisive stroke that led to a contract, you might ask. Well, not exactly. I closed my eyes and arbitrarily plucked another name from the directory of agents. This time my finger landed on one Jim Trupin of the firm JET Literary Associates. A letter to them was answered speedily and, as their name suggests, my hopes ascended when one week later I met Jim and his wife, Elizabeth, in their New York apartment. They were keen. They liked our proposal as it was (quite a relief) and after discussing it at length, Jim decided to arrange an auction amongst twenty publishers. . .exactly what our how-to book recommended. Perhaps we were on our way at long last.

While Jim busied himself sending our book proposal, which we had given the imaginative title *In Her Majesty's Service*, to all the big New York publishers, I left for Hawaii, while my movie producer landlord took possession of his Connecticut home for the summer.

I was staying at the Hotel Molokai, on the island of Molokai, a small, uncrowded haven in the Hawaiian chain. Malcolm was in England. The auction date had been set (to be conducted by telephone) and we agreed that I would call him with the news of our new publisher when word came through from New York.

Well, word did come through about eight o'clock in the evening on the appointed date (a Tuesday) and, to my amazement, I learned that every single New York publisher had turned the book down. Not only would they not pay several hundred thousand for it, but they wouldn't pay one cent! We were shocked and despondent to say the least. This resulted in the consumption of a number of killer mai tais on my part and a painful hangover the following day, not in the least helped by the scorching tropical heat, which necessitated further killer mai tais to see me through Wednesday. Thursday and Friday were dedicated strictly to recuperation.

By September 10, 1986, when I returned to the beautiful house on the lake in Litchfield, I felt renewed strength and vigor, and was determined that before the end of the year we would be in the bookstores. Malcolm, in the meantime, was winging his way across the Atlantic for the fresh assault on New York.

We met with Jim Trupin and his wife in New York a few days after Malcolm's return and chatted about the future of *In Her Majesty's Service*. Jim was still encouraging about its potential and gave us a file folder full of correspondence between himself and the publishers involved in the July auction. One said the book wasn't "enough of a trashorama" to work. Another felt it wasn't different enough to generate great sales.

But while we noted that no one was willing to invest any big money—we had set a floor of $150,000(US)—there were clear signs from at least four publishers that there *was* interest.

The problem, explained Jim, was essentially this: Following the high-flying early eighties when publishers routinely handed out huge advances to big names (and lost them on disastrous sales), they now insisted on *seeing* the finished manuscript before significant dollars were advanced. In short, he advised us to get down to work, actually *write* the book we had been talking about for so long, and take things from there.

Dinner later at the Waldorf was not tinged with the same

excited anticipation as on previous occasions when visions of shiny dust jackets bearing our names danced in our heads. But we still managed a bottle or two of fine wine and by dessert we were both full of optimism again, united in our determination to succeed. Malcolm reminded me of the encouraging letter from one publisher who mentioned that $150,000 was "slightly in excess" of what he wished to pay. Did that mean $125,000 *wasn't* in excess? It appeared so.

By 2:00 a.m. Malcolm feebly knocked on my bedroom door in the worst kind of agony with severe abdominal pain. I drove him to the emergency room of the Charlotte Hungerford Hospital in Torrington, where they treated him two hours later and discharged him with a good healthy shot of painkiller. It wore off around five that morning and once again we set off for the hospital, where this time they admitted him and kept him for a week.

During his absence, I made an attempt or two to get started on the book. When Malcolm returned, he had a go himself but after some stern reprimands from me over the pace of his progress, a huge dispute ensued and he shortly found himself booked on a flight out of Hartford back to London. Two weeks later, all was forgiven and he flew back to Connecticut. We celebrated his arrival and talked about our plans to "really get going" on the book this time and finish it by the end of the year.

We struggled through the remainder of October and November with the book but for some reason having the two of us work side by side just was not working out. We couldn't figure out what was wrong but put it down to the constant snowstorms and the drab New England winter.

I had invited Malcolm to stay with me over Christmas and on December 10 we flew to Bermuda, having written a staggering two pages. We had, however, done an awful lot of *talking* about what we were *going* to write and we thought that Bermuda was perhaps the place to get those creative juices flowing.

Alas, our Bermuda sojourn was decidedly unproductive. We left the island on January 12 but, as we had no desire to return to the snow and ice of New England right away, we flew to Molokai where we felt confident our writing would finally get underway. Yes...Hawaii was the answer, we agreed! The book would definitely happen now.

It did not. We were there for three months at the delightful Hotel Molokai but not a word was written. In April, I flew back to Connecticut and Malcolm to England where he was once again admitted to hospital complaining of stomach ailments. Once ensconced in Connecticut, I was determined to get underway with "the book."

When he was released from hospital, Malcolm refused to cross the Atlantic right away, even though I pleaded with him weekly. He was convinced our idea was never going to come to fruition. In June of that year my lease in Connecticut was up and I adjourned to my cottage in Bermuda. It was not until August that I was at last able to hound him into flying over. In September we finally bit the bullet and the writing began, with me on my computer in my bedroom upstairs, and Malcolm on his trusty typewriter downstairs.

We now realized what the problem had been all along. Of course, we should *never* have been working *together* on the book. Working *apart* was the answer. Now we each wrote our own share of the work, then regrouped at the end of the day to review the progress, with Malcolm correcting any factual errors I had made in my portion. Malcolm's fact-checking and correcting abruptly stopped when he disappeared for a brief hospital sojourn, again troubled with his stomach pains.

Our work was coming along nicely when, in Mid-October, we were awakened early one morning by the assistant manager of the hotel next door pounding on my front door. Through tumultuous rain and growing winds, he informed me that Hurricane Emily was about to hit the island and he feared the tall tree outside my living room window might come crashing down through the roof.

That was all I needed to hear. We dressed in record time and fled to the safety of the hotel lobby next door where many of the elderly guests were already collected with Bloody Marys in their hands. Having never experienced the havoc of a real hurricane before, we were truly frightened, but the panic really set in when I remembered that my computer and disks were still in my cottage. Should they come to any harm, all our hard labor, and about half the content of the book, would be lost forever. I recall thinking stupidly at the time that I would rather risk injury than come through the hurricane without our disks (only authors know this sickening, sinking feeling). I made a dash into the 160-km/hr winds back to my cottage where I retrieved the disks, then struggled through the trees back to the hotel.

The wind was whipping into a frenzy now and, above the lobby, in the hotel rooms, we could hear the intermittent shattering of glass as window after window cracked under the strain. Malcolm was the only person in the hotel lobby who was not fully dressed in proper clothes. He was more than a little self-conscious in his pajamas and dressing gown as the elderly hotel guests suspiciously gazed at us.

At its peak, the hurricane winds reached 190 km/hr and did millions of dollars in damage, but as unexpectedly as it had arrived, by noon it was all over and we were able to return to my cottage.

Unfortunately, things move rather slowly in the tropics

273

and we were without electricity or telephone lines for two weeks. Since computers require a steady flow of power, we resorted to continuing with the book by hand, in candle-light. This simple solution led to Malcolm being hospitalized once more: the constant burning of the candles had aggra-vated his asthma. However, since the hospital was full, he had to take a room in the children's ward, which caused a good deal of mirth at Malcolm's expense amongst his friends. Still, by Christmas of that year we had finished writ-ing the book. . .at long last. On January 5, 1988, full of expec-tation, we shipped it off to our New York agent and waited for his response.

New Yorkers are an odd lot. I suppose when you have more homeless living on the streets than the population of most large Canadian towns, and murders measured by the minute, you become rather jaded, but Jim's response to what we considered a sensational manuscript was excruciatingly reserved. But he said he and his wife liked it enormously. It was a great read and, with some minor alterations to the manuscript, another telephone auction was arranged for early February.

One week before the auction took place, Jim called us bearing (for the first time) some exciting news. The editor-in-chief of a large publishing firm was raving over the book (by this time known as *Officially Speaking*). In fact, he had taken the book home that weekend and Monday morning called Jim Trupin personally to say that he was transfixed by it to the point that he could not put it down. "I think we're going to see a sizeable offer from them," Jim predicted enthusiasti-cally. (As I've mentioned, Jim never gets overly excited about anything so naturally our hopes skyrocketed at his pro-nouncement.)

On the day of the auction, Malcolm and I waited nervously by the phone. At two o'clock we received the call we had been expecting from Jim. The news was not good. It was dismal. None of the publishers wanted to bid and the editor-in-chief was not returning his calls.

A day or two later, when he managed to make contact with the editor-in-chief, he told us that while *he* wanted to go with it, his colleagues had managed to persuade him otherwise, using the same stale old argument that it just would not work, that the market was too tiny for a book on this subject matter. The end result, now well into our third year of the venture, was a big, fat, robust zero!

Around this time we began to realize that with the exception of one or two publishers no one was actually reading our manuscript. It wasn't for lack of trying on our agent's part though. In fact, Jim Trupin had been awarded the much-coveted most-persistent (read obnoxious)-agent-of-the-year prize by Simon and Schuster for his efforts on our behalf. We discovered what was really happening from the editors themselves, both verbally and in letter form. For instance, when we heard comments such as "Their revelations have been reported before," and "I don't see how it differs from all the other tell-tale books on the Royal Family," we naturally became suspicious. I mean, where in the world had it been reported that a senior official to the Queen had buried his wife under the floorboards of his palace apartment? Where had it been reported that the Queen was knocked down the stairs by a drunken member of her staff and even kept his job? Who had revealed that male prostitutes on staff were working the lavatories to supplement their incomes?

In reality, most of the editors Trupin approached had not read one page of our book and those who had skimmed through it in minutes before rendering judgment.

Our suspicions were proved when we pointed out some of the most startling bombshells we'd uncovered. Their response was usually "Oh? I didn't see that," or "I must have missed those. What page did you say?" or (and this was the most annoying) "I wasn't told about those stories!"

The picture that began to emerge was that very little of the *reading* is actually done by the editors themselves, the people who ultimately make the buying decisions. In New York, this important task is frequently handed down to poorly paid assistants who will take a manuscript home for the night, then give their bosses a synopsis the next morning, accompanied by their opinions on its potential.

Can you imagine! These underlings unofficially making the calls on multi-million dollar decisions! Well, in our case, it is true. Being armed with this new information only made us all the more determined to take a detour round the seemingly impenetrable forces of the literary business in New York.

It still made no sense. We had written a blockbuster book by the highest-ranked employee of the Queen ever to talk openly. A prominent editor-in-chief said he could not put the book down. Interest in the Royal Family had never been higher. And yet we still could not elicit even a modicum of attention. To be honest, I had moments where I wanted to bury the nightmare once and for all. What was the point? After all, the world is full of sardonic, unpublished authors claiming the world has done them a grave injustice by not recognizing their genius. So why should we be any different?

We had our moments of self-doubt but they never lasted for long, especially since the book had taken on new meaning for us. It was no longer merely a collection of witty anecdotes about life in the Royal Household. It had become a kind of cause. I remember leaning back in my chair one day in late 1987 while we were writing and saying to Malcolm, "You know, it really is unacceptable, isn't it? Why are these *creatures* working for the Queen of England?"

It was at this point that we started to take some real pride in our work, whereas before it was, truthfully, just another way to make money. If nothing else, perhaps our book would shake the Royal Household out of its disgraceful apathy and into something that resembled a trustworthy organization responsible for the safety and care of an anointed Queen. The press can say what they like, bitter lot that most of them are, but we sincerely believed we had something important to say. And so the battle to unearth a publisher continued.

We concluded that if we were ever to interest the Americans we would have to slip in through the back door. If New York was convinced our book would not sell, then we would have to prove them wrong, and the best way to demonstrate this was to sign a deal with a major publishing house in another country. Surely publishers in the Commonwealth would jump at the opportunity, right?

Wrong. Publishers in Canada were just as negative as their counterparts in the U.S. We were sent rejection letter after rejection letter, but at least the Canadians were more polite than the Americans. They wrote back!

Next, our agent organized a telephone auction in Australia, aiming to include about twenty-five publishers, and set a date for early April, 1988. Again, we were full of hope and expectation, and confident the Australians would kill for this book given their bitter-sweet relationship with the mother country. On top of that, our book had all the makings of another *Spycatcher*, which had had its global launch courtesy the Aussies.

The auction day came and went. No one telephoned to make an offer, A couple of weeks later only two letters had trickled in from Australia, saying that editors had read the book but did not feel it was "revelatory enough." We were dumbfounded. Not revelatory enough? They were sounding frighteningly similar to the New Yorkers.

We spent the spring testing and re-testing the waters in America, Canada, Australia and England, seeking the usual advance against royalties for the hardcover rights. In London, our agent was Abner Stein, whose roster of illustrious clients included the likes of John le Carré, but even *he* was unable to secure a publisher for us. English publishers seemed either totally indifferent toward it or salivated over its potential while remaining fearful of the legal reprisals.

Understandably, we were now approaching burnout with the project, and we wearily gave our agent the go-ahead to sell the work on a royalty basis only (I adore that term), which meant that a publisher could own it without paying any money up front, thereby reducing its risk and investment. We were sure someone would go for it now. But no. They would not accept it on this basis either in any of the above mentioned countries. We now told Jim to advise publishers around the globe that we would pay *half* the printing costs ourselves if they would add the book to their list. That is how confident we were that it would sell. Again, no one bought.

In desperation we now agreed to pay *all* the printing costs up front ourselves, thereby reducing a publisher's risk to absolute zero. Even if the book did not sell *one* copy (and that was extremely unlikely) the lucky publisher would not be out of pocket one red cent. Talk about a sweetheart deal! But, believe it or not, we could not even *pay* someone to publish the book! Oh, there were a couple of promising publishers, but one concern we could not overcome was the fear of libel suits. To counter this objection, we offered to take full responsibility for all legal action and judgments taken against the publisher and agreed to put that in our contract. But this did not satisfy the few that expressed interest either. In most cases, after reading the manuscript, their lawyers convinced them the gamble was too great. As one well-known Canadian tycoon once erupted in the course of some tense negotiations: "You bloody lawyers...always complicating everything!" How true.

While we were figuring out our next move, one New York publisher unexpectedly indicated he was willing to talk to us. At last!

It was about May, 1988, when we met in the publisher's Madison Avenue offices in New York. The president of this small but respected publishing house was a personal friend of our agent, and chairman of a major publishing company before leaving them to form his own company. A slight but distinguished man, he was constantly on the phone during our meeting. It was extremely unsettling when every time we started to say something important he would be buzzed and we'd be put on hold while he dealt with some other matter. When he was not on the telephone, we naturally talked about the book, our difficulties in finding a publishing house, Malcolm's background, the legal aspects and, lastly, the terms under which we were prepared to sign a contract. The president's sleepy eyes widened when we explained that if the Queen chose to ban our book in England, a great deal of publicity might ensue.

By the end of our hour-long meeting we left the offices content in the knowledge that we had struck a good deal: no advance, we would share the printing costs, and, in return, we would be paid a twenty percent royalty on all sales. The publisher would take care of distribution and promotion. As a bonus, we would have a measure of control over various aspects of our book (such as jacket design and layout) that ninety-nine percent of authors never dream of having. We obviously wouldn't make anything unless the book had robust sales, but if it performed even one tenth as well as we had predicted, we stood to end up in the black.

The president said he would have contracts prepared within a week and he set a tentative release date there and then—October/November, 1988. It was going to be a tight schedule considering it sometimes requires twelve months to launch a major book in the United States, but we were both eager. Malcolm and I were elated over the fortunate turn of events, our agent was thankful he was at last able to place the manuscript, and we all agreed that, while it had been a long haul—more then three years—it had still been worth it. We were going to be authors!

Back in our suite at the Waldorf, we began receiving unsettling telephone calls from a reporter claiming to be from London's *Daily Mirror*. He had somehow discovered that a deal was in the works. Fortunately, the hotel would not give him our room numbers and, as he had no idea at that point what Malcolm looked like, he was somewhat lost. Mysteriously though, he managed to discover we were booked on a plane to Montreal the next morning. Along with two photographers, he boarded the same Air Canada flight to pursue us. We found out later that an assistant of a London agent had irresponsibly provided the *Mirror* with our itinerary.

Once we arrived in Montreal, the news hound telephoned our suite at the Four Seasons constantly but, again, connected by the house telephone and unaware of our suite number. We continued to decline his request for an interview. At one point Malcolm told him it would cost $1 million for us to speak with them, believing this would make the point that we had no desire to chat with a tabloid like the *Daily Mirror*.

I had to fly to Boston on another matter the following morning and arranged to meet Malcolm back in Nova Scotia. He arrived at the Air Canada check-in and no sooner was he handed his boarding card than the *Daily Mirror* reporter and photographers popped out of the crowd and demanded an interview. Malcolm was ruffled by this unexpected appearance and sharply told them they were wasting their time as he briskly marched towards his departure gate. They followed him and frantically began snapping pictures as though he were a male model strutting down a Paris fashion runway. In desperation, Malcolm sought the aid of a policeman patrolling the airport. The policeman led him to a security office where he was at last free from the press. The *Daily Mirror* appeared unwilling to follow him to Nova Scotia or perhaps their budget would not allow it, but one week later the following front-page headline appeared in the Sunday edition of the tabloid, with a picture of a startled Malcolm Barker staring out at their legion of subscribers:

QUEEN'S FURY OVER PALACE SEX SECRETS TELL-TALE
NEW ROYAL RAT SET TO MAKE A MILLION

It is sad, but true, that the entire press corps would now—and later—miss the whole thrust of our book. Yes, there were indeed some juicy sex scandals involving the Royal Household, but tales of sex represented an infinitesimal fraction of what we had written. If only the press had *read* the bloody thing instead of writing third- and fourth-hand opinions emanating from others who hadn't read it.

Two weeks later, I placed a routine call to Jim in New York questioning him about our contract with the publisher. When could I expect it? The president had said it would take only a week. Jim said he didn't know what was going on. I hung up and tried to reach the president myself. When I did, he seemed very vague and indicated he was having second thoughts about the whole thing. This did not sound good.

The next day, Jim called to say that he now knew why he was being so evasive: his company was declaring bankruptcy and, irony of ironies, filing for protection from its creditors under the infamous "Chapter 11." Our deal was now off for good.

It was a great disappointment but we consoled ourselves with the knowledge that the situation could have been far worse had we signed before the crunch. Jim told us a few months later that authors lost thousands of dollars in unpaid royalties and hadn't much hope of ever seeing another penny.

Thus began another mad scramble to locate another publisher.

During the remainder of 1988 our agent continued his battle to uncover someone—anyone—willing to talk to us about the book. Malcolm and I did the same.

In March 1989, we struck it lucky with a casual call to a small New York publishing house which expressed some interest in taking a look at our project. I flew to New York and met with the president and his assistant. They both liked the book and the assistant in particular was rhapsodic about its potential. He convinced his boss that it was a winner. They would not give me an absolute "yes" but said they would get back to me within the week. I flew home and waited.

One month later they finally responded with a fax saying they had discussed it further and had changed their minds. When I called the assistant to ask why, he explained their concern had strictly to do with the legalities and the $25,000 advance we had talked about. I told him we would be happy with a royalty basis only, no advance, and we'd sign a letter taking full responsibility for any legal suits. I flew down to New York again to make my pitch and convinced them it was a winner. With this, we shook hands and the deal was on again.

Another month or two later, they cancelled our verbal agreement via the fax machine. Again I flew to New York to quell their apprehensions and again I was successful in talking them back into a deal.

In September, we hired Jack Ground, another Toronto lawyer specializing in the publishing and entertainment field, and together we flew down to New York to hammer out the contract. Jim Trupin was also present. The two-hour meeting went well. We came to a mutually satisfactory arrangement over the contract, shook hands and set May 1990 as the release month. Now, incontrovertibly, the book seemed destined to appear in print.

Two weeks later, Jack Ground called me inquiring if I had heard the news. "What news?" I asked. He told me that the New York firm had faxed a letter to him indicating it was no longer interested in the book. The reason? They were not happy with the contract we had negotiated! I was furious but, to be truthful, nothing surprised me anymore. We had been so close so many times, and been let down for inexplicable reasons, that I would have been shocked had the deal actually gone through without any hitches. I read between the lines and knew the "legalities" excuse was only a pathetic way of backing out. Quite obviously, they did not fully believe in the book. I did not have the energy this time to talk them out of their decision.

Clearly there was now no use in searching for another publisher. Time was passing quickly and Malcolm and I had made a blood oath that if the book was not released in 1990, we would put ourselves out of our own misery and bury it once and for all.

We cooled it over Christmas. Then in January, 1990, we re-christened the book *Courting Disaster* and wrestled with the future. (We came up with the title one afternoon while waiting for the elevator in a Maui hotel, nursing monstrous hangovers.) Even if we did publish the book ourselves we still needed the help of the industry in the form of distribution, and no one would come to our rescue. All the big distributors in Canada and the U.S. took the same attitude as the publishers, that it was not worth handling because they did not believe it would sell. In short, we were royally screwed and totally shut out. No one would publish it, no one would distribute it, no one would stock it in their bookstores, no one would even take our money to print it! But we would not give up. We knew in our hearts it was a winning formula. Apparently we were the only ones who felt this way.

Then, quite by happenstance, I was introduced to an editor in Halifax named Elizabeth Eve, who saw the merit in our project and talked me out of throwing in the towel and into publishing it ourselves. Between her and our London attorney, a former publisher himself, they induced us to forge ahead. Eventually, they said, established publishers in other countries were bound to pick it up once it took off.

By this time we were thoroughly soured on the publishing business. However, after much discussion and soul-searching, Malcolm and I decided to take their advice and print a limited run of books. We truthfully did not think anything would come of it since it took clout to get in the bookstores. How could we possibly make a success of the book if we could not even get shelf space? Still, we consoled ourselves, at least we would have the satisfaction of seeing over four and a half years of struggle translated into a finished product—even if the only readers might be friends and colleagues who had listened to us wail about our literary hopes for so long.

To accomplish our objective we required a multitude of talent, from a graphic designer to devise the jacket to the right printer to print the books. Finding a cost-effective printer required a lengthy search in the U.S. and central Canada. It was an incredible eye-opening experience and we gained first-hand knowledge of just how much cheaper the book business is south of the border. For instance, would you have imagined that in Canada it costs as much as $4 to print one hardcover book, compared to $1.20 in Virginia?

At the same time, we developed a professional marketing campaign following exactly the same plan our former would-be publisher(s) had outlined to us. Shiny colour posters of the book jacket were printed to accompany the book orders (if we received any), as well as glossy brochures with ordering details for mailing to all the trade bookstores in Canada, England and the states of New York and California. In total, there were roughly seven thousand bookstores to solicit.

We knew that, alone, we could never handle distribution in a country the size of the U.S. In Canada, yes. America, definitely not. The market was just too vast. We hoped this limited distribution in two major states would act as a catalyst; we hoped to mimic the fortunes of the "Trivial Pursuit" inventors, who, when no one believed their board game would succeed, raised enough money amongst family and friends to manufacture a small number of the product. The rest, as they say, is now history.

While the book was being printed in Virginia, we sat back and awaited the retail response. Meanwhile, a public relations firm we had hired was having success in procuring several lucrative serialization deals for us in the U.S., Canada, Australia, France and Germany at tens of thousands of dollars a pop. A three-part serialization contract with *Star* magazine in New York, for example, paid us $40,000 alone! By the time the book was ready to be distributed we had already earned over $100,000(US) from serialization alone. We were now counting on this to raise interest from the big American publishers. Alas, not a creature stirred in the U.S., Canada or Australia.

By June 1990, twenty thousand copies of *Courting Disaster* were supposed to be ready for shipping to Canada, but two days before they were due to be released, I received a call from the printing plant in Virginia to say there was a problem: the gold foil used for the jacket lettering was running and what should they do? If they stopped now to correct the problem, which could mean some re-designing, the printing might be set back by as much as six weeks. Press time must be booked weeks ahead of time and, like an aircraft missing its takeoff slot, we would have to go all the way back to the end of the queue and wait our turn. Obviously, our timing would be off-kilter if we halted the presses, so I hopped on a plane to Virginia to take a peek.

I was not entirely happy with what I saw, but the problem was rectified as well as we could manage and I gave the go-ahead to print.

Ten days later, the books were shipped to Canada, but due to a heat wave in the U.S. about half the books arrived with a mysterious scattering of white flecks on the jackets. What a mess! The foil was obviously not designed to travel in stifling heat. We skimmed off the really bad ones, replaced as many as possible with spare jackets the printer had included (even most of those had been damaged) and hoped no one would comment on the less than pleasing results. No one did, publicly at least. However, in their haste to stock the book once it had become news, many stores made use of express shippers unused to handling hardcover books. Apart from having white flecks on the dust jackets, a number of copies appeared on stands torn and tatty as well!

Still, we perservered. In the interim, we had received a response from our brochures. Out of the seven thousand that we had sent out, twenty-three bookstores placed orders for a total of fewer than one hundred books. Wow!

Near the end of June, I made an important personal decision. Malcolm had spent the previous two years helping me out with another business venture in Nova Scotia and we decided that with its closure we both desired to live elsewhere. Malcolm wished to return to England; I set my sight on Bermuda, where I could continue with my writing interests.

In early July, after *Courting Disaster* had been available for about a month, we flew to London. I rented an apartment for the summer while my new cottage in Bermuda was being readied, and Malcolm returned to his home in Yorkshire. By this time, we both had resigned ourselves to the fact that *Courting Disaster* was never going to be a hit. It was time to get on with our lives.

For all the headaches, we knew *Courting Disaster* was well written, very funny, and an important statement on the British Royal Household.

With these feelings of satisfaction, I relaxed in London and started another book, one that had nothing to do with

royalty, while Malcolm trotted around the Yorkshire countryside, visited his family and friends and put some thought
into what he should do with his life now that he could never
count on a reference from Buckingham Palace.

As the days passed, we mused on the peculiarities of the
book business, where it's thought your book cannot be
taken seriously if you happen to use your own money to
publish it! Name one successful entrepreneur who hasn't
had to start their business on their own. That is why they are
called *entrepreneurs!* The book industry is another matter,
however. "How *dare* you print your own book!" was the
attitude expressed towards our venture. "How dare you
indeed question the judgment of Bantam or Doubleday or
Macmillan Canada!" Well, we had done just that.

Our book seemed destined to fade into obscurity now
but for one black cloud on the horizon—a letter we received
from the Queen's lawyers.

The letter claimed that Malcolm had breached a confi-
dentiality agreement when he was hired at Buckingham Palace in 1980. As a result, the lawyers said the publication of
Courting Disaster in England would be unacceptable.

This letter would serve to mark the start of a full-scale
international uproar.

2

On Wednesday, July 25, 1990, I was awakened by the jarring
ring of British Telecom and groggily answered the phone by
my bed.

"Hello. Tim?" our public relations man in England
inquired.

"Yes, Barry. How are you?"

He wasted no time. "Fine. Have you seen the papers this morning?"

"Papers?" I asked still half asleep, the furthest thing from my mind being *Courting Disaster*. "Which one?"

"All of them!" He sounded excited.

I was now fully awake and erect in bed (sitting up, that is). "Why? What is going on?"

"*Courting Disaster*, that's what's going on. Its all through the press. *The Daily Telegraph* and *The Times* have you on the front page."

I told him I'd call him back after I had seen them. Dressing quickly, I raced to the news agents just up the street on Park Lane where I purchased at least ten newspapers and returned home. They described how censors at the border in England had intercepted some 10,000 copies of *Paris Match* magazine and spent the night ripping out every page that contained excerpts from our book. The press was going berserk. To further enrage the Queen, *Paris Match* had published explicit photographs of her in bed and another of Princess Margaret standing with nude men on a tropical beach. The press automatically assumed they had come from our book! They had not.

Although many believed this blatant blockage of the fundamental freedoms to read and write was only happening in archaic Britain, copies of *Paris Match* reaching Canada also arrived with the offending pages missing. This was never mentioned in the press in Canada as far as I am aware, but it happened. I imagine because the circulation is relatively small in English-speaking Canada it went unnoticed, but it is interesting to note that copies in French, distributed in Quebec, *did* contain the book excerpts in full!

Freedom of the press needs no explaining here. Nowadays, incidents such as this inevitably cause a sensation. But to add to the drama, the censorship of *Courting Disaster* coincidentally occurred on the very day the civil list was published. The civil list, for those not familiar with the term, details the annual income allotted to individual members of the Royal Family by the government. The juxtaposition of the $15 million the taxpayers would be forking over per annum for the upkeep of the Royal Family, with the blatant censoring of a former employee's book detailing how these very funds were being squandered was too much to ignore. The papers were swamped with news of *Courting Disaster* and the censorship story.

Even the British House of Commons discussed the censorship issue. One Labour MP described the ban on *Courting Disaster* as "draconian," while a Tory MP welcomed the ban, saying "it is quite right that this sort of thing should be stopped."

In Canada, the censorship story was the lead news item across the country. Whereas twenty-four hours earlier we could not *give* the book away as the door prize at a provincial flea market, by nine o'clock in the morning Nova Scotia time, Fleetwood's phones were ringing non-stop with requests from the press for interviews and bookstores for books.

By noon of July 25, Fleetwood—Malcolm and I named the company after the English town in which we attended school together—had sent out book orders amounting to $600,000. By five o'clock orders totalled $1.3 million, or $150,000 per hour, and we were forced to telephone our printer in Virginia to print additional copies due to the overwhelming demand. The following morning we were already discussing the possibility of a third print-run because of the mounting interest in the U.S. That morning, too, our London lawyers were notified by the Queen's lawyers that we had two weeks to prepare for a hearing—a hearing in which they would be seeking a permanent injunction blocking the sale of the book in the United Kingdom.

People have asked us how we managed to handle distribution of the book when we had essentially been shut out of the industry. The answer is simple. When the story broke in the press, everyone who had previously given us the cold shoulder now appeared on our doorstep begging forgiveness—the major distributors, the national book chains, the giant airport and hotel concession shops. They all wanted to stock *Courting Disaster* and they wanted it now! We had many irate calls from book chains furious that we could not supply them as rapidly as they wanted. In fact, one Nova Scotia newspaper told how copies of *Courting Disaster* were being scalped on the street for forty percent above the cover price of $26.95.

Courting Disaster was hot property not only in Canada at this early stage. Bermuda bookstores telephoned Fleetwood to say the island had sold out entirely in two days and they pleaded for more, even offering to cut their own commission if it meant speedier delivery. What we were able to send them sold out in one day.

Bookstores, I mused, really must be the best businesses going. I know of no other where you can fill your entire store with free merchandise (most books are "sold" to bookstores on a consignment basis), keep it as long as you like, earn forty to fifty percent commission when a book is sold, remit the money to the publisher when you feel like it and, if any of your suppliers get too uppity and demand payment forthwith, simply send back enough books for credit to equal the amount your creditors are requesting!

In London, the pace was just as frantic. Malcolm and I taped a number of important broadcasts: CTV National News, Canada AM, CBC, CBC Newsworld, followed by live radio shows the next morning out of Toronto, Montreal and Halifax. We were supposed to appear on the CBC's *Journal*, but at the last minute they axed us for another fast-breaking story involving the Indian standoff at Oka, Que. They telephoned us just as we were going out the door to catch a cab to their London studio, where the segment would be aired live late in the evening. They offered us CBC *Midday* instead, but when we told them we were not keen to stay up past midnight to film that show, they became irked, claiming that our dropping-out would cost them $4,000 for the satellite time they had booked. We still refused, confident the capital loss would not, in all probability, put the CBC under. However, from that point on the CBC seemed to disregard us. While every other news medium in the country wanted to talk to us regularly over the next two to three months, the CBC remained strangely silent.

The pace was so hectic that Malcolm and I had to divide up the interviews, which actually worked well because it seemed that the Canadian media were more anxious to talk with *me* than with him! Perhaps this was to accentuate the "Canadian" side of the story. I do not know for sure. We barely had time to eat, I know that.

On July 27, our lawyers were informed that the Queen's lawyers were going to court *immediately* to seek an injunction banning the book. We had only two days to prepare our case.

Advising us was Tony Yablon, a senior partner with the firm Jaques and Lewis, and David Fowell, who represented us in court for the first hearing. Malcolm and I did not attend as we wished to avoid the media crush. Instead, we were sequestered away in the offices of the law firm. On the court steps a few blocks away, the BBC and ITV cameras, along with masses of photographers and reporters, were gathered, hoping to catch a glimpse of Malcolm.

We lost our bid to halt the injunction and decided to appeal.

That evening, the book injunction was national news in England and international news everywhere else. The story heralded still more interviews on television, on radio and for magazines. Malcolm and I were now going night and day doing interviews. We had to decline more than we accepted because there simply were not enough hours in the day.

I would have to say that the media was split fifty-fifty on the matter of the high handed measures of the Crown. While we were strongly denounced by some, we were praised and supported by others.

Meanwhile, Mr. Fowell had to be replaced due to other commitments so Jaques and Lewis brought in one of the top trial lawyers in England, a gentleman by the name of David Pannick, to handle our appeal. Mr. Pannick was experienced in banned books and had been involved with the famous *Spycatcher* case. We had to laugh a bit now at the collection of names on our legal team: "Pannick, Fowell and Gay" (Tony Yablon signed all his correspondence with his initials only— G.A.Y.). How could we possibly lose with a crack legal team like that?

On July 29, the day before the appeal hearing, the Queen's lawyers were furious with us because they thought we had sold excerpts to the Scottish newspaper, *Scotland on Sunday*, which printed a full page of our revelations, in direct defiance, it seemed, of the initial ban which applied to the entire United Kingdom. Indeed, we sent a fax to the Queen's lawyers the next day telling them that we had in no way authorized this publication.

Mr. Pannick argued our appeal most eloquently for ninety minutes but, alas, we were unsuccessful. This resulted in the well-publicized "world-wide ban" ruling.

If you have ever thought the wheels of the judicial system turn slower than molasses pouring onto pancakes, this situation most definitely does not apply to the Queen of England when she is seeking legal retribution. We must be the only case in history that has enjoyed a full trial—*and* an appeal—all in the space of four days!

I do admit the appeal was interesting as I and our battery of lawyers sat in the frighteningly sterile atmosphere of the High Court, facing three elderly and rancorous Lords.

Had it not been for Mr. Pannick's reputation and the respect even the Lords who heard the appeal had for him, I doubt the trial would have lasted more then ten minutes, such was the picture of outrage and determination on the three judges' faces. This was hammered home when they rendered their decision at the conclusion of the hearing. Lord Donaldson said: "My abiding impression of this case is that I have confirmed my admiration for counsel (Mr. Pannick) for the defendants as an advocate in his ability to dress up the wholly unarguable as if it had a scintilla of a basis for reason."

The injunction made legal history in Britain and would appear in the October issue of *The All England Law Reports* as the lead case. Quite an honor! We were glad it was only a civil matter otherwise we may have got thirty years, or a term in the Tower.

From July 31 onwards there were non-stop interviews to deal with from Canada, the U.S. and around the world. The demands were brutal but we were not complaining. After all, the success of our book was what we had dreamed of for nearly five years. We were, however, grateful for the help and management of our PR company who dealt with all media inquiries. You name it, we did it: in-depth magazine interviews, radio, talk shows, and all the Canadian, American, British and French newspapers. In Canada, the country was hotly debating the issue of a foreign monarch telling Canadians what they could and could not read.

As the Kitchener-Waterloo *Record* remarked in an August 3 editorial: "Britain's courts have every right to interpret the law within their own borders. It is more than passing strange, however, to ask these same courts to restrict the reading rights of residents of other nations on their own soil...The judges of the United Kingdom seem to have forgotten that the empire dissolved a long time ago."

One of the most memorable interviews involved *People* magazine, who arrived at my flat in London for a chat which lasted well over three hours. They wanted to know every single detail about the book and, naturally, everything to do with the trial.

We thought the *People* interview went very well, although they insisted that Malcolm pose in front of Buckingham Palace for a photo session. He refused, quite rightly, on the grounds that Lord Donaldson had explicitly forbidden him from discussing and promoting his banned book. Posing in front of the Queen's London home holding a copy of *Courting Disaster* for one of the largest American magazines in existence most assuredly defied this edict! But the *People* reporter told us that unless Malcolm complied they would not run the story. Malcolm still declined and, in the end, they kept their promise and dropped the feature story, claiming their readers "needed the visual."

The *New York Times* did a lengthy story on the book. It amazed us how friendly and chatty reporters could be on the phone and in your presence, then calmly proceed to run a story that bore no resemblance to the one they had promised. In our case, their story was also factually wrong. They reported that the Queen had been successful in stopping the book world-wide. Technically she had been, but did anyone really expect that *Courting Disaster* would no longer be sold outside the United Kingdom?

The outcome of the hearing, as much as it fueled the sale of books abroad, put us in a highly awkward position. We had the attention we always thought our book merited. At the same time, Mr. Pannick was warning us either to stop giving interviews and distributing books, or to leave the country immediately. He was concerned that should we "flaunt" the ban, we might be found in contempt of court. That could mean a jail term for Malcolm, and a heavy fine.

We were truly torn. Could Mr. Pannick be, in fact, panicking? (We had to get that one out of the way.) Or was he just being sensible? What a predicament! Here we had a judgment from the High Court to stop selling books, yet *Courting Disaster* had all the makings of another *Spycatcher*, maybe even something bigger. According to one Toronto bookseller, *Courting Disaster* was going to be "bigger than *The Satanic Verses* or *Spycatcher*."

It really was a Catch-22 situation. We needed to do interviews to sell books but, if we did continue with promotion, the chances seemed very real that Malcolm may end up in serious trouble with the British courts.

In the meantime, the Queen's lawyers were fretting about the 20,000 copies of *Courting Disaster* that already had been printed. How many had been distributed, and how many were still in storage, they enquired.

As you may have guessed, the final resting place of the 20,000 books was in bookstores across Canada and more were on their way from the printer! They most certainly were not housed in some warehouse collecting dust as Her Majesty's lawyers so earnestly seemed to believe.

Following the drama of the appeal, the press attention intensified. Even Dutch Television phoned to set up an interview with Malcolm. We laughed at his new star status when they told him they were going to fit him in between Katharine Hepburn and Meryl Streep. They even offered to fly a crew over to another country if he felt uncomfortable speaking in England. Talk about feeling like Mary Queen of Scots! We could not decline the opportunity, especially as several Dutch publishers were now considering the book. But whether real or imagined, neither of us felt comfortable defying the ban ruling so blatantly. While it was highly improbable an author of a book would be sent to prison nowadays, we nevertheless were always looking over our shoulder to see if we were being watched. Paranoia was setting in and it did not feel comfortable in the least.

The precarious situation became quite unnerving. At one point I was threatened with eviction by the management of my apartment building on Park Lane because it was tired of all the reporters hanging around outside. A scruffy man from the *Daily Mirror* in particular just would not give up. He even began chatting up the doorman in the hope that he would pass a message to me.

Another annoying reporter kept telephoning us from *People* newspaper in London. How he got my number I will never know. The *People* reporter would call early in the morning and late at night. I would tell him "No" and then slam the phone down. The next day he would try again, as though it were the first attempt, and I'd slam down the telephone again. He never gave up.

Eventually, even *talking* about the proceedings with our public relations firm in Canada by telephone made us uncomfortable. As a consequence, we asked a "spy shop" called The Counter Spy Store in Mayfair, conveniently situated around the corner from my flat, to test our lines for wire taps.

Meanwhile, we decided to continue distributing the book in Canada, the U.S. and Bermuda and to grant interviews to the media. The only situation which turned slightly nasty was a feature interview with our "friends" from France, *Paris Match*. They asked us to meet them in a London hotel to discuss the case. We agreed only because we felt it might attract a French publisher. However, until such time as we left England, Malcolm was being careful not to talk openly about his employment with any publication available for purchase in the U.K. It was on this understanding that we agreed to the *Paris Match* interview and *Paris Match* was advised that any question directly related to the Royal Household would be answered by me. (This was a clever manoeuvre thought up by our advisors, since *I* had not been banned by Lord Donaldson's decree from discussing the book.)

We were led to believe the interview would be conducted in the reporters' hotel room. When we arrived, the two of them were seated in the oriental restaurant in the hotel basement having lunch. They had apparently just flown in. We felt uncomfortable discussing such sensitive material under an international restraining order in such a public place as a hotel restaurant, especially since the reporters' command of the English language was very limited and we had to explain our comments over and over to them. It was patently obvious that the hotel staff recognized Malcolm since the story was in all the papers, and we got the distinct feeling they did not approve of us.

The interview at last neared an end and we prepared to depart. As a last request, the female reporter asked us to pose with a copy of the book. As with *People*'s request to shoot Malcolm outside the Palace we did not think it a wise move, but they were most insistent and we reluctantly agreed, desperate to be rid of them for good. We had to dash back in a cab to my flat to retrieve a copy of the book and then, since it was really Malcolm they were interested in, he went back to the hotel alone to be photographed.

When he returned to my flat an hour later, he was pale and nervous. He explained how half way through the shoot a terrible argument developed between *Paris Match* and the hotel general manager over the picture taking. Outside, where he was posing with the book, the *Paris Match* reporters suddenly turned very nasty and started pointing at the anonymous men dressed in grey suits sitting in their cars watching the scene. "See!" he pointed to the men. "You are being watched. They are investigators following you!" Malcolm realized they were not joking when he spotted them with walkie-talkies in their hands and saw them shift uncomfortably in their seats at their discovery. With that, he ended the photo session abruptly and hailed a cab and jumped in.

By the middle of August, *Courting Disaster* was at the top of every major bestseller list in Canada, including those of the *Globe and Mail* and *Maclean's*. We were starting to climb the charts in the United States as well.

September and most of October saw us on a continuous book tour of Canada and the U.S. The highlights had to be the *Larry King Live* show and *The Joan Rivers Show*. We were given the opportunity to see first hand what goes on behind the scenes on some of the biggest programs in the country. This was an unexpected treat, on top of having a hit book.

But before appearing on the above mentioned programs we kicked off the U.S. section of the tour with a number of other popular television productions, such as *Hard Copy*, a nighttime show on CBS that follows *Entertainment Tonight*. We were flown to New York and a crew came in from Los Angeles especially for the taping. I sat on the sidelines and watched the interview unfold.

It was done extremely early in the morning and everyone, including the chap who interviewed Malcolm, looked exhausted. It lasted two or three hours as Malcolm answered one in-depth question after another—all this for just an eight-minute segment on the actual program. Once taped, the camera was then repositioned to film the interviewer asking all the questions over again while Malcolm had to pretend it was the first time, as he nodded his head when directed. The interviewer was most impressive when he recited from memory all the questions in the exact order they had originally been asked without any prompting whatsoever.

It was about this time that we began experiencing our only real problems with Buckingham Palace. They were so furious with Malcolm for what he had done that they refrained from giving out much information about his tenure at Buckingham Palace. In the meantime, rumors were circulating that he had occupied the *lowliest* of positions in the Royal Household. Some of the media unfortunately lapped up this misinformation. One Canadian paper quoted an unnamed Palace source stating that Malcolm was responsible for counting empty Coke bottles in the kitchen! Finally, a press secretary confirmed that, yes, Mr. Barker had, in fact, achieved the status of an Official within the Master of the Household's Department.

After a hectic schedule in New York, it was time to do *The Joan Rivers Show*. Although it is regularly broadcast in the afternoon, the actual show is taped at the ungodly hour of

9 a.m. in Manhattan. Everyone connected with her was extremely pleasant, fun and co-operative. Along with Malcolm, Joan had as guests a female editor from *People* magazine and another royal watcher who had written her own Royal exposé which, much to her annoyance, was not nearly as successful as *Courting Disaster*.

Each person was allotted about five minutes alone with Joan and then the next guest joined the panel. The two women obviously did not appreciate being usurped from the spotlight by someone who had actually worked for the Queen. They seemed truly to think *they* were more reliable experts than he! At one point Malcolm shared an insight with the audience only to have the author say that he was wrong and attempt to correct him! Malcolm had only worked in the Palace for several years. The closest the author would ever come to the Queen would be in using Pears soap, emblazoned with her Royal Warrant!

Still, the show was great for sales and the major chains were stepping in with big orders as *Courting Disaster* entered the Top Ten ranking on American bestseller lists.

Without question, the big highlight of the tour was doing the *Larry King Live* show in Washington, DC. It is surprisingly controlled very little by the King himself. He has a coterie of underlings who make all the decisions on who appears and he often has no say in the guest lineup.

Larry King Live had expressed interest in Malcolm as far back as early August but would never commit to a time. First the show was on, then it was off. Just when we thought it was finally going to happen, we would be replaced with the Iraqi Ambassador or other officials offering their opinions on the impending war in the Gulf. As Malcolm's father noted sarcastically at one point, "This invasion of Kuwait is cutting into your coverage, isn't it?"

Still, what could one do? With a nightly audience estimated in the tens of millions, a spot on his show is worth its weight in gold.

Larry had this one booking agent who phoned us to see if we were "suitable" for his show. She prefaced the conversation with, "Now just let me warn you that what you tell me during this call will decide whether or not we want you. So, make sure you give me all the dirt! I want all of it!"

Apparently, we gave her enough dirt because one day we finally got the call we had been anxiously awaiting and Malcolm was placed on stand-by. It did not seem to faze them one bit that he was standing by in Bermuda! In the end, it was a go, and after the confirmation call at noon he rushed to Hamilton airport to catch the 2:00 flight from Bermuda to Washington, DC.

The show went extremely well. Larry was more than cooperative and when you get a thumbs up from him you are on your way. It also didn't hurt when, in front of millions, he said, "This is sure one book I intend to read, let me tell you." That one statement translated into sales and within days we had become an American bestseller, reaching the Number Three spot on the Doubleday National Best Seller list. We even edged out Donald Trump's *Surviving at the Top*, which, we were delighted to see, was Number Four.

Meanwhile, in Canada, *Courting Disaster*, the book that everyone proclaimed would never sell, continued its ride on the *Globe and Mail* bestseller list for three consecutive months. It became the sixth biggest-selling book in Canada for the entire year of 1990, even though it only went on sale mid-year. Had we had the additional books to fill the overwhelming demand in the heat of the press attention, there is every chance we would have been the biggest-selling book for that year. A *Maclean's* representative told an executive from our PR firm that while they kept no statistics, it appeared *Courting Disaster* was "the fastest selling book in Canadian history," meaning that more copies had been sold in a specific period of time than any other.

As I write this afterword the book has been translated into many languages and is being released by other publishers later this year in Holland, France, Germany, Italy and even China. So far, excerpts have been serialized in Canada, America, France, Germany, Italy, Japan and Australia. We are currently working on the film rights and, even more exciting, a possible television series based on the book.

But that is really only the beginning. Auctions for the rights to the book are planned in Australia, Ireland and Scotland, and as far away as Japan. No doubt one will be able to pick up a copy of *Courting Disaster* in a dozen or more languages over the next two to four years.

The Attorney General of Great Britain dropped all legal action against Malcolm and the book upon being granted a final and permanent injunction that would ensure *Courting Disaster* would never appear in print in the United Kingdom. They had at least learned one important lesson from the government's unsuccessful pursuit of Peter Wright and *Spycatcher* in the Australian courts. To our knowledge, *Courting Disaster* in the only book in history to have a world-wide ban issued against it. Many books have been banned in specific countries over the years, but none so far-reaching as our own.

Ironically, we thank the stars above that we did not accept any of the inconsequential offers from American or Canadian publishers over the years. On average, authors earn between seven and ten percent of the cover price of their book, the rest landing in the publishers', distributors' and bookstores' pockets. Because we ended up publishing the hardcover edition ourselves, we earned *fifty* percent!

But apart from the story of how the book came to be, the ensuing legal drama, the world-wide ban and its ultimate international success, we wanted this afterword to inspire those hundreds of writers out there struggling to find someone willing to take a risk and publish them. Perhaps, like us, you have been rejected so many times that you have often doubted your own skills and abilities. To you we would say, don't ever give up. Sure, you may not have the added lure of the Queen of England banning your book, but if you believe that your manuscript is truly well written, fresh and unique, then keep on pushing even if it takes *five* years. One thing is clear in this business: if it is good, then it will eventually be recognized. As Helen Heller, literary agent to the late Northrop Frye, said to me once,"You can usually tell from the very first sentence if the manuscript is going to be of any worth."

So take heart! Don't accept "no" from anybody. Publishers are frequently wrong. This book is proof of that.

T.C. Sobey
April 1991